is and evaluation of the role
cy in c
ives a
the

perience from 1935 to 1947, the Taft-
Hartley Act and the duty to bargain, and
with case histories, the impact of the
duty to bargain. An eighth chapter
which evaluates the duty to bargain, con-
cludes Professor Ross's cogent and effective nonconforming treatment of a subject of importance to lawyers, judges,
personnel administrators, political scientists, economists, and many others.

An associate professor of economics and
business administration at the Graduate
School of Business of the University of
Pittsburgh, Philip Ross holds a doc-
torate from Brown University, where he
studied under the distinguished labor
historian Philip Taft. Mr. Ross's firsthand
knowledge of labor relations stems from
his experience as a field examiner with
the National Labor Relations Board and
subsequently consultant to its chairman,
executive secretary of the National Enforcement Commission of the Wage
Stabilization Board, regional director of
the United Hatters, Cap and Millinery
Workers International Union, and labor
consultant to the state of Pennsylvania.
He was recently awarded a Ford Foundation fellowship for research in business.

THE GOVERNMENT AS A
SOURCE OF UNION POWER

BROWN UNIVERSITY BICENTENNIAL PUBLICATIONS
STUDIES IN THE FIELDS OF GENERAL SCHOLARSHIP

THE GOVERNMENT AS A
SOURCE OF UNION POWER

THE ROLE OF PUBLIC POLICY
IN COLLECTIVE BARGAINING

BY PHILIP ROSS

BROWN UNIVERSITY PRESS
PROVIDENCE RHODE ISLAND

DESIGNED BY DAVID FORD

TYPE SET IN 11/13 LINOTYPE CALEDONIA
  AND PRINTED ON UNIVERSITY TEXT
  BY THE CRIMSON PRINTING COMPANY

BOUND BY THE STANHOPE BINDERY, INC.

PREFACE

This book attempts to analyze the nature of government activity in the field of labor-management relations, and is centered upon the public policy in support of the principle of collective bargaining. It is shown that this government intervention works most effectively through the employer's mandatory duty to bargain in good faith with the union representing a majority of his employees. The aim of this work is to trace the development of this policy of government intervention, and to evaluate its implications.

This work does not purport to set forth in detail the entire range of governmental activity which adds to or detracts from union power. As far as the Wagner and Taft-Hartley Acts are concerned, the writer is convinced that the heart of the matter is the duty to bargain, and the aids to unions specified in other unfair labor practices are accordingly only alluded to briefly. Unlike the duty to bargain, which directly establishes certain rights of labor organizations, nearly all other protective labor legislation in the United States and abroad is designed to further the interests of individual employees. There has been no attempt to evaluate state and local laws encouraging unions, such as licensing laws; while they are important for the unions involved, they lack the sweep and reach of the federal law. Except inferentially in the discussion of the Taft-Hartley amendments, there has been no systematic attempt to measure the influence of recent anti-union statutes, particularly the secondary boycott provisions of the Taft-Hartley and Landrum-Griffin Acts.

If the book has an overriding thesis, it is that understanding of public policy in its influence upon behavior can best be reached by examining the specific way in which the law works. In other words, the prime method of approach has been empirical. The author confesses an uneasiness when confronted with generalizations about the behavior of unions and employers which are not only inconsistent with his experience but are not supported by probative evidence.

It is hoped that this work may be useful to students in various disciplines. To begin with, there is a correction of the view maintained by practically all scholars and by the courts, including the Supreme Court, that the Congress which passed the Wagner Act had no notion of the meaning of the duty to bargain. It is demonstrated that this proposition is not merely probably wrong but utterly erroneous. More specifically, there is an effort here to answer for the historian the question of how the Wagner Act aided unions. It is easy to assert that the Wagner Act was passed and that therefore the labor movement expanded in numbers and strength; but the particular way in which this result came about appears to have been generally ignored. The study of a merit unfair labor practice charge, as well as the treatment of the economic consequences of legal standards, may aid the economist in understanding the ways in which the law affects union power through the supply curve of labor. And for political scientists and lawyers, an attempt is made to assess the meaning of legislation by examining the consequences of a violation in its historical setting. Although the book is a product of original research, the author has hoped, unrealistically as it may prove, that the practice of scholarship has not marred its readability and made it inaccessible to the general reader.

It is difficult to list all the help that has been received in the research and writing of this volume. Grateful acknowledgment must be made of the assistance of the staff of the

National Labor Relations Board in getting the empirical data. The author feels greatly indebted to the imaginative understanding and co-operation of Associate General Counsel H. Stephan Gordon; Clarence Wright, Director of the Division of Administration; Edward Goodstein, Assistant Director; Martha Dunleavy, Assistant Chief of Organization and Methods Branch; and the personnel of the Statistical Analysis Branch. The former General Counsel, Stuart Rothman, was always helpful and co-operative during the author's investigation, as was his successor, Arnold Ordman. In addition, valuable insights into board operations were furnished in the course of many discussions with Board Member Gerald A. Brown and his Chief Counsel, Ralph Winkler; by the former Assistant to the Chairman and now Professor of Law at the University of North Carolina, Daniel H. Pollitt; by the board's Solicitor, William Feldesman, and his associate, Saul J. Jaffe; and by Arthur Leff, former Trial Examiner and presently Chief Counsel to the Chairman. Harry Brickman, formerly of the agency's Operations Analysis section and presently head of the board's research unit, was always a constant and reliable source of information and helpful suggestions. I am also particularly obligated to my good friend Howard W. Kleeb, Associate Executive Secretary, for giving me the benefit of his sound judgment and long experience. My friends Thomas Kennedy, Assistant General Counsel, and Thomas Healy, Associate Director of Information, were helpful in more ways than they may have realized.

Furthermore, the directors and staff of the various regional offices of the board invariably extended their courtesy and co-operation. In particular the author wishes to thank Henry Shore, Director of Region 6, Pittsburgh, and Bernard L. Alpert, Director of Region 1, Boston, for having borne the brunt of his regional visits, and for having shared their experience with him. The author also wishes to thank Jerome H. Brooks, Acting Director of Region 7, Detroit; Philip Fusco, Director of Region 8, Cleveland; Walter C. Phillips, Director of Region 10, Atlanta; John L. LeBus, Director of Region 15, New Orleans; Hugh E. Sperry, Director of Region 17, Kansas City; C. Edward Knapp, Director of Region 18, Minneapolis; Roy O. Hoffman, Director of Region 20, San Francisco; and Ralph E. Kennedy, Director of Region 21, Los Angeles.

But above all, the author wishes to express his deepest appreciation to two remarkable men, Frank W. McCulloch, Chairman of the NLRB, and Ogden W. Fields, the board's Executive Secretary. Mr. McCulloch is a man of extraordinary qualities of mind and character whose commitment and devotion to the public interest are beyond praise. Mr. Fields is more than a prototype of the very best in the American civil servant: his integrity and moral courage have earned for him the reputation among his associates of being "the conscience of the board."

It goes without saying that this work does not reflect in any way the views, official or unofficial, of the NLRB or any of its officers. All the opinions, interpretations, conclusions, and errors are the responsibility of the author alone.

The writer also wishes to thank Professor Ivan Rutledge, Professor of Law at Ohio State University, for reviewing the book in manuscript and for his many valuable contributions. The author is grateful to his former dean, Dr. Marshall Robinson, and to his present dean, Dr. William Frederick, for having made the University of Pittsburgh's Graduate School of Business a congenial and hospitable environment for research. The author's colleague at the University of Pittsburgh, Professor Edward Sussna, has also been a friendly sounding board and critic for many ideas.

It is very difficult to express the writer's debt to Professor

Philip Taft, who has served not only as a teacher but as a colleague and guide in the world of scholarship. More than he can possibly know, his knowledge, insights, and critical standards have shaped not only this work but the direction of the author's professional life.

The real cost of this book has been borne by my family. For my wife, Julie, and for my son, David, no acknowledgment is possible of the full measure of their love, patience, and forbearance.

CONTENTS

1   INTRODUCTION   1
    The Meaning of the Duty to Bargain   2
    Hostility to the Duty to Bargain   4

2   THE ORIGIN OF THE DUTY TO BARGAIN   8
    The Role of the Duty to Bargain During World
        War I   10
    The Railroad Industry Experience   18
    The Newlands Act   24
    The Adamson Act   25
    Wartime Administration of the Railroads   28
    The Transportation Act of 1920   32
    The Railway Labor Act of 1926   42
    The 1934 Amendments to the Railway Labor
        Act   47

3   THE LEGISLATIVE HISTORY OF THE WAGNER ACT—THE
    DEVELOPMENT OF THE NEW DEAL COLLECTIVE
    BARGAINING POLICY   49
    The First Wagner Bill, 1934   57
    Public Resolution No. 44   62
    The First National Labor Relations Board   64
    The Effectiveness of the National Labor
        Relations Board   69
    The Wagner Bill, S. 1958   71

4   THE LEGISLATIVE INTENT AND THE DUTY TO BARGAIN   87
    Scholars' Attacks on the Duty to Bargain   89
    Other Attacks on the Duty to Bargain   94
    Congressional Intent in the Wagner Act   96

xi

5   THE WAGNER ACT EXPERIENCE, 1935–1947   101
    The Statutory Basis for Collective Bargaining   101
    The Employer's Duty to Meet with the Union   103
    The Duty of the Employer to Negotiate   104
    The Subject Matter of Collective Bargaining   105
    The Duty to Bargain in Good Faith   108
    Positive Action Required of Employers   112
    Refusal to Supply Relevant Information upon
        Request   116
    Positive Acts in Derogation of an Employer's
        Duty to Bargain   118
    Bypassing of the Union   120
    Bypassing of the Union–Individual Bargaining   120
    Acts Designed to Dissipate a Union's Majority   122
    The Effects of the Destruction of a Union's
        Majority upon the Employer's Duty to
        Bargain   123
    The Terms of a Collective Bargaining Agreement
        and the Test of Good Faith   124
    Defenses to the Duty of Good-Faith Bargaining   127
    Refusal to Bargain on the Inappropriateness of
        the Unit   130

6   THE TAFT-HARTLEY ACT AND THE DUTY TO BARGAIN   133
    The Background of the Taft-Hartley Act   133
    Legislative History of Section 8(a)(5) of the
        Taft-Hartley Act   134
    The House Bill on the Duty to Bargain   137
    The Senate Majority Report   146
    The Taft-Hartley Act and the Employer's Duty
        to Bargain   148
    The Development of Board Doctrine on the
        Duty to Bargain–Duration of Designation
        of Union   149
    Appropriateness of Unit   151
    Individual Bargaining and Unilateral Action   152

The Duty to Bargain as Affected by Section
8(d)   153
The Duty to Bargain as Affected by Unlawful
or Unprotected Conduct of Employees   154
Refusal to Furnish Information   154
Mandatory Subject Matter for Collective
Bargaining   155
Good-Faith Bargaining in General   159
The Duty to Bargain in Good Faith as Affected
by the Imposition of Conditions on
Bargaining   163

7   THE IMPACT OF THE DUTY TO BARGAIN   170
Introduction   170
The Existing Evidence of the Effectiveness of
the Duty to Bargain   172
The Impact of the Duty to Bargain—The
Empirical Evidence   179
Dr. Brown's Study   180
An Empirical Analysis of the Duty to Bargain   182
Meritorious Formal Cases which Resulted in
Contracts or Other Compliance   184
Meritorious Formal Cases which Did Not
Result in Contracts   195
Cases Closed in Compliance with an
Intermediate Report   203
Meritorious 8(a)(5) Cases, Closed upon Com-
pliance with an Intermediate Report, in which
Contracts were Signed   204
Meritorious Refusal-to-Bargain Charges which
Did Not Proceed to a Formal Hearing   210
Informally Adjusted Meritorious Cases, Involving
Recognition as a Major Issue, in which
Contracts were Executed   210
Informally Adjusted Meritorious Refusal-to-Bargain
Charges Involving Recognition which Did Not
Result in a Contract   214

Informally Adjusted Meritorious Refusal-to-Bargain
Cases, Involving Unilateral Action, which Resulted
in a Contract   217
Informally Adjusted Meritorious Refusal-to-
Bargain Charges on the Major Issue of Bad-
Faith Bargaining   220
Meritorious Cases in which No Contract Was
Signed   227

8   AN EVALUATION OF THE DUTY TO BARGAIN   231
The Impact of the Board upon Employer
Behavior in Cases Before the Board—
The Legal Sanction   239
The Impact of the Board upon Employer
Behavior in Situations where Court Enforcement
was Not Invoked   248
An Appraisal of Non-Compliance   257
The Strategic Role of the Duty to Bargain   260
Conclusion   262
NOTES   267
SELECTED BIBLIOGRAPHY   301
MAJOR CASES CITED   309
INDEX   315

CHAPTER 1 · INTRODUCTION

The Wagner Act was passed in 1935. The effects of this statute, with the rather minor amendments added by the Taft-Hartley and Landrum-Griffin Acts, have been extensive and widely recognized. There appears to be little doubt that the Wagner Act promoted a spectacular increase in union membership and played a fundamental role in the subsequent development of collective bargaining. Indeed, the influence of the national labor law has been so pervasive that it requires an effort to envision contemporary collective bargaining without the rules and standards established and enforced by the government.

But it must be emphasized that the passing of the Wagner Act was not the first step by which the government has involved itself in labor-management affairs. It must also be recognized that the Wagner Act was not an unusual example of government promotion of collective bargaining. The forty years which preceded the Wagner Act witnessed many state and federal laws specifically designed to aid trade unions.

The uniqueness of the Wagner Act lay not only in its permanence but in the particular way in which the public policy promoting collective bargaining was carried out. As was anticipated in prior legislation, the act forbade employers to interfere with, restrain, or coerce employees who wanted to engage in concerted activities, and similarly outlawed the discriminatory treatment or discharge of union-minded employees. These prohibited activities were specified as unfair labor practices in Sections 8(1) and (3) of the Wagner Act. But Congress went one step farther. It specifically required an employer to bargain with the union which represented a majority of its employees in an appropriate unit. The duty to bargain was incorporated in Section 8(5) of the Wagner Act and the principle of majority rule was spelled out in Section 9(a). In order to emphasize the obligation of an employer to deal only with an uncoerced majority of its employees, unions dominated, established, or assisted by the company were also banned under Section 8(2) of the act.

THE MEANING OF THE DUTY TO BARGAIN

The duty to bargain can best be approached by examining some of its constraints upon an employer. Once an employer is confronted with a majority union, his freedom of action is seriously limited. The employer must meet with the union at reasonably frequent intervals at a mutually agreeable time and place. He must refrain from bypassing the union and negotiating directly with his employees. He must not refuse to discuss the mandatory subjects of collective bargaining, which, under National Labor Relations Board doctrine, include not only wages and hours but merit increases, bonuses, sub-contracting, work rules, pensions, stock-purchase plans, and any other subject which affects the terms and conditions of employment.

In negotiating with a union, an employer must make a bona fide effort to come to terms with the union and cannot legally avoid the duty to bargain by "surface bargaining," "shadow boxing," or prolonged futile discussion. While concessions are not required, an employer must in good faith so conduct his negotiations that his acts of commission and omission are consistent with the inference of a desire to reach an agreement.

In the course of contract negotiations and during the life of a contract, an employer has certain specific obligations under the duty to bargain. He must, on request, furnish relevant information concerning facts peculiarly within his knowledge, such as wage classifications, rates of pay, cost of fringe benefits, and the like. If an employer states that he cannot afford to pay higher wages, he must provide the union with specific information, by opening his books, for instance, or by preparing special reports to justify his claim. In no event, except after a bona fide impasse, may an employer change any of the terms or conditions of employment without the agreement of the union.

At any time that a union represents his employees, an employer may not engage in acts designed to dissipate the union's majority. In the event that an employer, by refusing to bargain or by other improper means, does succeed in destroying a union's majority, he is not permitted to benefit from his past misconduct but is required to deal with the union despite its minority status.

The historical significance of the duty to bargain cannot be exaggerated. In an early decision, the National Labor Relations Board noted that the protection to organization of employees given by the other unfair labor practices was intended to make possible the fostering of collective bargaining under Section 8(5).[1] The Supreme Court, on a number of occasions, has also emphasized the importance of the duty to bargain. For example, the court has stated, "It was believed that the other rights guaranteed by the Act would not be meaningful if the employer was not under an obligation to confer with the union in an effort to arrive at the terms of an agreement."[2] On another occasion the court took an even broader view, observing, "Enforcement of the obligation to bargain collectively is crucial to the statutory scheme." [3]

From a statistical and operational point of view, the duty to bargain has always played an important role in the administration of the Wagner and Taft-Hartley Acts. Second only to discriminatory discharge of employees, breach of this duty has always been a source of most employer unfair labor practices. Indeed, the proportion of charges alleging a violation of an employer's duty to bargain has recently increased to a point where it now constitutes about one-quarter of all cases.

HOSTILITY TO THE DUTY TO BARGAIN

Notwithstanding this, it is curious to note that most labor scholars remain dubious about the value of an employer's statutory obligation to bargain. Professor George Taylor has recently asserted that the duty to bargain "has been one of the greatest mistakes in public policy in this area." [4] Professor Davey has said that the determination of the scope of collective bargaining by board decisions "raises some serious questions for the future of private bargaining relationships." [5] On the same point, Professors Shultz and Coleman have asserted that board doctrine in this area "has carried us much closer toward settlements by government fiat than we may wish to be." [6] And Professor Gregory gloomily foresees a trend which would "eventually end in a drastic modification of our economic system itself." [7]

The roll call of writers who agree that the duty to bargain is deleterious and should be drastically modified or eliminated includes Professors Cox and Dunlop, who see the question as one of undesirable government regulation of the collective bargaining process, and Professors Northrup and

4

Bloom, who assert that good-faith bargaining cannot be legislated and that the law "is wholly unrealistic." [8]

Late in 1961, a committee of distinguished scholars headed by Dr. Clark Kerr issued a very important report on the duty to bargain. The report stated:

The original intent of this provision was to ensure a minimal degree of recognition so that efforts to decide the question of representation by an orderly process would not be frustrated. Senator David I. Walsh, then Chairman of the Senate Committee on Education and Labor, in arguing for this provision in 1935, said:

> When the employees have chosen their organization, when they have selected their representatives, all the bill proposes to do is to escort them to the door of the employer and say, "Here they are, the legal representatives of your employees." What happens behind those doors is not inquired into, and the bill does not seek to inquire into it.

Senator Walsh's objective was a sensible one, and an appealingly simple one, too. Unfortunately, as time has passed, the simplicity has been lost. It has been succeeded by a flood of litigation and an increasingly complex set of regulations stemming from amendments of the original provisions and from interpretations by the NLRB and the courts. The efficacy of the process in achieving a more ambitious objective—to compel the parties to bargain in good faith—is at best doubtful.

Parties have been told that they must bargain in good faith, and elaborate tests have been devised in an attempt to determine "objectively" whether the proper subjective attitude prevails. The limitations and artificiality of such tests are apparent, and the possibilities of evasion are almost limitless. In the light of the realities of the bargaining situation, distinctions between matters that are subject to "mandatory bargaining" and those that are not have a hollow ring. Basically, it is unrealistic to expect that, by legislation, "good faith" can be brought to the bargaining table. Indeed, the provisions designed to bring "good faith" have become a tactical weapon used in many situations as a means of harassment.[9]

The significance of the report by the Committee for Economic Development goes beyond the eminence of its sponsors. It must be recognized that the report expresses a consensus of the informed academic community on the appropriate role of public policy in this area. The arguments against the duty to bargain advanced in the report, while unsupported by documentation, rest upon prior scholarly investigations and effectively summarize the prevailing climate of opinion.

In effect, the report recommends that the duty to bargain should be abandoned for the following reasons: (1) It goes beyond the original intent of Congress. (2) It is "unrealistic," "artificial," and of doubtful efficacy. (3) It involves an undue and undesirable intervention by the government in the bargaining process.

The first two reasons are questions of fact, and the third is a judgment derived from the others. To a very large extent, the contemporary issue of government intervention in collective bargaining is centered upon the various rules adopted by the NLRB and enforced by the courts in the interpretation of an employer's duty to bargain. And it should be observed that the conclusions expressed in the report, as well as those articulated by other scholars, are based upon an appraisal of experience, i.e., on the actual operations and consequences of the law.

However, an examination of the literature for the evidence in support of the hostility to the duty to bargain yields the surprising result that there is practically none. The present state of knowledge in this area consists of thousands of articles in law and economics journals which describe and evaluate the government's role with scant reference to the empirical evidence. As Harold Davey observed, "Notwithstanding this surfeit of academic literature. . . , it remains possible to acknowledge the worthwhile empirical studies of the [Taft-Hartley] Act's operational effect on collective bargaining in one academic note." [10]

6

As early as 1953, Sumner Slichter commented that "Surprisingly little is now known about how [the Taft-Hartley Act] is actually operating. . . . Until much more is known about the actual operation of the law, Congress is not in a good position to revise it." [11]
More recently, D. V. Brown confessed:

For many years I have been plagued by the uneasy feeling that, while I was ready at the drop a hat to make pronouncements on desirable public policy in the area of labor-management relations, I was woefully ignorant of the actual impact of existing policies, let alone of policies as yet untried. . . . What, in fact, do we know about what happens after an order of a court or an administrative agency has been duly issued? . . . When the National Gadget Company is directed to bargain with the union of its employees, is the result one big happy family? A search of the literature revealed an almost dearth of studies throwing any light on the answers to questions such as these, at least in the area encompassed by the Wagner and Taft-Hartley Acts. [12]

We are here confronted with a dilemma. Despite the absence of data, there has been no shortage of scholarly conclusions. Explicit appraisals of the effectiveness, value, and wisdom of government intervention have been made on the basis of experience, but the nature of this experience has been either assumed or set forth in general, non-verifiable terms.

Accordingly, it appears useful to take the following steps: review the development of the public policy which led to the establishment of the duty to bargain; describe and analyze the nature of this legal duty; examine the effectiveness and consequences of this policy; and finally, evaluate the merits of the contemporary hostility to the duty to bargain.

CHAPTER 2 · THE ORIGIN OF THE DUTY TO BARGAIN

In 1916, a minority of the membership of a Commission on Industrial Relations recommended to Congress that an administrative body be established which would prosecute and adjudicate certain unfair trade practices. These practices were specified in two particulars: "(a) Refusal to permit employees to become members of labor organizations. (b) Refusal to meet or confer with authorized representatives of employees."[1]

The basis for this recommendation was the history of rejection by most employers of collective bargaining. This rejection was noted time and again by both state and federal governments in various legislative reports on the causes of industrial unrest. Typical of such reports was the recommendation of the Industrial Commission in 1902 that "fair dealing" by employers was imperative to the practical success of collective bargaining, which it endorsed.[2]

The major issues that precipitated most strikes hinged upon the acceptance of collective bargaining by employers. During this period, employer opposition took the form of non-recognition of the union. As a government commission observed:

> Some employers say to their employees: "We do not object to your joining the union, but we will not recognize your union nor deal with it as representing you." If the union is to be rendered

impotent, and its usefulness is to be nullified by refusing to permit it to perform the functions for which it is created, and for which alone it exists, permission to join it may well be considered as a privilege of doubtful value.[3]

A characteristic result of the refusal to bargain was recited in a subsequent inquiry, which concluded:

We find that the direct and proximate cause of the killing of men, women, and children, destruction of property, and looting of the homes of the striking miners in the southern Colorado coal fields during the strike therein was the arbitrary refusal of the coal-mine operators to meet and confer with the representatives of workers in their several mines.[4]

The opposition to government intervention by imposing a duty to bargain upon employers was vigorously stated by the majority members of the Commission on Industrial Relations. It was primarily based upon the logical ground that, in order to be effective, the government would have to go all the way to compulsory arbitration.

It seems appropriate to reproduce this line of thought:

The first step in strategy of collective bargaining is recognition of the union; that is, recognition by the employer of the representatives of the union by consenting to confer with them. How important this preliminary step is considered by both sides is shown by the meaning which they give to the term "recognition." To "recognize a union" is considered to not merely hold a conference with its agents, but also to investigate grievances and demands, to negotiate concerning the terms of a collective agreement, and even to employ union men on terms consented to by the union. Strictly speaking, these are not "recognition" but are steps in collective bargaining that follow recognition. Recognition in the ordinary sense of the term (the one here used) would be merely a conference in which the employer meets certain individuals, not as individuals but as recognized agents of the union authorized to speak on behalf of his employees. But it is so well understood that recognition, even in this limited sense, will be followed by other steps, that the decisive battle is often fought out at this point. . . . The mere compulsion on employers, through prosecutions, as proposed by our colleagues, to compel employers to confer with unions, can have no result, unless it be accompanied by compulsion to investigate, as in the Canadian and Colorado Acts, or to arbitrate, as in Australia. If employers are compelled merely to confer, they can, of course, reject all propositions, and the nominal recognition of the union thereby secured would only be a further opportunity for declaring their determination not to recognize the union. If such a law is intended to accomplish anything it should go further and compel the employers to submit to compulsory investigation or compulsory arbitration, and this would mean compulsion also on the unions to confer and testify or to arbitrate.[5]

It must be understood that this rejection of the duty to bargain was not based upon hostility to collective bargaining. On the contrary, the commission was united in agreeing upon the superiority of collective bargaining to individual bargaining. But the only effective method of securing the growth of trade unionism was considered to be "through the influence of public opinion without force of law."[6] In other words, the essence of the majority's conclusion was that a legal duty to bargain would be only nominal if employers so chose, and that effectiveness could be achieved only by an inadmissible grant of power to the government to prescribe the terms and conditions of employment. As we shall see, this view was taken up time and again during the evolution of the present law.

THE ROLE OF THE DUTY TO BARGAIN
DURING WORLD WAR I

By the time of the entrance of the United States into World War I, there had been numerous legislative attempts to promote collective bargaining. These ordinarily took the form of protecting the right of employees to join unions. As early as 1898, in the Erdman Act, the federal government made it a crime for a railroad carrier to discriminate against its employees for their union activities. At about the same time, some twenty-two states passed little Erdman Acts extending the same protection to most employees in manufacturing and other industries.[7]

Prevailing judicial principles did more than undermine legislative efforts to promote collective bargaining. Court decisions on both the state and the federal level restricted union conduct and activities by the regulation of strikes, picketing, and boycotts and, on the whole, constituted active government intervention in labor-management affairs.

It was not until the establishment by executive order of the National War Labor Board and other agencies in 1917 that a national policy to promote collective bargaining was inaugurated. This policy, even to the words in which it was embodied, has been continued until the present day: "The right of workers to organize in trade unions and to bargain collectively, through chosen representatives, is recognized and affirmed. This right shall not be denied or abridged, or interfered with by the employers in any manner whatsoever."[8]

However, it should be noted that the board's policy fell short of actively expanding the role of unions in achieving collective bargaining. Where an existing union had won the union shop and other goals, these conditions were to be maintained. But, in the absence of past contractual relations, the failure of an employer to recognize a union was not considered to be a breach of public policy. Still, the right of workers to organize was protected and the right of collective bargaining was construed as requiring the employer "to recognize and deal with committees after they have been constituted by the employees."[9]

In the actual award or recommendation by the board, the following clause usually appeared:

The principles upon which the National War Labor Board is founded guarantee the right to employees to organize and to bargain collectively, and there shall be no discrimination or co-ercion directed against proper activities of this kind. Employees in the exercise of their right to organize shall not use coercive measures of any kind to compel persons to join their unions, nor to induce employers to bargain or deal with their unions. As the right of workers to bargain collectively through committees has been recognized by the Board the company shall recognize and deal with such committees after they have been constituted by the employees.

The difference between an employer's having a duty to deal with representatives of his employees and his being required to recognize a union was a very thin one. The board consistently maintained that employers had to deal with shop committees "regardless of the fact that they may be elected at meetings of employees who are members of a union." [10] The basis for the board's position was put in the following way: "In meeting committees of employees so elected the company does not necessarily recognize the union nor deal with it as such. What they are dealing with is committees of employees and not with the union." [11] It is possible that employers felt that this rationale was excessively ingenuous.

Awards establishing collective bargaining were made even when the parties in a case had had no previous experience with it and required the assistance of the board in installing shop committee systems. Plans were accordingly devised by board representatives which provided for the election of department and general committees of employees. In addition, these committees were furnished with constitutions and bylaws in accordance with local needs and desires. Of course, this procedure was invoked only when there was no union involved.[12]

Employees' freedom to choose their representatives was

usually safeguarded. In a number of cases in which elections of department committees were ordered, the board specified the conditions under which the elections should be conducted, including the place and time of election. Furthermore, provision was usually made for a secret ballot election in which all female as well as male workers in the appropriate classification were eligible to vote.[13]

In one case, the board inspected an existing shop committee plan in order to determine whether the election was fairly held and whether the plan in operation provided for amendments in the event that employees so desired. When necessary, the board set up machinery for changes in any functioning plan by new election as circumstances warranted.[14]

Many awards stipulated the subjects of bargaining between employers and shop committees. Among the subjects of mandatory bargaining were the establishment of job classifications, discharge cases, wage scales (including the setting of minimum rates and handling of inequitable rates), health and safety, hours of work (including overtime), holidays, weekly work periods, piecework rates, payment for special services, payment of less than minimum rates to the physically handicapped or to beginners, apprentice systems, and working conditions in general, including matters not specifically included in the award.[15] In one case involving a single employer, the board went farther and proposed industry-wide bargaining for settling grievances and negotiating wage agreements.[16]

In its decisions, the board not only forbade discrimination against union membership but required reinstatement with back pay for employees who were discriminatorily discharged. Black-listing was banned and the right to participate in strikes was protected. Company-dominated unions were disapproved of, and union members were so well protected that an employer was forbidden to object to the wearing of a union button. Furthermore, employers were required to permit union members to take time off without pay to attend union conventions.[17]

The specific meaning of the government's protection of collective bargaining can be seen from a typical award:

The right of the workers of this company freely to organize in trade unions, or to join the same, and to bargain collectively, is affirmed, and discharges for legitimate union activities, interrogation of workers by officials as to their union affiliations, espionage by agents or representatives of the company, visits by officials of the company to the neighborhood of the meeting place of the organization for the purpose of observing the men who belong to such unions, to their detriment as employees of the company, and like actions, the intent of which is to discourage and prevent men from exercising this right of organization, must be deemed an interference with their rights as laid down in the principles of the board.[18]

The significance of such an award is not the mere cataloguing and outlawing of employers' traditional methods of combatting union organization. The abiding importance of the War Labor Board was twofold. In the first place, it was effective and promoted phenomenal gains in union membership. As a demonstration of the efficacy of government aid to unions, it was highly successful. Second, the principles established by the board anticipated the methods and techniques of promoting collective bargaining, even to the statutory language that was later to become a permanent part of the legal environment.

The strategic role of the duty to bargain was clearly evident in postwar events. In 1919, President Wilson convened an industrial conference for the purpose of reaching "some common ground of agreement and action with regard to the future conduct of industry" and to work out "a practical method of association" between management and labor.[19] In attendance at this meeting were representatives of labor organizations, bankers' associations, farm organizations, the National Chamber of Commerce, the National Industrial Conference Board, and other groups. The public interest was presumably represented by such prominent persons as Bernard Baruch, Robert S. Brookings, John D. Rockefeller, Jr., Dr. Charles W. Eliot, and Judge Elbert H. Gary.

The union representatives, led by Samuel Gompers, introduced the following resolution on collective bargaining:

The right of wage earners to organize in trade and labor unions, to bargain collectively, to be represented by representatives of their own choosing in negotiations and adjustments with employers, and in respect to wages, hours of labor, and relations and conditions of employment, is recognized.

The public representatives promptly and unanimously voted in favor of this resolution with the proviso that an employee has the right "to refrain from joining any organization or to deal directly with his employer if he so chooses." [20]

The employer group rejected these principles. Its position was:

There shall be no denial of the right of an employer and his workers to voluntarily agree that their relation shall be that of the "closed union shop" or of the "closed non-union shop." But the right of the employer and his men to continue their relations on the principle of the "open shop" shall not be denied or questioned. *No employer should be required to deal with men or groups of men who are not his employees or chosen by and from among them.* [Emphasis added.][21]

There were two major though related issues in the deadlock. The first was the nature of the relationship between employers and employees, the question of collective bargaining. The second was the question of public policy, which involved a consideration of the desirability of government intervention. The kinship between these issues was revealed in the remarks of Frederick P. Fish, chairman of the National Industrial Conference Board and former president of the American Telephone and Telegraph Company, on the nature of collective bargaining. After describing collective bargaining as a vague phrase, incapable of definition, Mr. Fish observed:

As I understand the attitude of most of the employers in this country and the attitude of the employers in the group which is here in this conference, they are in favor of collective bargaining, but they do not feel that this conference should take any action which indicates that it imposes as a burden upon all the manufacturers and industrialists of this country that they should engage in collective bargaining, with the representatives of the men who are other than selected from the employees themselves.[22]

The employers' objection to the legal duty of bargaining rested mainly upon its compulsory nature. Related to this was the further rejection of any involuntary dealing with a union which was independent of the employer. But several important points must be emphasized. First, the employers as a group did not protest against legal restriction of their right to discharge, coerce, or discriminate against their employees because of their union activities. In other words, there was agreement by management representatives on what later was to be incorporated in Section 8(1) of the Wagner Act.

The second point is that a government-enforced duty to bargain was opposed because of its presumed effectiveness. One management spokesman viewed the right of a union to be recognized as a symbolic right which, once granted by employers, would result in a vast increase in the number of unions.[23] Another employer representative prophesied that a legal duty to bargain would have the following effect: "Practically, what this means is that the men to be selected by the shop employees, the establishment employees, outside of their number, are to be labor union men." [24]

The right to representation was the critical issue in the conference. The reaction of the labor representatives to management's position was bitter. There were frequent references to the right of organization given to trade unions by the government during World War I and to the inconsistency of management's endorsement of collective bargaining with its rejection of recognition rights. Finally the labor representatives withdrew from the conference.

The official report on the conference summed up the proceedings by noting:

An analysis of the heated controversies that are current with reference to collective bargaining indicates that the employees place the emphasis on the right of wage earners to bargain collectively, and that the employers place the emphasis on the right of employers to bargain or to refuse to bargain collectively at their discretion.[25]

The import of the employers' position on collective bargaining soon appeared in subsequent events. The labor movement's postwar organizational efforts were met by the "American Plan," the success of which began with the failure of the 1919 steel strike. Judge Gary, speaking for the steel industry, told Congress: "It has been my policy and the policy of our corporation, not to deal with union labor leaders . . . at any time. And the reason is we do not believe in contracting with unions. When an employer contracts with the union labor leaders, he immediately drives all his employees into the unions. . ." [26] With the experience of the war years in mind, we do not find here an appeal to logic or legal ineffectiveness.

But the best evidence we have on the effectiveness of the government policy of protecting unions is the change which took place in union membership, as shown in Table 1.[27]

TABLE 1

AVERAGE ANNUAL MEMBERSHIP OF UNIONS
1913–1924

1913	.	.	.	.	.	.	.	.	.	2,716,300
1914	.	.	.	.	.	.	.	.	.	2,687,100
1915	.	.	.	.	.	.	.	.	.	2,582,600
1916	.	.	.	.	.	.	.	.	.	2,772,700
1917	.	.	.	.	.	.	.	.	.	3,061,400
1918	.	.	.	.	.	.	.	.	.	3,467,300
1919	.	.	.	.	.	.	.	.	.	4,125,000
1920	.	.	.	.	.	.	.	.	.	5,047,800
1921	.	.	.	.	.	.	.	.	.	4,781,300
1922	.	.	.	.	.	.	.	.	.	4,027,400
1923	.	.	.	.	.	.	.	.	.	3,622,000
1924	.	.	.	.	.	.	.	.	.	3,536,100

The rise and fall of union membership appear clearly to result from

the *abnormal* and forced nature of the preceding expansion. If we examine the figures of growth from 1917 to 1919, we shall find that the war policy of the government was by far the greatest factor, for it was the government that opened the doors to unionism in industries heretofore closed—not that unionism *forced* the doors open by its own strength. The government, by virtue of its war time power and prestige, gave the unions the all-important right to organize against a temporarily confounded and half-rebellious employing group. . . . On the contrary, the unions which best maintained their membership strength were those which had received no or only incidental aid from the government during the war.[28]

THE RAILROAD INDUSTRY EXPERIENCE

The evolution of the duty to bargain took a different course in the railroad industry than elsewhere. The conspicuousness and unpopularity of railroad disputes, and the unquestioned power of Congress to regulate interstate commerce were major reasons for the statutory regulation of railroad labor since 1888. But the industry's distinctive characteristic, the one which led to government intervention, was the strength of its labor organizations.

The importance of the early railroad labor legislation was due to the explicit recognition of the role of collective bargaining as the method of determining the conditions of employment. The first national labor law, the Act of 1888, provided two main methods of settling disputes. The first was a system of voluntary arbitration in which the government power was invoked in the form of a Board of Arbitration with the authority to subpoena witnesses and to receive testimony and records. The arbitration award was to be transmitted to the Commissioner of Labor, whose duty was limited to publishing it. It is important to emphasize that arbitration was wholly voluntary, in both the submission of a dispute and compliance with the terms of the award. Not surprisingly, in the ten-year life of the statute this provision was never employed.[29]

At the suggestion of President Cleveland, the statute also incorporated a second provision which, although little noticed at the time, was to become a standard feature of later government action in labor disputes. This was the authorization for the President to appoint an investigating committee at the request of either party to a dispute, at the suggestion of a state governor, or on the President's own motion. This committee "shall constitute a temporary commission for the purpose of examining the causes of the controversy, the conditions accompanying, and the best means for adjusting it."[30] The commission's report was to be transmitted to the Congress and the President, and presumably publicized. Although the recommendations were to have no enforceable power, President Cleveland thought they would have "a most salutary influence in the settlement of disputes between conflicting interests."[31]

This provision of the law was to be invoked only once, after the unsuccessful ending of the Pullman strike in 1894. The strike itself had been occasioned by the discharge of three members of an employees' grievance committee and the subsequent refusal of the company to deal with the union.[32] A sympathy strike undertaken by the American Railway Union led to the dispatching of federal troops to prevent the obstruction of the mails which was a by-product of the strike, and to enforce court orders against the strike leaders. The recommendations of the strike commission inferentially condemned the conduct of the Pullman Company by proposing a permanent government commission with enforceable powers, by endorsing the principle of collective bargaining, and by recommending that pending investigation of a dispute, and for six months following an award, a railroad should not be allowed to discharge employees except for certain specified reasons.[33]

Widespread dissatisfaction with the Act of 1888 led to the passage of the Erdman Act in 1898; it passed both houses of Congress by overwhelming margins.[34] The act was not a hasty measure hustled through a reluctant Congress, but one which had been debated for over three years, with many hearings held during this time. All succeeding labor legislation passed by Congress in the railroad and other fields has been influenced in some way by the epoch-making features of this act.

The abiding significance of the Erdman Act was twofold. To begin with, it inaugurated a government policy for the mediation and conciliation of labor disputes. Unlike the Act of 1888, it provided that either party alone could invoke the aid of the United States Commissioner of Labor and the chairman of the Interstate Commerce Commission in the event of any controversy, and the commissioners were required to "put themselves in communication with the parties to such controversy and . . . use their best efforts, by mediation and conciliation to amicably settle the same." [35]

In the event that these efforts failed, the commissioners should attempt to get the parties to agree to a voluntary arbitration of the dispute, and the act provided a detailed procedure for such arbitration. Once arbitration had been agreed to, the award was to be final and binding. While the arbitration proceeding was pending, the status quo was to be maintained, with the carriers forbidden during this time to discharge employees and the unions required not to strike. Also, for three months after an award, thirty days' notice was required before employees were permitted to leave their employment or the carriers were free to discharge any employee. The award itself was to be binding for one year from the date of the rendering of the decision. Furthermore, the arbitration board was given authority to administer oaths and compel testimony through the use of subpoena power.

The second very important feature of the act was the protection to labor organizations contained in Section 10. It was made a misdemeanor for an employer to require the execution of an oral or written yellow dog contract from any employee as a condition of employment, to threaten or discriminate against any employee because of union membership, to require employees as a condition of employment to contribute money to any fund, to require employees to agree to release the employer from liability for accidents on the job by reason of the establishment of a contributory injury fund, and to black-list an employee for any reason after discharge.

It is remarkable that the strongest opposition to the Erdman Act came from the American Federation of Labor. The 1897 convention came out strongly against its passage [36] and Gompers inveighed against the bill as follows:

The Erdman Administration Bill, so called, is a piece of legislation destructive of the best interests of labor, ruinous of the liberties of our people; a step in the direction for the creation of an autocracy or an empire on the one side and a class of slaves and serfs on the other. Against such a condition of the affairs the whole sentiment . . . the entire interest of wage workers should be directed.[37]

Gompers finally withdrew his opposition in deference to the enthusiastic support given to the measure by the railroad brotherhoods, but only after succeeding, with the help of Andrew Furuseth, in removing seamen from the act's coverage.[38]

Very quickly the positive protection given to labor by Section 10 was held to be an unconstitutional violation of the right of contract of both employees and employer. The Supreme Court's majority opinion stated that "the employer and the employee have equality of right, and any legislation that disturbs that equality is an arbitrary interference with the liberty of contract which no government can legally justify in a free land." [39] The court also found no link between interstate commerce and the prohibited acts which would justify such a public policy: ". . . we hold that there is no such connection between interstate commerce and membership in a labor organization as to authorize Congress to make it a crime against the United States for an agent of an interstate carrier to discharge an employee because of such membership on his part."

Several curious features of the act reflected contemporary views on the role of unions. For example, arbitration awards were not binding upon individual employees who were not union members unless they assented in writing to being parties to the proceedings. Also, the act required that any union incorporated under an enabling act of Congress passed in 1886 had to expel any union member who was guilty of force or violence during a labor dispute.[40]

Until 1905, the mediation and conciliation provisions of the law were invoked only once and this case ended in failure since the carrier involved refused to participate. However, from 1906 to 1913, when the law was superseded by the Newlands Act, it was successfully invoked on sixty-one occasions covering 250,000 employees. Most disputes were settled by mediation, although there were ten cases of mixed arbitration and mediation and six disputes which were settled by arbitration alone. All arbitration awards were observed by the parties.[41]

It is interesting to note that congressional hearings on the operations of the act indicated that application for mediation was made by unions in those cases where the number of employees was small and the union felt that it could not win a strike. On the other hand, where the number of employees was large, the rule was for the carrier to invoke the mediation services.[42]

Between the passage of the Erdman Act and its replacement by the Newlands Act of 1913, both the railroads and the unions changed their views on the nature and desirability of government intervention. Early in this period, the leadership of the railroad unions wholeheartedly endorsed arbitration of labor disputes, including legislation providing both the mechanism and the sanctions to make it effective. E. E. Clark, Grand Chief Conductor of the Order of Railway Conductors, summarized this position in a speech in 1900 in which he said, "We have submitted a good many cases and disputed points to arbitration and our experience has been such as to commend the employment of that agency in settling such disputes." [43]

But in a period of only ten years the attitude of management and labor to government intervention had shifted. As early as 1911, the president of the Wabash Railroad expressed the general opinion of railway management by supporting the creation of a permanent arbitration court with sufficient authority to compel arbitration and to enforce the award.[44] The following year a poll taken by the organ for railroad management revealed that "a large majority of the managers expressed themselves in favor of some plan for the fixation of wages of railway labor by the government."[45] The response of labor was hostile. The president of the Brotherhood of Locomotive Firemen and Enginemen stated:

I know of no proposition which would be so distasteful to working people in any class of employment as compulsory arbitration, even though it could be legally enforced. Without assuming the role of a ghoul and digging from history's graveyard the skeletons of the working men a century old, it can be readily shown that when the courts dictated the wages and working conditions of the working people they enjoyed but little greater privileges than those of serfs.[46]

The reasons for this shift in sentiment are not difficult to fathom. Not only had union membership increased considerably but the railway brotherhoods had begun systematically to combine together and present their demands as a unit. As one observer put it, ". . . the employees formerly felt that they were too weak to secure their demands by the strike and that it was necessary to look to some higher authority in order to secure justice. Therefore, they preferred to risk their case in the hands of a board working under government supervision."[47] The change in relative economic strength which resulted in a complete shutdown of a railroad during a strike appears to be sufficient explanation of the changes in attitude toward government intervention in general and arbitration in particular.[48]

THE NEWLANDS ACT

The passage of the Newlands Act in 1913 did not represent any new departure in public policy. A permanent Board of Mediation and Conciliation was established to perform the duties previously carried out by the Commissioner of Labor and the chairman of the ICC. These duties consisted of bringing the parties together for the purpose of settling a dispute and, if this step was unsuccessful, of inducing the acceptance of arbitration. But the new law went one step farther in another direction. In the event of a dispute as to the meaning or application of any agreement that had been negotiated under the mediative auspices of the board, either party had the right to apply to the board for an expression of opinion on the merits of the issue. Although the board was required to render an opinion, there was no sanction other than public opinion to enforce the award.[49] In effect, this made the Mediation and Conciliation Board "a quasi-judicial body for interpreting and applying agreements reached through mediation."[50]

Under the operation of the Newlands Act from 1913 to the end of 1919, the board handled 148 cases involving 586 railroads and covering 620,810 employees. Twenty-one cases were settled by a combination of mediation and arbitration, nineteen were adjusted by mutual agreement after the invocation of the act's procedures, and seventy were handled by mediation alone. The services of the board were requested by the railroads in twenty-nine cases, by individual employees in seventy-four cases, by joint request of management and labor in twenty-seven instances, in response to public request in two cases, and by the board acting on its own behalf in sixteen cases.[51]

THE ADAMSON ACT

The increasing economic strength of the unions based upon concerted action led to the formulation in 1916 of a demand for an eight-hour day. The response of management was a counterdemand for arbitration either under the

Newlands Act or before the Interstate Commerce Commission. This was rejected by the unions, which also refused to join the railroads in submitting the dispute for mediation to the Board of Mediation and Conciliation, preferring direct negotiation.

The difference in position of the unions and the railroads on government intervention was dramatically demonstrated in the events that preceded and followed the passage of the Adamson Act. The reluctance of the unions to use the services of the board was in large part based upon dissatisfaction with prior action, particularly with the standards used in the selection of neutral abritrators.[52] It is probable that the alacrity with which the carriers endorsed government intervention was based upon appraisal of the same experience from the point of view of management interests. As early as 1914, the head of the Southern Pacific Railroad, who was at that time president of the American Railway Association, proposed drastic changes in the Newlands Act which came close to requiring compulsory arbitration under government auspices.[53]

The breakdown of negotiations for the eight-hour day resulted in the intervention of President Wilson, who secured a promise from the unions not to strike provided a law was passed granting an eight-hour day. With extraordinary speed the legislative machinery was set in motion. The presidential request for an eight-hour day was made before Congress on August 29, 1916, and by September 2, after hearings and debate, both houses passed the bill introduced by Congressman Adamson, which was then signed into law on September 3. Although the Adamson law was to go into effect on January 1, 1917, a district court ruling of its unconstitutionality resulted in a renewal of the strike threat. Ignoring the provisions of the Newlands Act, the President appointed an *ad hoc* committee consisting of the Secretary of the Interior, the Secretary of Labor, the president of the Baltimore and Ohio Railroad, and the president of the American Federation of Labor. With the aid of the committee, negotiations between the brotherhoods and the carriers resumed and ended in a settlement granting the employees the eight-hour day, despite the fact that the constitutionality of the Adamson Act was still in the courts.[54]

The Supreme Court heard argument and issued its decision upholding the constitutionality of the Adamson Act with a celerity which matched its passage through Congress. On the same day that an agreement was reached with the aid of a presidential committee, the court sustained the act. But the sweep of the court's decision renewed the growing split between the brotherhoods and the carriers on the desirability of government intervention. Chief Justice White, speaking for the court, stated that:

We are of opinion that the reasons stated conclusively establish that from the point of view of inherent power the act which is before us is clearly within the legislative power of Congress to adopt, and that in substance and effect it amounted to an extension of its authority to compulsorily arbitrate the dispute between the parties by establishing as the subject matter of that dispute a legislative standard of wages operating and binding as a matter of law upon the parties. . . .[55]

Although railroad management resented the President's intervention during the negotiations which resulted in a settlement of the dispute, they were on the whole pleased by the court's decision. It seemed to them to justify the hope that further legislation might be expected in which compulsory arbitration would become part of collective bargaining. The organ for the railroads commented in this regard:

The important question now is, will our politics-ridden Congress have the patriotism and the courage to enact the legislation for the passage of which the Supreme Court has opened the way, and which the brotherhoods have so conclusively demonstrated is vitally necessary for the protection of the public?[56]

Despite the fact that union leadership had endorsed the passage of the act during the hearings on the bill,[57] the implications of the court's decision provoked dismay. The president of the Brotherhood of Locomotive Engineers testified in a congressional hearing that the unions had only acquiesced in the bill's passage and did not really want it. He further said, "But it was not our law; we did not have anything to do with the framing of it; we did not want it, and it was simply choked down our throats as a settlement of the case . . . and it never tasted good, and it does not taste good yet. I want to make that clear."[58] Although this sentiment may overstate the attitude of labor to the law, it appears to reflect accurately labor's reaction to *Wilson v. New.* Another statement to the same affect was the answer of the president of the Brotherhood of Railroad Trainmen when asked whether he had ordered a strike before the enactment of the Adamson Act. He said, "Absolutely; and now I wish to God that, regardless of the Adamson law, I had never recalled it."[59] President Gompers of the American Federation of Labor was outraged by the decision and viewed the consequences as heralding the end of the right to strike.[60]

WARTIME ADMINISTRATION OF THE RAILROADS

In accordance with prior statutory authorization, President Wilson took over the railroads on December 31, 1917, and appointed the Secretary of the Treasury as Director General of Railroads. In one of the first acts of government administration, a General Order was issued which forbade discrimination because of membership or non-membership in a labor organization.[61] The effect of this order was to secure the confidence of organized labor in the new administration, as well as to increase union membership greatly.[62]

Inasmuch as the government was now the employer, methods had to be devised for fixing and adjusting wages. An initial adjustment of wages was based upon the recommendation of a special commission composed of four eminent men.[63] Machinery was also created to handle all further wage questions by the establishment of a Board of Railroad Wages and Working Conditions, whose duties included the investigation of and submission of recommendations on wage inequalities, rules, working conditions, and "other matters affecting wages and conditions of employment referred to it by the Director General." [64]

During the first year of government operations, the Director General entered into national agreements with the brotherhoods incorporating the wage awards of the Board of Wages and Working Conditions as well as covering rules, hours, and other working conditions. These national agreements extended "to the whole transportation system the main rules and working conditions of the agreements formerly made with separate carriers.[65]

Similar national agreements were "negotiated and signed with the shop crafts organizations, stationary firemen and oilers, clerks and freight handlers, maintenance-of-way employees, and signalmen." [66]

The consequences of national agreements were dramatically improved working conditions for many employees, particularly for non-operating employees. The establishment of an eight-hour day and premium pay for overtime took place at a time when most non-operating employees worked a basic ten-hour day without punitive overtime. In addition, the standardization of working conditions resulted in the creating of job classification systems which made arbitrary employer action much more difficult and made the recognition of seniority the principal basis for promotions and layoffs.[67]

Another wartime innovation which was to have a permanent effect upon further legislation was the procedure set up for the handling of disputes about agreements and awards. Following the precedent of the presidential commission which settled the eight-hour day issue, Railroad Boards of Adjustments were set up for the purpose of settling "all controversies growing out of the interpretation or application of the provisions of the wage schedule or agreements which are not promptly adjusted by the officials and employees on any one of the railroads operated by the Government." [68] Three Adjustment Boards were set up, the first covering engineers, firemen, conductors, and trainmen, the second having jurisdiction over shop craft employees, and the third covering telegraphers, switchmen, clerks, and maintenance-of-way employees.

These boards were composed of an equal number of representatives of union officers and management officials, and a majority decision was necessary in order to dispose of the dispute. In the absence of a majority, a final decision was to be made by the Director General. In practically every case an agreement was reached by the board and few if any cases were submitted to the Director General. Altogether, 3,753 cases were handled by the boards, and of the number not withdrawn or compromised, the carriers won 1,799 decisions and the employees received favorable awards in 1,369.[69]

The creation of the Adjustment Boards was aptly described as a recognition of the principle of collective bargaining. Not only were the boards themselves a product of negotiations between the unions and the railroads, but the requirement that no dispute could be referred to the boards until it had been "handled in the usual manner by general committees of the employees up to and including the chief operating officer of the railroad" emphasized the duty of bargaining. Director General Hines stated, "On many of the largest roads all the disagreements had been settled by conference without having to bring them to the attention of the Adjustment Boards at all."[70]

The unions were particularly delighted with the operation of the Adjustment Boards. Not only did the procedure avoid compulsory arbitration but it institutionalized the national organizations as the legitimate spokesmen for employees. A former president of one of the brotherhoods, who was also a prominent member of the Railroad Administration, summed up the unions' position in stating:

> The work of these boards demonstrates not only the advisability of the creation of such boards, but the necessity of their continuance, either under Federal control of railroads or thereafter. The fact that boards are bipartisan without any "umpire" or "neutral member" and all of which members are experts in railroad agreement matters have led both officials and employees to have confidence not only in the fairness of decision reached but as to the technical ability of the members of the board to pass intelligently upon all controversies submitted for decision.[71]

Another measure of government aid to the railroad unions was the appointment of the president of the Brotherhood of Locomotive Firemen and Enginemen as the head of the Division of Labor within the Railroad Administration. The duties of the director of this division included general supervision over all labor matters as well as specifically assigned functions. Those involved acting for non-union employees in all controversies ranging from wages to working conditions.[72]

The consequences of the government operation of the railroads can be viewed in different ways. As an answer to the problems of a wartime government, its success seems clear. Strikes and other interferences with production were minimized and the average increase of wages appears to have been less than for the country as a whole. The conclusion of the Director General that labor peace was not purchased at the price of excessive wage increases appears justifiable.[73] But one conclusion remains indisputable: The unions rejoiced over and management resented the results of the government administration of the railroads.

THE TRANSPORTATION ACT OF 1920

As might be expected, the unions and the carriers presented different legislative proposals to handle labor matters. The extraordinary gains won by the unions during the war resulted in a complete reversal of their attitude toward government ownership of the railroads and united them behind the Plumb Plan, the essence of which was that "the operating and management of the railroads would in fact be virtually placed in the hands of the classified employees and railroad officials."[74] Although most of the leadership of the American Federation of Labor opposed government ownership, the railroad unions felt, as the head of the Machinist Union said, that labor had achieved more in three years of government control than in twenty-five years of private management; and this view resulted in an endorsement of the principle of government ownership by the 1920 convention of the federation.[75]

The views of management were more ambivalent. There was widespread resentment of the Railroad Administration's making use of union leaders and, above all, of the administration's negotiations and execution of national agreements. Former President Taft expressed their attitude by writing that the railroads propose that each company shall be permitted to deal collectively with the men in its employ and shall not be required to deal in the first instance with the national heads of labor organizations. This is real collective bargaining. . . . The primary unit of action is the shop railroad system in which the dispute arises. . . . Experience has shown that with full liberty to deal with their respective employees by themselves, many railway executives can fully and satisfactorily adjust working conditions, and wages, too. In such matters, local self-government is the essence of collective bargaining and not a straw should be put in the way of it.[76]

Despite the wartime experience, the railroads were not disposed to forgo government intervention. In particular, the appeal of compulsory arbitration to management was still strong. The proposal which unions fought most strongly, the Cummins bill, which passed the Senate, not only provided for compulsory arbitration over all disputes but made strikes a crime.[77]

The law which was finally passed, the Transportation Act of 1920, transferred the railroads back to private ownership and set up a new procedure for settling disputes in Title III.[78] Born in compromise and presenting no consensus on what the public policy should be, the provisions of the act have been described as

vague in their purposes, capable of a multiplicity of interpretations, and uncertain in their legal authority. They reflected an oversimplification of the problems of labor relations, as if disputes and strikes were the only evils involved and if these could be removed by decisions of a board or a series of boards on which all interests, including the public, were represented.[79]

The essence of the act consisted of an exhortation to labor and management to settle disputes among themselves; in the event of a failure to do so, all unresolved cases were to be referred to a new agency, the United States Railroad Labor Board. In view of the significance of the statutory language for future legislation, an examination of the statute appears appropriate.

Section 301 of the act expressed the legislative mandate as follows:

It shall be the duty of all carriers and their officers, employees, and agents to exert every reasonable effort and adopt every available means to avoid any interruption to the operation of any carrier growing out of any dispute between the carrier and the employees or subordinate officials thereof. All such disputes shall be considered and, if possible, decided in conference between representatives designated and authorized so to confer by the carriers, or the employees or subordinate officials thereof, directly interested in the dispute. If any dispute is not decided in such conference, it shall be referred by the parties thereto to the Board which under the provisions of this title is authorized to hear and decide such dispute.

On the basis of this principle, the structure of the act resembled closely the pattern of wartime regulations. Sections 302 and 303 provided for the establishment by mutual agreement of adjustment boards to "decide any dispute involving only grievances, rules, or working conditions, not decided as provided in Section 301 . . ." Section 304 set up a tripartite Railway Labor Board whose duties were to hear and decide all disputes involving grievances, work rules, or other working conditions not otherwise settled by conferences or adjustment boards. The board also had exclusive jurisdiction over all disputes involving changes in wage rates.

It is instructive to observe the way in which the new board read into the statute principles which were later to be incorporated into a general legal duty to bargain. The specific standards of behavior in bargaining which the board took to be required by the statute can be seen in the following decision:

. . . the conference . . . on the side of the carriers was merely a perfunctory performance of the statute. Nor was the action of the organizations with regard to the individual carriers more than per-functory. Naked presentations as irreducible demands of elaborate wage scales carrying substantial increases, or of voluminous forms of contract regulating working conditions, with instructions to sign on the dotted line, is not a performance of the obligation to decide disputes in conference if possible. The statute requires an honest effort by the parties to decide all matters in dispute in conference. . . .[80]

It is clear that the duty to avoid disputes and to meet in conference was considered to demand certain kinds of behavior. Certain acts were held to be inconsistent with the concept of negotiation: "perfunctory performance," "naked presentations of irreducible demands," insistence that the other party had "to sign on the dotted line" without more ado—all were departures from the statutory mandate. The development of the concept of good-faith bargaining is but an imperceptible step beyond the requirement that the parties engage "in an honest effort" in negotiations.

The board also decided that the statute required adherence to certain principles in making collective bargaining agreements: among others, that employees had the right to organize without interference, that there should be no discrimination against employees because of their membership or non-membership in a labor organization, that employees should have the right to be consulted before a decision adversely affecting their wages or working conditions was made by management, and that a majority of any class or craft of employees should choose the organization to represent them.[81]

It should be noted that the activities proscribed by the board were not specified as unlawful in the act; they were condemned as inequitable and inconsistent with the general tenor of the statute. For example, pursuant to these principles, the board early decided that the discharge of employees because of their union activity was "unfair, unjust and unreasonable" and ordered reinstatement with full back pay and restoration of all seniority rights.[82]

The board also had occasion to rule on the practice of contracting out work. To evade earlier board decisions on rules and wages and the necessity of negotiations, the carriers increasingly began to contract out certain kinds of construction work, such as bridge building and grading, to independent construction companies and to subsidiaries of the carriers. In a number of cases, the contracting included such traditional railroad work as repair of maintenance-of-way equipment and freight handling. The consequences of the carriers' action were the discharge of many union members and establishment of lower wages and more onerous working conditions for the employees who were assigned the work. The unions protested on the grounds of unilateral action and alleged a violation of board decisions. The board held in a series of cases that such contracts were violations of the Act of 1920 and directed the carriers to reinstate employees so displaced.[83]

The inability of the board to enforce its awards was soon demonstrated in the court decisions that followed the action of the Pennsylvania Railroad in establishing a company union and abrogating the bargaining rights of System Federation No. 90, which was affiliated with the AF of L. The railroad proceeded to hold an election for employee representatives with whom it negotiated and executed a contract on a company-wide basis. The System Federation conducted its own election and requested relief from the board. The board found that the railroad had violated its method for selection of representatives,[84] but before its decision could be published, the railroad secured a permanent injunction from a federal district court prohibiting the board from issuing its decision.[85] Subsequently the Supreme Court issued its decision which permitted the board to publish its decisions but interpreted the act as merely imposing a moral duty on the parties which was not enforceable through the courts. In the language of the court,

The decisions of the Labor Board are not to be enforced by process. The only sanction of its decision is to be the force of public opinion invoked by the fairness of a full hearing, the intrinsic justice of the conclusion, strengthened by the official prestige of the Board, and the full publication of the violation of such decision by any party to the proceeding.[86]

The reluctance of the government to raise wages after the war and before the return of the railroads to private management resulted in wage negotiations soon after the passage of the Act of 1920. The pressure for higher wages was exacerbated by the rapid rate of increase in the cost of living during this period. The breakdown of negotiations resulted in transfer of the issue of wage increases to the Railway Labor Board, which, after investigation and hearing, ordered wage increases averaging about 22 per cent for all employees. The basis of the decision was the finding

that the scale of wages paid railway employees is substantially below that paid for similar work in outside industry, that the increase in living cost since the effective date of General Order No. 27 and its supplements has thrown wages below the prewar standard of living of those employees, and that justice, as well as the maintenance of an essential industry in an efficient condition, require a substantial increase to practically all classes.[87]

This award was made in July, 1920, and was complied with. Soon afterward a serious recession took place which resulted in a management request for an immediate wage reduction, abrogation of the rules negotiated by the administration, and an end to national agreements. In June, 1921, the board issued an award which reduced wages by an average of about 12.2 per cent. However, the impact of the reduction was not uniform. Maintenance-of-way employees lost practically their entire increase won in the prior award, while other classifications fared somewhat better.[88]

In the following year the railroads applied to the board for additional cuts in wages, which were granted effective July 1, 1922, for non-operating employees. The superior economic strength of operating personnel enabled their unions to reach agreements which maintained the existing pay scale.[89] The labor members of the board vehemently dissented from the wage reductions and accused the board of being "unable to separate themselves from the partisan struggle long enough to perform the function for which they were appointed; and consequently it tends to absolve the employees from any limitation which the existence of a judicial board was intended to impose." To this criticism the majority responded with heat, "It is something new for labor members of the board to issue incendiary arguments to employees in favor of striking against a decision of the board. The minority are sowing some of the tiny seeds that have germinated and blossomed into industrial anarchy in Russia . . ."[90]

The same lack of unanimity characterized the board's decisions on rule changes; they vacillated between continuing national agreements and the wartime rules, as urged by the unions, and making changes requested by the carriers, and the net effect was a loosening of the principle of national agreements and the granting of numerous changes in rule schedules. The shop craft employees especially resented the change which ended premium pay for work on Sundays and holidays and the reinstitution of piecework.[91]

Events quickly moved to a head. Following the last wage reduction made by the board, the shopcraft unions wired a strike ultimatum to the carriers which protested against the refusal to establish adjustment boards as prescribed by the Act of 1920, and against the past violations by the railroads of board decisions in cases involving discrimination, establishing of company unions, and contracting out of work. The unions insisted upon a continuance of the current wage level regardless of the board reduction, and restoration of the wartime rules. The strike itself began on July 1, 1922; it involved 400,000 shop employees and was not only the greatest railroad strike in history but the first nation-wide strike.[92]

The first official action undertaken by the board occurred two days before the strike. It called for an immediate meeting of the unions who had threatened to strike and also of twenty-three carriers who had been previously charged with violating past board decisions on contracting out work. President Grable of the United Brotherhood of Maintenance-of-Way Employees and Railroad Shop Laborers testified that the wage reduction was not the only reason for the strike. Other reasons included

prior decisions of this Board not being carried out properly by the carriers; decisions of the Board being ignored on some properties in their entirety; rehearings had and decisions not yet carried out or applied; the contract labor propositions, which arbitrarily reduced maintenance-of-way employees' rates of pay; the matter of the eight-hour day, which some properties are trying to make a ten-hour day as a regular proposition—all these different things influenced the vote in favor of a strike.[93]

The next action of the board followed on the heels of the carriers' decision to recruit strike replacements who were promised permanent jobs. Strikers were also threatened with loss of seniority and other rights and would only be taken back, if at all, as new employees.[94] On the third day of the strike, the board issued a resolution which harshly condemned the strike and stated that inasmuch as the strikers were no longer employees, it was incumbent upon the carriers, the employees, and the strike replacements to form new organizations in order to carry out the purposes of the act.[95] The resolution considered the strike as one directed at the board's decisions and declared in strong terms that strike replacements

> are not strike breakers seeking to impose arbitrary will of an employer on employees; that they have the moral as well as the legal right to engage in such service of the American public as to avoid interruption of indispensable railway transportation; and that they are entitled to the protection of every department and branch of the Government, State and National.[96]

Although the board immediately issued two subsequent resolutions which to some extent undercut the impact of the "outlaw" resolution, the damage had already been done. One commentator said that it not only justified the strike-breaking activities of the carriers but "practically forced them to take such a stand. Moreover, it injected the issue of seniority into the controversy, which later became the most serious stumbling block in the way of a settlement."[97] The board soon lost all contact with the parties and the influence of the government on the strike came from other sources.

On the basis of long conferences with the unions and carriers, President Harding proposed a settlement plan with three points: all parties to agree to the validity of board decisions and to live up to them, the decisions of the board which occasioned the strike to be resubmitted for further hearings, and all employees to be returned to work with full seniority. The unions accepted the President's plan but the carriers objected to the third point, which would require the discharge of the strike replacements. The carriers based their objections upon the claim that the promise of permanent jobs for the strike replacements was "justified by the authoritative utterances of the Labor Board" and that the strikers were no longer employees of the railroads. Harding then refashioned his proposals to end the strike by having the board decide the question of seniority. This plan was rejected by the unions.[98]

As the strike continued, the original issues faded into the background. The most important issues were now the questions of seniority and national agreements.[99] Despite the hiring of strike replacements, the increase in the number of breakdowns resulted in a serious shortage of freight cars. There was reason to believe that the unions were justified in hoping that their terms would be met if the situation continued.[100] However, the Attorney General of the United States intervened and secured a sweeping injunction from a federal district court which prohibited all activity in furtherance of the strike. The injunction was directed not only at union officers and members but at "all persons acting in aid of or in conjunction with them." The order banned picketing and any communication whatsoever between any individual, whether or not a union member or officer, and any other individual for the purpose of continuing the strike. Furthermore, the union officers were directed not to issue any instructions, requests, public statements, or any other suggestions to their members to further the strike and a prohibition was obtained against the use of any union money for the same purpose. The original order was slightly amended several weeks later in order to permit the use of union money to help strikers' families and to permit meetings of union members for purposes other than that connected with the strike itself.[101]

The strike was effectively broken. A historian has summed up this episode by writing, "It was a period when the postwar reaction was in full force, and the government was plainly on the side of employers in their efforts to push back the unions to their less powerful prewar positions."[102] One of the casualties of the shopmen's strike was the Railway Labor Board. In part, this was due to the departure in the

Transportation Act of 1920 from the principles of mediation which had been worked out in the prior legislation. And notwithstanding the substantive merits of the board's decisions, its lack of enforceable authority reduced it to futility.

THE RAILWAY LABOR ACT OF 1926

The absence of any machinery to handle labor disputes in the railroad industry created pressure for new legislation. Experience had taught both management and labor that government intervention was not always predictable.

On December 6, 1923, the President stated in a message to Congress:

The settlement of railway labor disputes is a matter of grave public concern. The labor board was established to protect the public in the enjoyment of continuous service by attempting to insure justice between the companies and their employees. It has been a great help, but is not altogether satisfactory to the public, the employees, or the companies. If a substantial agreement can be reached among the groups interested, there should be no hesitation in enacting such agreement into law. If it is not reached, the labor board may very well be left for the present to protect the public welfare.[103]

In response, conferences were held between the railroads and the railroad unions which resulted in an agreement on what was to be the Railway Labor Act of 1926. This act has been described as "written under the direction and approval of hard-headed, practical, successful men. It was not the academic product of a mythical brain trust. It was the expression of the agreed opinion of substantially all the employers and employees of one of our greatest, most essential industries."[104]

No railroad appeared before the congressional committees to oppose the bill and it was supported by all the standard railroad unions.[105] The basic reason why the law was passed in almost the form agreed upon by the carriers and unions was expressed in a congressional report:

The proponents of this bill have assured the committee of their conviction that the methods for voluntary settlement of disputes with the aid of Government mediators are so well adapted to insure the adjustment of differences, either through conference, mediation, or arbitration, that it should be seldom, if ever, necessary for the President to exercise the power conferred upon him to appoint an emergency board. The records of the success of mediation and arbitration under the Erdman and Newlands Acts considerably justify this conviction, which is also supported by the obvious good faith, the spirit of fair play, and of genuine regard for the public interest which characterized the negotiations of the parties and their presentations before the committee.[106]

The structure of the Railway Labor Act of 1926, like all its major substantive features, had its origin in the prior railroad legislation. In effect, the act represented a distillation of past experience, and the only novelty was the particular combination of procedures incorporated in it. In brief, the act can be viewed as affirming the principle of collective bargaining in the railroad industry, making the duty of bargaining legally enforceable, and providing certain procedures as instruments of this policy.

The protection to labor organizations first extended in the Erdman Act and later put in practice by the United States Railroad Administration during the war found expression in Section 2 of the act. This section stated:

It shall be the duty of all carriers, their officers, agents, and employees to exert every reasonable effort to make and maintain agreements concerning rates of pay, rules, and working conditions, and to settle all disputes, whether arising out of the application of such agreements or otherwise, in order to avoid any interruption to commerce or to the operation of any carrier growing out of any dispute between the carrier and the employees thereof.[107]

Further support of the principle of collective bargaining

43

was spelled out in Section 2. In the language of the statute, all disputes "shall be considered, and, if possible, decided with all expedition, in conference between the representative designated and authorized so to confer, respectively, by the carriers and by the employees thereof interested in the dispute."

In addition, representatives for the purposes of collective bargaining were to be chosen "without interference, influence, or coercion, exercised by either party over the self-organization or designation of representatives by the other." This provision was clearly aimed at the company-dominated unions which were flourishing in many railroads, particularly among the shop crafts.

The rest of the act spells out alternative procedures to be followed by the carriers and the unions in the settlement of all disputes. For example, all disputes arising out of grievances or the interpretation or application of collective bargaining agreements could be handled in the following ways. First, a duty was imposed upon both parties to confer about such a dispute within a time not to exceed twenty days from the receipt of a request for negotiation. A second method of adjusting grievances was contained in Section 3, which provided that boards of adjustment "shall be created by agreement between any carrier or group of carriers, or the carriers as a whole and its or their employees." The procedure provided for the invocation of a board of adjustment only after prior negotiations had failed to settle the matter. Furthermore, the statute stipulated that the numbers of representatives from labor and management were to be equal. However, adjustment boards were not considered to be an exclusive method of settling disputes, since Section 3 also provided that alternative methods independent of adjustment boards could be arrived at by agreement.

The third method of adjusting disputes was the creation

of a Board of Mediation, whose functions had already been developed in large part by the mediatory provisions of the Erdman and Newlands Acts. The jurisdiction of the Mediation Board covered all disputes, specifically including those arising out of grievances not successfully settled by agreement or through adjustment boards, bargaining issues such as changes in wage rules and working conditions, and finally, "any other dispute not decided in conference between the parties." In the event that the Mediation Board was unable to bring the parties together, the statute required it "to induce the parties to submit their controversy to arbitration in accordance to the provisions of this act." The Mediation Board was also authorized to issue an advisory opinion on the meaning or application of any contractual provision under dispute, at the request of either or both parties.

The arbitration provisions of the act covered in considerable detail the powers of the arbitration board and the procedure to be followed. The agreement to arbitrate had to be in writing, to stipulate that the arbitration was to be under the act, to spell out the size of the arbitration board, to state specifically the issues to be submitted to the board, and, among other details, to provide that the award should be final and conclusive. Any disagreement as to the meaning or application of the arbitration award itself was to be arbitrated.

The unions' resistance to compulsory arbitration resulted in a proviso that the failure or refusal of any party to arbitrate a dispute was not a violation of any legal obligation imposed by the act. However, in the event that an unsettled dispute threatened to "interrupt interstate commerce to a degree such as to deprive any section of the country of essential transportation service," the Board of Mediation was authorized to so notify the President, who could, at his

45

discretion, "create a board to investigate and report respecting such dispute."

Section 10 also provided that there should be no change "in the conditions out of which the dispute arose" after the creation of the board, which had to make a report within thirty days of its formation, and for an additional thirty days after the issuance of its report. The Congress clearly intended this provision to prohibit a strike during the sixty-day period.[108]

Past experience was also reflected in the procedure and powers of the emergency board. In the first place, each board was to be an *ad hoc* body in order to avoid the accumulated hostility which rendered the Railway Labor Board ineffective. In order to assuage labor sensitivity to compulsory arbitration, the emergency board was not given the subpoena power. In any case, the Congress did not think this important because of "the practical fact that the merits of the case will turn on large and easily ascertained considerations and that neither party could decline to give all the information desired by the board without the certainty of the concentration of public opinion against that party."[109]

Without question, the unions were reluctant to accept the emergency board. One commentator noted that the waiting period was "the first time that organized labor ever agreed to such a postponement of action by a strike."[110] Labor's attitude was summed up in a Senate report which stated that it had been "informed that in agreeing to the emergency board the representatives of the employees had gone further than they had ever gone before in the history of their organizations, that they could go no further as a matter of agreement."[111]

The act also provided in Section 6 for the procedure to be followed in changing wages, rules, and other working conditions. Thirty days' notice of intention of making such a change had to be given to the other party, and negotiations had to be arranged within thirty days of such notice. The carriers were forbidden to change wages or working conditions until the various alternative procedures specified in the act had been invoked.

THE 1934 AMENDMENTS TO THE RAILWAY LABOR ACT

The onset of the depression and a concomitant shift in the climate of opinion resulted in additional legislation. Since the protection accorded to unions by the Norris-LaGuardia Act did not apply to railroads run by receivers or operating under court control, Senator Norris succeeded in incorporating an amendment to the 1933 Bankruptcy Act which in effect prohibited such railroads from interfering with the organizational methods of employees, outlawed the yellow dog contract, and ended company assistance or domination of unions.[112] The labor provisions of the Bankruptcy Act were extended to the entire railroad industry in the Emergency Transportation Act of 1933.[113] Upon the pending expiration of this act, hearings were held which resulted in the 1934 amendments to the Railway Labor Act. The essential principle of the amended act was its repeated emphasis on collective bargaining through labor organizations. The basic changes were setting up of national adjustment boards to handle grievances growing out of the interpretation of contracts, the specific provision for the holding of elections, the establishment of the majority rule principle, and regulation of specific unfair labor practices on the part of employers which includes the prohibition of the company-dominated union, the ending of the yellow dog contract, and a specific imposition of a duty to bargain.

The hostility to company unions was so strong that the

1934 amendment prohibited the union shop and dues deduction in the form of checkoffs. Although the national labor organizations would have preferred to retain union security, they consented to the ban.[114]

The principles established by the amended act have been described as

the culmination of 45 years of experience with legislation to govern the relations of employers and employees on the railroads and to promote peace and order in those relations as a means of preventing interruptions to interstate commerce . . . These principles would be mere verbiage and incapable of effective, practical operation if the act did not endow the parties with definite legal rights and impose corresponding duties on them. Thus for about a hundred years wage earners in this country have had what has been called a "right" to organize. But because no corresponding duty was imposed on employers to refrain from trespassing on that right, and they were free to refuse to deal with organized employees and to destroy labor organizations by any means at their command, the so-called right of the employees was meaningless except as they could enforce it by strikes and other means of industrial warfare.[115]

The evolution of public policy in railroad labor relations served more than the needs of the industry. The stage was set for a wider application of certain fundamental principles promoting the institution of collective bargaining. It must be noted again that the chief characteristic of the transportation industry was the strength of its labor organizations. The effect of a mandatory duty to bargain in such circumstances was to strengthen its role in industries where collective bargaining either was non-existent or had a fragile foothold.

CHAPTER 3 · THE LEGISLATIVE HISTORY OF THE WAGNER ACT—THE DEVELOPMENT OF THE NEW DEAL COLLECTIVE BARGAINING POLICY[1]

In order to understand the Wagner Act, some acquaintance with its legislative history is essential. Indeed, the Supreme Court has stated that to interpret the act "We must look . . . to the language of the statute, read in the light of its purpose and its legislative history."[2] Another court has used the preamble to the act as evidence of congressional intent.[3]

However, it would be inadequate and misleading to treat Senate Bill 1958 (74th Congress, 1st Session), which was enacted into law as the "Wagner Act," without some discussion of the New Deal collective bargaining policy of which this was the culmination.[4]

The first New Deal measure relating to collective bargaining was Section 7(a) of the National Industrial Recovery Act, which was signed into law on June 16, 1933.[5] For our purpose, the pertinent part of Section 7(a) was the following:

Every code of fair competition, agreement, and license approved, prescribed, or issued under this title shall contain the following conditions: (1) that employees shall have the right to organize and bargain collectively with representatives of their own choosing, and shall be free of the interference, restraint, or coercion of employers of labor, or their agents, in a designation of such representatives or in self-organization or in other concerted activities for the purpose of collective bargaining or other mutual aid or protection; (2) that no employee and no one seeking employment shall be required as a condition of employment to join any company union or to refrain from joining, organizing, or assisting a labor organization of his own choosing and (3) that employers shall comply with the maximum hours of labor, minimum rates of pay, and other conditions of employment, approved or prescribed by the President.

After the passage of the act, the question immediately arose whether employers subscribing to the code were obliged to bargain with unions. In the view of one commentator the vagueness of the statutory language appeared to allow an interpretation which would not "force the making of collective agreements, compel union agreements . . . did not rule out individual bargaining; . . . did not designate trade unions expressly as the agents for collective bargaining; it did not call for wage agreements, bilaterally binding . . ." [6] Another writer believed that in Section 7(a) employers' bargaining with the union was reaffirmed as a privilege "rather than newly set up as a right imposing upon employers the definite duty to bargain collectively with their employees." [7] This writer could see nothing in Section 7(a) which "lays upon the employers any duty, even to recognize, much less to bargain with, and still less to make a bargain with, their employees." [8] Still another writer could not find that Section 7(a) established any duty of an employer to recognize or deal with unions. [9] However, considerable legislative history indicated that the draftsmen of the bill expected to encourage the process of collective bargaining. [10]

A review of the legislative history of Section 7(a) discloses no clear-cut, definite congressional intent as to its meaning. Of some forty-five witnesses who appeared at the hearings before the House Ways and Means Committee, only four or five referred to Section 7(a).[11] The witnesses who spoke on Section 7(a) were either labor leaders such as President William Green of the American Federation of Labor, or supporters of protective labor legislation such as Senator Robert F. Wagner. On the floor of the House, Section 7(a) received very hurried consideration. Only two references were made to the provision, both by supporters. A representative comment was that made by Congressman Kelly of Pennsylvania, who stated that the import of Section 7(a) can be summed up as follows: ". . . we are here frankly recognizing the right of workers to organize and bargain collectively. It is an inherent God-given right, and granting it without equivocation will put a solid foundation under the structure of industrial justice." [12]

Although testimony in the hearings before the Senate Committee on Finance dealt with Section 7(a) at more length, it did not generate a consensus on its meaning. Industry spokesmen generally attacked this section, while witnesses friendly to labor supported it. One witness, Donald Richberg, who had played an active role in drafting the entire bill as well as the Railway Labor Act of 1926 and the Norris-LaGuardia Act of 1932, gave his view that the bill would mean "that the employee would have in such an industry the right to bargain with management as to the terms or conditions affecting labor." [13]

It seems safe to conclude that the provisions of Section 7(a) were sufficiently vague to have different meanings to different men. One commentator, indeed, sums up the background and philosophy of Section 7(a) as follows: "It is entirely accurate to say that Congress in the adoption of the Section had in mind no clear-cut ideas of collective bargaining." [14]

The vagueness of the statute immediately gave rise to conflicting interpretations. On the day that the act was

51

passed, President Roosevelt stated: "Workers, too, are here given a new charter of rights long sought and hitherto denied." [15] In general, union spokesmen felt that the bill as enacted into law protected and encouraged collective bargaining and provided for its use in the making of codes. [16]

At issue was what kind of collective bargaining was envisaged in the section. Many employers in such industries as iron and steel, rubber, chemicals, and automobiles immediately formed company unions, holding the view that they were not only permitted but encouraged by the statute. By November, 1933, 400 manufacturing and mining companies out of 653 surveyed had established company plans involving bargaining between the employer and a company-sponsored union. [17]

On August 5, 1933, President Roosevelt approved the proposal of NRA Industrial and Labor Advisory Boards to create a National Labor Board. Although its enabling authority was vague, the purpose and major functions of the board was to administer and enforce the provisions of Section 7(a). The board had three members with Senator Wagner as its chairman. Initially, its major work was to mediate and conciliate labor disputes. [18] The deluge of cases which immediately began to flood the board necessitated the creation of regional boards.

The board was confronted with the task of interpreting on a case-by-case basis the meaning of Section 7(a). Primarily, this meant definition and elucidation of the employer's duties under the statute. The problem before the board has been aptly stated by Professor Spencer:

[The Board] might have said that the statute merely protects workers in their right to organize for the purpose of effective bargaining with employers, or that the statute requires an employer to bargain collectively with employees and reach an agreement with them. Under the first interpretation, the right to organize is the important fact, and the matter of collective bargaining is an incident. Under the second, the employer's duty to make collective agreements is the important fact, and the right to organize is an incident.[19]

The first case arising under the National Labor Board in which the board found that the employees' right to bargain collectively imposes a corresponding duty on the employer was decided on February 21, 1934. In this case a majority of the employees had formed a federal labor union. The president of the union and an active member were discharged, and a strike soon followed. The employees urged the company to recognize their rights under Section 7(a) and offered to return to work if the company would agree not to discriminate against any of the strikers. This offer was met by a company counterproposal which restricted the statutory rights of the employees.

A mediator from the Department of Labor entered the dispute at the request of the National Labor Board. His proposal that the strike be ended, that all strikers be reinstated without prejudice, and that the employees afterwards choose representatives for the purposes of collective bargaining was met by a company offer to reinstate old employees and to employ new workers at its own discretion. In addition, the company refused to take back fourteen designated employees on the grounds of their activity in the union. The company also insisted that representatives chosen by its employees for purposes of collective bargaining be limited to employees of the company. The union rejected this point as inconsistent with the law.

In the meantime two injunctions had been secured by the employer, and the employees had returned to work. The company thereupon helped form a company union which included assistant foremen among its officers. Negotiations between the federal labor union and the company were completely blocked by the company's inflexible position.

53

The board's decision on the statutory duty of the employer in this case ran as follows:

The collective bargaining envisaged by the statute involves a quality of obligation—an obligation on the part of the employees to present grievances and demands to the employer before striking, and an obligation on the part of the employer to discuss differences with the representatives of the employees and to exert every reasonable effort to reach an agreement on all matters in dispute. Negotiations should precede rather than follow the calling of the strike. But no matter how grievous the fault of the employees may have been in striking before exhausting every possible means of reaching an amicable adjustment of differences, there was and can be no justification for the infringement by the employer of the statutory rights of his employees.[20]

Upon making a specific finding that the employer had interfered with the rights of its employees to organize and bargain collectively, the board ruled that the strike should be called off immediately; that all strikers who wished to be reinstated should be placed without discrimination on a preferential hiring list before any new employees were hired (with the exception of employees guilty of misconduct during the strike, as determined by the board after a hearing); and that an election should be held to choose representatives for the purpose of collective bargaining. All strikers were to be eligible to vote in this election.[21]

In another case in which the board interpreted Section 7(a) as imposing a similar duty on the employer, the board stated:

The record reveals a deplorable misconception by the company of the nature and meaning of collective bargaining. Peaceful relations between management and labor can only result from a display of mutual trust and confidence. Agreement is possible wherever the will to agree is present. The peremptory rejection of the employees' proposal and the refusal to enter into negotiations with the representatives of the employees are repugnant to the very concept of collective bargaining.[22]

In another case, the board stated "that Section 7(a) . . . creates rights in employees and imposes reciprocal obligations upon employers."[23]

Still another case in which the board found a duty of the employer to bargain was the *Matter of Whatcom County Dairymen's Association.*[24] In its decision the board commented:

It is unseemly for the Association to resent the exercise by its employees of the right of self-organization which the Association itself enjoys under the sanction of the law. Individual bargaining is fair only where equality of economic power prevails. Where there is disparity in bargaining power, there must be pooling of the resources of those suffering from the inequality in order to place them upon a parity in their bargaining relationships.[25]

The meaning and content of collective bargaining were gradually worked out as the cases reached the board. In one case, bargaining by an employer was considered to require the making of "an earnest, genuine, and conscientious effort to arrive at an agreement on the matters in controversy."[26]

In language indicative of what was to come, the National Labor Board stated in another decision:

The statute requires the employer to meet with the duly chosen representatives of its employees, whether an employee or an outside union, and to negotiate actively in good faith to reach an agreement. . . . Summary rejection of employees' demands and restriction of communication to others do not constitute compliance with the statute.[27]

In an earlier case, the board made this significant comment upon the objective of the statute:

The objective sought by the law is the making of collective agreements. The obligation of the statute is satisfied if both parties approach the negotiations with a sincere intention to agree and if every reasonable effort is made to reach an agreement. The nature and contents of the collective arrangement are matters for negotiation.[28]

This decision went on to hold that a company had violated Section 7(a) by refusing to make an agreement with the union as such rather than reaching an agreement with its employees or with individuals representing its employees.

In a number of other cases, the board has held that employees may select any representatives of their own choosing as their agents for collective bargaining and that the employer may not restrict this statutory right.[29] Of great interest was the wording of a decision of the Petroleum Labor Policy Board on the relationship between an election and collective bargaining. The decision stated: "The election of representatives is merely incidental to the exercise of the right to bargain collectively, because it is through representatives that a collective bargain is arrived at."[30]

The principle that the majority of the employees within a given plant or department was the exclusive collective bargaining agent for the entire plant or department was established in a number of decisions.[31]

The board had often recommended that when an agreement had been reached between a union and an employer it should be reduced to writing and executed.[32] The board has also held that Section 7(a) established new rights for employees which cannot be impaired by a company union.[33]

The ambiguity and vagueness of the authority of the National Labor Board resulted in an executive order on February 1, 1934, to provide for the enforcement of Section 7(a). This order gave the board authority, when a question of representation existed, to conduct elections and to "publish promptly" the names of the representatives chosen by a majority of the employees voting. Exclusive representational rights were granted to the majority organization. Moreover, once the majority of the employees had chosen their representatives and the National Labor Board had certified the names of these representatives to the employer, authority was given to the board to determine on the basis of a complaint or on its own motion whether

such an employer has declined to recognize or to deal with said representatives, or is in any way refusing to comply with the requirements of said Section 7(a), and the Board shall report its determination promptly to the Administrator for Industrial Recovery for appropriate action.[34]

Because of a growing split within the administration on the question of the universal application of the principle of majority rule, this executive order was amended on February 23, 1934, by removing from the administrator of the NRA his discretionary powers to enforce the board's order and by providing that the board may "report such findings and make appropriate recommendations to the Attorney General or to the Compliance Division of the National Recovery Administration."[35] This executive order, of course, confirmed the National Labor Board's interpretation that Section 7(a) imposed a duty upon an employer to bargain with representatives of his employees.

THE FIRST WAGNER BILL, 1934

Widespread non-compliance with the decisions of the National Labor Board resulted in activity designed to embody the board's principles in a permanent statute. The culmination of these activities was Senator Wagner's introduction in the Senate of a labor disputes bill, S. 2926. This bill, unlike other New Deal legislation, was not drafted in the executive departments but in Senator Wagner's office with the aid and consultation of public officials and representatives of the labor movement.[36]

The preamble of the bill stated that its purpose was "to equalize the bargaining power of employers and employees." Section 5 of Title I established unfair labor practices; in

Section 5(2) an employer was forbidden "to refuse to recognize and/or deal with representatives of his employees, or to fail to exert every reasonable effort to make and maintain agreements with such representatives concerning wages, hours, and other conditions of employment." [37]

In introducing the bill Senator Wagner said that its purpose was to "clarify and fortify the provisions of Section 7(a) of the National Industrial Recovery Act, and to provide means of administering them through the legislative establishment of a National Labor Board with adequate enforcement powers." [38] After stating that the greatest obstacle to collective bargaining was the company-dominated union, Wagner asserted that a

major defect of Section 7(a) is that it guarantees employees the right to organize, but not the right to recognition. My six months' experience as Chairman of the National Labor Board has proved conclusively to me that the second guarantee should be firmly established by Congress. Over 70 per cent of the disputes coming before the Labor Board have been caused by the refusal of employers to deal with representatives chosen by their workers. The new bill, if enacted into law, will remedy this evil. It is modeled upon the successful experience of the Railway Labor Act, which provides that employers shall actually recognize duly chosen representatives and make a reasonable effort to deal with them and to reach satisfactory collective agreements.[39]

In the hearings which followed the introduction of the bill, considerable testimony was given on the duty to bargain imposed by paragraph 2 of Section 5. Professor Slichter was opposed to it because he thought it merely expressed a pious wish which was not only meaningless but patently unenforceable.[40] Other witnesses, however, relied heavily upon experience of the National Labor Board in defense of this section. A member of the National Labor Board, Dr. Francis J. Haas, testified as follows:

58

Again and again cases have come before the National Labor Board in which the employer flagrantly violated Section 7(a) but took refuge in the claim that he observed the language of the statute. He made the defense that he met, received, and conferred with representatives of his employees. In one extreme instance an employer came to the National Labor Board and held that he had observed the law, although it was clear that he has had no intention of coming to an agreement. He had held conversations with the workers' representatives extending over several weeks and climaxed a 2 days' negotiation with them in Washington by throwing them along with their attorney in jail on their return home. Paragraph 2 of Section 5 of the bill is therefore of utmost importance, especially that passage which requires the employer "to exert every reasonable effort to make and maintain agreements" with representatives of the employees.[41]

Strong support for the measure came from such labor union leaders as John L. Lewis, who also adverted to the experience under the National Labor Board.[42]

The members and staff of the National and Regional Labor Boards cited cases in explaining their support for Section 5(2). For example, Dr. John A. Lapp, Chairman of the Bituminous Coal Labor Board of Division 2, referred to his experience in giving his view of what collective bargaining means. Dr. Lapp stated:

Meeting the employees is one thing and bargaining is quite another thing. We have had ever so many instances—not in the coal business, because that is organized—but in the other lines of industry where men have said, "Yes, I will meet my men; I have always been willing to meet my men; I will meet a committee of my men at any time—" but they have added, "I will not agree with them, I will not bargain with them, I will not do as they ask me to." In other words, in advance agreeing that they will disagree on anything that is proposed by the employees. . . . Now, it is essential that we have some means by which men who are required to have collective bargaining go beyond the mere meeting and discussion, and the bill does specifically provide that they must observe every reasonable effort to bring about collective bargaining. That is to my mind the most essential fact, and the machinery set up in this bill will have its main duty in

59

seeing to it that the bargain is actually made or that every reasonable effort is exerted to make that bargain.[43]

Another witness, Dr. William Leiserson, Chairman of the Petroleum Labor Policy Board, strongly disagreed with Professor Slichter on Section 5(2). Dr. Leiserson pointed out that this section was copied from the Railway Labor Act and stated that if labor were given the right to organize but no corresponding obligation to deal with the union were imposed on the employer, then the act would mean nothing at all. He further commented:

Now, I think it is exceedingly important that it should stay in the bill. It should not be thrown out on the theory "Well, you cannot enforce that anyway." If we can say, if the administrators of the law can say to an employer, "Now, you really haven't tried to agree with them, so that we will avoid a strike. They have elected their representatives. Now sit down and make an honest effort, the way the law says." [44]

Employer representatives also discussed Section 5(2) and made their opposition to it clear. A witness representing the National Association of Manufacturers thought that an employer should deal with the union only if he saw fit.[45] Another employer representative considered this section one of the most vital provisions of the act. He furthermore interpreted Section 5(2) in the light of existing decisions of the National Labor Board, saying, in part, that the National Labor Board has taken it "on themselves to decide a matter of intent, and to decide that the employers are stalling in making agreements, or not using every endeavor, or not using good faith in agreeing to a proposal." [46] Moreover, the witness feared that this section would be held like a club over the heads of all employers so that a failure to reach an agreement for whatever reason would be made an unfair labor practice.

For a number of reasons, S. 2926 was reported out of committee with drastic revisions.[47] One of the provisions eliminated was the duty to bargain, although the bill, which could be fairly described as the Walsh bill, contained a prohibition of employer activity which interfered with the right of employers to "engage in concerted activities for the purpose of collective bargaining."

The absence of an explicit duty to bargain was not accidental. The evidence indicates that although Senator Walsh believed in protecting the right to join a union, he placed less emphasis on the government's role in protecting and fostering collective bargaining.[48] Senator Walsh's view of the bill's purpose is illustrated by the following remark:

> The bill indicates the method and manner in which employees may organize, the method and manner of selecting their representatives or spokesmen, and leads them to the office door of their employer with the legal authority to negotiate for their fellow employees. The bill does not go beyond the office door. It leaves the discussion between the employer and the employee, and the agreements which they may or may not make, voluntary and with that sacredness and solemnity to a voluntary agreement with which both parties to an agreement should be enshrouded.[49]

However, the report which Walsh submitted to the Senate with his bill gave a number of indications that the duty to bargain was not completely lost. For example, the Senate report discussed at some length the wealth of precedents upon which the Walsh bill had drawn, including the experience of the National Labor Board with specific reference to Executive Order No. 6580 of February 1, 1934, and to the Executive Order No. 6612-A of February 23, 1934, which asserted and affirmed the NLB's authority to require employers to bargain.

Also cited in support of the Walsh bill was Section 2 of the Railway Labor Act, which made it mandatory for employers "to exert every reasonable effort to make and maintain agreements" with the representatives of their employees. And, significantly, the Walsh report stated that "the policy of the Government is founded upon the theory of democratic collective bargaining" which "means the exchange of ideas." It is extremely difficult to conclude that any law which affirms and protects the right of organization would be satisfied if an employer only agreed mechanically to meet with a union and to do nothing more. Indeed, the Walsh report stated that an "employer will presumably make a reasonable effort to reach an agreement with his workers or their representatives when and if they seek to negotiate with him; but the terms of that agreement are for the parties to settle by collective bargaining." [50] Senator Walsh never addressed himself to the question of whether or not his bill reached those employers who failed to make a reasonable effort to reach an agreement. Taking into consideration the precedents established by the National Labor Board with a far weaker mandate, it is not unlikely that in the administration of a statute similar to the Walsh bill, the affirmation of the right to join unions would have generated a corollary duty of employers to bargain in good faith.

PUBLIC RESOLUTION NO. 44

The inability to secure passage of the Walsh bill in the closing days of an election year resulted in the introduction of Public Resolution No. 44. This resolution was personally drafted by President Roosevelt on the basis of drafts prepared by two aides.[51] Its essence was a grant of authority to hold secret ballot elections without the consent of the employer. The resolution has been described as ". . . at bottom a compromise which avoided the basic issues raised by the NLB's efforts to interpret and apply Section 7(a)," [52] and as "... a bland and ineffectual stop-gap measure which many believe sounds the death knell of the Wagner Bill." [53]

But stop-gap measure or not, the legislative history of the resolution provides some fascinating insights into the congressional treatment of the duty to bargain. In the debate on the resolution, Senator Walsh repeated his interpretation of the Wagner bill as requiring nothing more from an employer than reception of his employees and conference with their representatives. He stated:

> The moment they entered the employer's door, their deliberations and their acts were as sacred as in any tribunal in the world. Furthermore, the employer did not have to make an agreement with them if he did not see fit, but he did have to recognize the right of men in his own employ to confer with him.[54]

Immediately afterward, however, Senator La Follette offered an amendment as a substitute of the Joint Resolution. This resolution stated in Section 3(1) that it should be an unfair labor practice for an employer "to refuse to recognize and deal with such representatives for the purpose of collective bargaining." [55] Senator La Follette's substitute bill, which in effect was the Wagner bill prior to the Walsh amendment, incorporated the amendments which Senator Wagner intended to offer had the Walsh measure been given consideration.[56]

In his explanation of Section 3, La Follette stated that his purpose was to define and enlarge the rights already embodied in Section 7(a). More specifically, he stated that "the right to bargain collectively through representatives of their own choosing are words which had come to have a definite meaning." [57] Of course, he was referring to Section 7(a) as interpreted by the National Labor Board. He referred to the experience of the National Labor Board and the other special labor boards in administering Section 7(a),

63

as well as the experience with the Railway Labor Act of 1926, as the basis for the specific unfair labor practice provisions, including the one imposing a duty to bargain. Senator La Follette concluded his explanation of the unfair labor practices in his proposed amendment by stating:

What boots it, Mr. President, if representatives are chosen by the employees or if elections are held as provided by the joint resolution, if after those representatives are chosen the employers refuse to meet with them? In instance after instance, after representatives were chosen by the wage earners, employers have contended that they have complied with their obligations as to collective bargaining when they permitted representatives to enter their offices but have declined to consult with them further.[58]

La Follette then inserted into the Senate record as part of his remarks a summary of the National Labor Board's principles and excerpts from press releases about specific case decisions. Included in his statement was the following remark on collective bargaining:

The Board has held that the employees' right to bargain collectively imposes a corresponding duty on the employer. Collective bargaining has been construed to mean the exertion of every reasonable effort to reach an agreement. The Board has deprecated the calling of a strike without attempt of negotiations or the presentation of grievances, on the part of the employees.[59]

However, La Follette's substitute for Resolution 44 was withdrawn at the request of Senator Wagner, who stated that he felt obligated to follow the leadership of the President and defer consideration of a more permanent bill until the next session of Congress to allow more study, experimentation, and experience.[60]

THE FIRST NATIONAL LABOR RELATIONS BOARD

On June 29, 1934, the National Labor Relations Board was created by the President in an executive order by virtue of both the National Industrial Recovery Act and the Joint Resolution. The board's authority was

to investigate disputes involving or affecting commerce, to order elections, conduct hearings and issue findings of fact in cases of alleged breach of the statute, issue regulations subject to Presidential approval, arbitrate in disputes voluntarily submitted, and subpoena in election cases.[61]

The new labor board promptly affirmed and extended the old board's interpretation of the duty to bargain contained in Section 7(a). In a landmark decision, *Houde Engineering Corporation*, 1 NLRB 35, the board affirmed the principle of majority rule and elaborated upon an employer's duty to bargain. In view of the subsequent importance of this case in the legislative history of the Wagner Act, it seems appropriate to quote extensively from this decision. The board interpreted the fundamental purpose of Section 7(a) as follows:

The right of employees to bargain collectively implies a duty on the part of the employer to bargain with their representatives. Without this duty to bargain the right to bargain would be sterile; and Congress did not intend the right to be sterile. The National Labor Board in a series of decisions, and the Petroleum Board in one of its most important cases,[62] have established the incontestably sound principles that the employer is obligated by the statute to negotiate in good faith with his employees' representatives; to match their proposals, if unacceptable, with counter-proposals; and to make every reasonable effort to reach an agreement. Collective bargaining, then, is simply a means to an end. The end is an agreement. And, customarily, such an agreement will have to do with wages, hours and basic working conditions, and will have a fixed duration. The purpose of every such agreement has been to stabilize, for a certain period, the terms of employment, for the protection alike of employer and employee. By contrast, where all that transpires is a demand by any employees for better terms and assent by the employer, but without any understanding as to duration, there has been no collective agreement, because neither side has been bound to anything. Section 7(a) must be construed in the light of the traditional practices with which it deals, and the traditional meanings of the words which it uses. When it speaks of "collective bargaining" it can only be taken to mean that long-observed process whereby negotiations are conducted for the purpose of arriving at collective agreements governing terms of employment for some specified period. And prohibiting any interference with this process, it must have intended that the process should be encouraged, and that there was a definite good to be obtained by promoting the stabilization of employment relations through collective agreements.[63]

The board commented upon the company's practice of meeting with the union committee and discussing matters of only secondary importance, such as toilet facilities, safety measures, coat racks, slippery stairs, etc. Such discussion, in the view of the board, could not be considered collective bargaining since the employer refused to discuss "the recognized subjects of collective bargaining; namely, wages, hours and basic working conditions." [64]

Other activities of the company were held to impair the effectiveness of collective bargaining, since it appeared indisputably clear that the company policy was to prevent

any arrival at collective agreements in the sense intended by the statute. The Company's conception of its duty was merely this: That the Company should periodically receive each committtee, listen to its suggestions, discuss them politely and then act upon them or not, as it might see fit. If that be all that the statute requires, the Company was within its rights, but, as has been pointed out, the statute calls for more than that. It was not enacted to promote discussions. Such an anemic purpose was foreign to the Recovery Act. The statute was enacted to promote the making of collective agreements covering terms of employment for definite periods, as an integral part of the process of stabilizing industry upon a new and juster basis.[65]

The board then laid down the principle of majority rule, relying upon precedents established under the National War Labor Board, the railway legislation beginning with the

Transportation Act of 1920, and the President's executive order of February 1, 1934. The board stated that once a majority representative had been established, "the Company's duty was to endeavor in good faith to negotiate and arrive at such an agreement."[66] The board concluded its decision:

When a person, committee or organization has been designated by a majority of employees in a plant or other appropriate unit for collective bargaining, it is the right of the representative so designated to be treated by the employer as the exclusive bargaining agency of all employees in the unit, and the employer's duty to make every reasonable effort, when requested, to arrive with this representative at a collective agreement covering terms of employment of all such employees.[67]

In succeeding cases, the board found further opportunity to expand its conception of an employer's duty to bargain. In one case the board decision stated:

The record shows beyond any doubt that the Company had no intention to negotiate in good faith with the representative of its employees duly chosen in appropriate industrial units, to match unacceptable proposals with counter proposals, settle points of difference if possible, and to arrive at a binding agreement whether oral or written, for an appropriate term.[68]

In another case, the board stated that

the Company's conception of collective bargaining seems to be that the obligation imposed by the statute is fulfilled if an employer receives the representatives of his employees, discusses terms of employment with such representatives, and acts upon such of the demands put forth as are satisfactory to him; and that the statute does not require that such action be embodied in an agreement.[69]

The board then cited *Houde* and made this further comment:

Section 7(a) therefore requires employers to go further than merely to receive the duly constituted representatives of their employees, to give ear to their demands, and to assent to such demands if they

THE GOVERNMENT AS A SOURCE OF UNION POWER

are satisfactory. The statute imposes duties consistent with its purpose. It contemplates that the demands of the employees, or modifications of such demands, if acceptable to the employer, be embodied in an agreement, and that such an agreement bind both parties for a certain period of time.[70]

In another case, the board described the company's conduct during negotiations:

The avowed position of the Company's officials throughout these proceedings may be summarized as follows: We will meet with the employees or their representatives at any time, "on any subject of their own choosing:" if they want to bargain some more, we will talk to them; we have "agreed" to some of the union's demands but not to all; from time to time in the future, "if anything comes up we can agree to, we will be glad to do it." This does not constitute a proper discharge of the Company's obligations under Section 7(a) to bargain collectively with the representatives of its employees.[71]

The decision went on to further elucidate the duties imposed upon an employer by Section 7(a) in the statement that "... the statute does not require an employer to acquiesce in particular demands; it does require he enter into negotiations with a sincere desire to reach agreement." [72]

As other cases reached the board, principles of good-faith dealing on the part of the employer were constantly repeated and amplified. Typical of such decisions was one in which the board stated,

As we have frequently pointed out, the Company's obligation under the circumstances here, was to enter into collective bargaining negotiations with an open mind, to match unacceptable proposals with counter proposals and to exert every reasonable effort to reach an agreement binding it for an appropriate term.[73]

In other cases the board held that a strike did not affect the employer's duty to bargain,[74] nor was the collective bargaining responsibility of the employer in any way affected by changes in corporate structure.[75] The board also held that an employer may not move his place of business in order to evade his obligation to bargain under Section 7(a).[76] The *Resnick* case also established the proposition that it is an interference with the right of organization for the employer to bypass the union and bargain directly with employees.

The subjects on which an employer must negotiate with the union were elaborated in a number of decisions. In one case, the board gave a sweeping definition of the subjects of collective bargaining, holding that any changes in the terms and conditions of employment were bargainable "whether forecast by a change in plant location, the introduction of a new line of products, or otherwise."[77] The board went so far as to state that the failure of an employee to pay a fine imposed upon him by the union was a proper subject of collective bargaining. In this case, the union requested the employer to lend money to the employee so that he could pay his fine. However, the refusal of the company to agree to this was considered proper by the board, since

The duty of the Company to bargain collectively did not require it to yield to the insistent proposal of the union that it help Schmeltz [the delinquent employee] with his fine; the process of collective bargaining had thus been carried to a point where an irreconcilable difference created an impasse.[78]

Other mandatory subjects of collective bargaining included the sharing of work,[79] vacations with pay, changes in pay period, and group insurance.[80]

THE EFFECTIVENESS OF THE NATIONAL LABOR RELATIONS BOARD

Between July 1, 1934 and March 1, 1935, 5,309 cases were filed with the regional labor boards. These cases involved about 1,500,000 employees. Francis Biddle, chairman of the National Labor Relations Board, had testified that the effectiveness of the law depended upon proper enforcement in the courts. He therefore examined the consequences of the formal cases which resulted in an NLRB finding of a violation. In this period, there were 111 such decisions and a violation of Section 7(a) was found in eighty-six cases.

In only 34 of these did the employer make appropriate restitution in accordance with our decision. In the remaining 52 of the 86 cases, such compliance was not obtained. In these 52 cases, therefore, it was necessary for the Board to attempt to obtain enforcement through the removal of the "blue eagle" or through court action. Of these 52 cases the Board referred 33 to the Department of Justice. The status of these 33 cases is as follows: In one case a bill in equity has been filed in a district court. Seven cases have been referred to the local United States Attorney, on the understanding that further evidence must be secured by him in cooperation with the Board before instituting suit. In none of these cases has suit been brought. In 9 cases the Department of Justice has advised the Board that further investigation on certain points is necessary before the case can be referred to the local United States Attorney, and in 3 cases the Department has advised that as a matter of law no suit is justified. In 13 cases, the Department has not proceeded for various reasons.[81]

It seems clear that the effectiveness of the National Labor Relations Board had broken down, despite its statistically impressive case load. Of course, there were successes. In less than six weeks after the passage of the NIRA, 360,000 miners joined United Mine Workers of America.[82] At least in the first few months of the operation of the first National Labor Board and the National Labor Relations Board, the appeal to public opinion and the prestige of board members resulted in fairly widespread compliance with Section 7(a).[83]

The major result of Section 7(a) appears to have been the rise of company unions. A 1932 estimate of union membership in company unions was 1,263,194; the estimate for early 1935 was 2,500,000.[84] The reasons for this growth are not difficult to find. As we have already mentioned, management construed Section 7(a) to mean that company unions were encompassed by the law's promotion of collective bargaining. There is other evidence on the way in which company unions were initiated. For example, in February of 1934 the National Association of Manufacturers sent to each of its members a copy of a manual on employee representation which "presents the merits of employee representation, problems involved in the introduction and subsequent life of any 'works counsel' or employee representation plan, and suggestions as to possible provisions of such a plan." [85]

THE WAGNER BILL, S. 1958

The unexpected midterm victories of the Democratic party in November, 1934, provided a legislative opportunity for the introduction of a new labor bill. On February 21, 1935, Senator Wagner introduced S. 1958, which he described as "designed to clarify the provisions of Section 7(a) of the National Industry Recovery Act and to invest a permanent National Labor Relations Board with adequate powers for their enforcement. It embodies, in perfected form, the main provisions of the labor-disputes bill which I introduced last year." [86]

In introducing the bill, Senator Wagner made some explanatory comments. He first stated that the breakdown of Section 7(a) was due to the lack of enforceable authority, and went on to say that the

Bill which I now propose is novel neither in philosophy nor in content. It creates no new substantive rights. It merely provides that employees, if they desire to do so, shall be free to organize for their mutual protection or benefit. Quite aside from Section 7(a), this principle has been embodied in the Norris-LaGuardia Act, in amendments to the Railway Labor Act passed last year, and in a long train of other enactments of Congress.[87]

S. 1958 differed in a number of ways from the Walsh bill as well as from Wagner's original bill in 1934. Although there was no specific unfair labor practice which made it unlawful for an employer to refuse to bargain collectively, the evidence is overwhelming that the intent of the bill was to make bargaining in good faith obligatory. To begin with, the declaration of policy in S. 1958 stressed the intention of encouraging the practice of collective bargaining, an intention which was not present in the Walsh bill. Much more important was the testimony of Senator Wagner, in which he stated that this bill "is an entirely new draft, in that it must not be interpreted in the light of whether or not it contains provisions that were in the bills upon the same subject before Congress last year." [88] Wagner also stated that his new bill "has benefited by an additional year of thought and by the additional problems and experiences of the present National Labor Relations Board in its fine work." [89] The importance of the duty to bargain was further emphasized by other testimony of Senator Wagner.

While the bill explicitly states the right of employees to organize, their unification will prove of little value if it is to be used solely for Saturday night dances and Sunday afternoon picnics. Therefore, while the bill does not state specifically the duty of an employer to recognize and bargain collectively with the representatives of his employees, because of the difficulty of setting forth this matter precisely in statutory language, such a duty is clearly implicit in the bill. To attempt to deal with his men otherwise than through representatives they have named for such purposes would be the clearest interference with the right to bargain collectively.[90]

Senator Wagner then cited verbatim the relevant language of the *Houde* case on the duty to bargain.[91] The import of

Wagner's explanation permits only one conclusion: The duty to bargain was to be an obligation of employers, even in the absence of a specific unfair labor practice requiring such a duty.

An examination of the legislative history easily demonstrates this. For example, immediately after Senator Wagner's statement of the implicit duty to bargain in good faith, Chairman Walsh asked: "There was nothing in this bill that permits the issue of an order or the inflicting of any penalty upon any employer who receives representatives of the employees and who conducts conferences with them, even if the conferences end in the inability of the employer to agree to the terms of the employee?"

Senator Wagner replied: "No; you could not do that very well. But I am sure there is in the legislation the implicit obligation upon the employer to bargain collectively."

SENATOR WALSH: "How are you going to reach that?"

SENATOR WAGNER: "These things are not very difficult in actual practice, because it is easy to ascertain whether an employer refused to recognize the process of collective bargaining."

SENATOR WALSH: "Whether he is acting in good faith?"

SENATOR WAGNER: "That is it exactly."

SENATOR WALSH: "Suppose he is not, what are you going to do with him under this legislation? He receives the representatives of the employees, sits in the conference room with them, and says, 'Thank you, gentlemen, but I cannot accept your proposition.' The only thing left is for the employees to strike, is it not? There is nothing in the law to compel the employer to do anything."

SENATOR WAGNER: "Of course, he need not reach an agreement. But if he evidenced bad faith by not really attempting to bargain collectively, that would be an unfair labor practice, because it would be interference with the right of employees to bargain collectively." [92]

What Senator Wagner had in mind was clearly the application of Section 7 of S. 1958 which was absent in the Walsh bill. Section 7 stated: "Employees shall have the right to self-organization, to form, join or assist labor organizations to bargain collectively through representatives of their own choosing and to engage in concerted activities for the purpose of collective bargaining or other mutual aid or protection." It is obvious that the failure to include a specific unfair labor practice imposing a duty to bargain was not based upon the substantive merits of such a duty, but rather upon the belief that the duty was already included implicitly under Section 7 and Section 8(1) of the Wagner Bill.

The suggestion that the specific duty to bargain be included as Section 8(5) of the bill was made by the chairman of the National Labor Relations Board, Francis Biddle, who testified:

The right of employees to self-organization and to collective bargaining is defined in Section 7 of the act. The National Labor Relations Board has in the Houde and other cases found a corresponding duty on the part of the employer to bargain collectively with his employees, since a declaration by Congress of their right would have been sterile without such a corresponding duty. Senator Wagner, in his testimony before the committee yesterday, argued along these lines—that the duty of the employer to bargain collectively was implied from the right of the employees to bargain, and that a failure to bargain would therefore be an interference with the right. However, there has been so much disagreement and confusion with respect to the employer's duty to bargain collectively that I believe this duty should be expressed in the act, and suggest that the following be added as subdivision (5) of Section 8, which section defines unfair labor practices: (5) to refuse to bargain collectively with the representatives of his employees subject to the provisions of Section 9(a).[93]

74

An interesting exchange thereupon took place between Senator Walsh and Biddle. Walsh asked what would constitute a refusal to bargain. Biddle replied:

When they turn them down flat and say, "I will not deal with the Union," that is the most obvious refusal of this, as we frequently have such cases. Or when they string them along without any real purpose of intent of bargaining. You may say that to tell a man he must try to make a contract does not mean much, but it means a great deal in actually dealing with these problems, because it means that the employer must make a bona fide genuine effort to come to an agreement.

Senator Walsh then asked, "Refuse to meet are the words you give?"

Biddle replied, "I said to refuse to bargain collectively with the representatives. I thought it could be very simply stated in that way."

Senator Walsh thereupon asked, "Why would it not be more definite and direct to say to refuse to meet and confer for the purpose of collective bargaining with his employees?"

Biddle responded, "I think that is an excellent suggestion, Senator."

Senator Walsh replied:

A man sailing direct in the face of his employees, certainly would be committing an unfair practice if it was so defined, if after they entered into his presence he refused to talk with them. It would be an unfair practice under such conditions, but if he sat in conference with them and permitted them to present their views and made an effort to confer with them it would not be an unfair practice.[94]

The first chairman of the National Labor Relations Board, Lloyd Garrison, strongly endorsed the addition of Section 8(5) as proposed by Francis Biddle. In his testimony Garrison said:

I personally regard that as absolutely essential to this bill. What is the purpose of going through all this detail forbidding discrimination and providing for elections and the selection of the majority shall speak for all if when all of that has been gone through with the employer can simply say, "Run along; I am not going to talk to you; I do not want to see you; I do not want to have anything to do with you." The whole end of this process is collective bargaining, and the bill which sets the stage for collective bargaining and then says nothing about it at all, to my mind, omits the very guts of the whole thing. It is true that the Board might interpret under Section 7 in the bill that employees shall have the right to bargain collectively as implying a correlative duty on the part of the employer. The National Labor Relations Board reached that result under 7 (a), and the old National Labor Board reached that result under 7 (a), and this new Board might reach this result under Section 7. But why leave it to possible interpretation by the Board when it is really to my mind the crux of the whole thing?

At this point Senator La Follette commented:

I have been told—I do not know whether it is true or not—that there were employers who thought they had complied with the provisions of 7 (a) when they met the representatives of the union in their office and said "nothing doing" when they suggested that they wanted to enter into a collective bargaining agreement. In other words, they contended that having met with the representatives that they had complied with the mandate of 7 (a) to provide collective bargaining.

Garrison replied:

Yes; there have been numerous cases where the employers met with the union, but have talked about the weather and everything else except collective bargaining, with no effort at all to try to reach some agreement. Of course, the statutes cannot compel an agreement. Nobody suggests that. But it does seem to me that Congress can say it is an unfair labor practice likely to lead to strikes and burdening interstate commerce for an employer to have nothing to do with the employees or with the representatives of the majority of his employees, and I think that Mr. Biddle's amendment is very well phrased, and I hope it will be adopted. I want to say I think not only from the point of view of the logic of the bill but from a very practical point of view it is an essential provision.[95]

Senator Walsh made no comments on the suggestion of Mr. Garrison. A few minutes later Garrison had incorporated into the record of the hearings most of the decision in *Houde* which not only discussed thoroughly the majority rule principle but contained the language previously cited on an employer's duty to bargain.[96]

It is striking that the testimony of all administrators connected with the earlier boards was unanimous in supporting the inclusion of a specific duty to bargain in the proposed bill. The former general counsel of the National Labor Board, Milton Handler, submitted a statement to the Senate committee which read as follows:

There is one omission in Section 8 which I believe to be fraught with danger. There is no explicit imposition of a duty upon employers, as in the Railway Labor Act, to bargain collectively with the chosen representatives of their employees and to exert every reasonable effort to reach agreement. I believe such a duty is implicit in the statute, but it would be wise policy to avoid controversy by making the obligation explicit. Without such an obligation, the rights conferred by the bill can be emptied of all significance.[97]

Opposition to the bill by management ran the gamut of tactics, from constitutional objections to specific attacks on any interference with company unions. One of the major objections was against the principle of majority rule. The ranks of opposition included the Communist Party, the American Civil Liberties Union, and Mr. Walter Lippman. Needless to say, their reasons for opposition differed.[98]

Since the bill as originally introduced did not have a specific unfair labor practice requiring an employer to bargain, there were no witnesses (apart from the instances already cited) who commented directly upon this duty. The sole exception that I have been able to find was the comment of James Emery, representing the National Association of Manufacturers, who stated that the "refusal to bargain collectively with an irresponsible, a Communistic, or a racketeering organization, is by definition as illegal as refusal of relations with a labor organization of reputation and integrity."[99] Emery was here referring to the implication in Section 7 that permitted a duty to bargain to be read into the bill.

Section 8(5) was added to the Senate Committee on Education and Labor Bill, which was reported to the Senate on May 2, 1935. However, in the course of the Senate hearings, an important change took place in the position of committee chairman Walsh. On the basis of personal interviews, Bernstein reports:

In the deliberation of the Senate Labor Committee Chairman Walsh reversed his 1934 position, delegating full responsibility to Wagner without asserting his own views. As a result Wagner was asked to prepare the report and was again assisted by Keyserling. They regarded this as a key opportunity to break with the 1934 report and, more important, to state congressional intent for the guidance of the Board and the Courts.[100]

In discussing this new Section 8(5), the committee report stated that the section did not require the making of agreements or permit government supervision of their terms. The committee report went on to state:

But after deliberation, the committee has concluded that this fifth unfair labor practice should be inserted in the bill. It seems clear that a guarantee of the right of employees to bargain collectively through representatives of their own choosing is a mere delusion if it is not accompanied by the correlative duty on the part of the other party to recognize such representatives as they have been designated (whether as individuals or labor organizations) and to negotiate with them in a bona fide effort to arrive at a collective bargaining agreement. Furthermore, the procedure of holding governmentally supervised elections to determine the choice of representatives of employees becomes of little worth if after the election its results are for all practical purposes ignored. Experience has proved that neither obedience to law nor respect for law is encouraged by holding forth a right unaccompanied by fulfillment.[101]

The addition of Section 8(5) was not an afterthought. The Senate committee report emphasized the importance of protecting the right to bargain in a number of other places. In describing the general objectives of the bill, the report stated that it was not intended to remove all causes of labor disputes, but it went on to say:

. . . many of the most fertile sources of industrial discontent can be segregated into a single category susceptible to legislative treatment. Competent students of industrial relations have estimated that at least 25% of all strikes have sprung from failure to recognize and utilize the theories and practices of collective bargaining, under which are subsumed the rights of employees to organize freely and to deal with employers through representatives of their own choosing.[102]

The report also noted that 74 per cent of all cases received by the regional offices of the NLRB during the second half of 1934 had been concerned with the issue of collective bargaining. Therefore, the committee concluded that it thought it feasible to remove the basis for a large proportion of the bitterest industrial disputes by giving definite legal status to the procedure of collective bargaining and by setting up machinery to facilitate it.[103]

The report went on to state that the committee's opinion was based upon the legislative experience in the United States, particularly the consequences of the railroad legislation and of the War Labor Board's protection of the practice of collective bargaining. On the basis of the experience under Section 7(a), the report expressed the view that a new law was required because of the weakness in the existing law. The weaknesses were described as basically consisting of an ambiguity and excessive generality in the statutory language. "While Section 7(a) states the principles of collective bargaining in general terms, it contains no particularities as to what practices are contrary to its purposes. This has greatly hampered not only administrative and enforcing agencies, but also all those subject to the law who wish to obey it." [104]

The report also discussed the background of the majority rule principle, which it traced through the National War Labor Board, the Railway Labor Board, Public Resolution No. 44, and the 1934 amendments to the Railway Labor Act. The report stated that the majority rule principle

is sanctioned by our governmental practices, by business procedure, and by the whole philosophy of democratic institutions. The object of collective bargaining is the making of agreements that will stabilize business conditions and fix fair standards of working conditions. Since it is wellnigh universally recognized that it is practically impossible to apply two or more sets of agreements to one unit of workers at the same time, or to apply the terms of one agreement to only a portion of the workers in a single unit, the making of agreements is impracticable in the absence of majority rule . . . Majority rule carries the clear implication that employers shall not interfere with the practical application of the right of employees to bargain collectively through chosen representatives by bargaining with individuals or minority groups in their own behalf, after representatives have been picked by the majority to represent all.[105]

On May 15, 1935, Senator Wagner, as the sponsor of the committee bill, formally presented the bill to the Senate and made a lengthy address explaining it. He opened his remarks by asserting that the "National Labor Relations Bill does not break with our traditions." [106]

Senator Wagner discussed the unfair labor practices and emphasized that Section 8(1) was based on long-established congressional policy and that its language

follows practically verbatim the familiar principles already imbedded in our law by Section 2 of the Railway Labor Act of 1926, Section 2 of the Norris-LaGuardia Act, Section 77 (p) and (q) of

1932 amendments to the Bankruptcy Act, Section 7 (a) of the National Industrial Recovery Act, and Section 7 (e) of the Act creating the office of the Federal Coordinator of Transportation.[107]

The duty to bargain collectively as envisaged in Section 8(5) was carefully explained. Wagner was emphatic in stating that this duty does not imply government regulation of wages or hours. However, "the right of workers to bargain collectively through representatives of their own choosing must be matched by the correlative duty of employers to recognize and deal in good faith with these representatives." [108]

On this point Senator Wagner went on to explain precisely the meaning of Section 8(5). He said:

Just what the duty to bargain collectively implies was clearly set forth by the present National Labor Relations Board in the *Houde Engineering Corp.* case, decided on August 30, 1934. There the Board said:

Without this duty the right to bargain would be sterile . . . The incontestably sound principle is that the employer is obligated by the statutes to negotiate in good faith with his employees' representatives; to match their proposals if unacceptable, with counterproposals; and to make every reasonable effort to reach an agreement.

Wagner concluded by observing, "The sound result which the Labor Board reached by interpretation of a vague law should be confirmed and protected by a clear definition of congressional policy." [109] On the following day, May 16, 1935, the committee amendment to insert the avoidance of the duty to bargain as an unfair labor practice was approved by the Senate. There was no discussion on this amendment.

As a matter of fact, the Senate debate on S. 1958 was quite limited, at least compared to debates in the preceding year. One commentator thought that this was due "first to the fact that the bill had been discussed for more than a year in Congress, in the press, and over the radio, and had been the subject of a flood of congressional mail . . . the second factor was that the opposition lacked a champion." [110] However, the brief debate elicted from Senator Walsh a number of general explanations of the bill. It seems essential to include all Walsh's statements since these are the basis for the contemporary view of the congressional intent in inserting Section 8(5) in the act.

In response to a question from Senator Vandenberg as to the rights of the minority if there existed a majority union, Senator Walsh stated:

If a labor union is going to be organized there has to be someone to speak for the employees and that someone must be the representative of the majority, but that does not prevent the other employees discussing their grievances with their employer. It means that for the purpose of collective bargaining, when the representatives of the employees knock at the door of the employer, he will say, "Do you represent a majority of my employees? If so, all right; come on and I will undertake to engage in collective bargaining with you as the chosen representatives of my employees," that is all it means.[111]

Shortly afterwards, again with respect to the question dealing with proportional representation and the right of minorities, Senator Walsh repeated his views on the nature of the bill:

There is nothing in this bill that compels any employer to make any agreement about wages, hours of employment, or working conditions with his employees. The bill does provide the means and manner in which employees may approach their employers to discuss grievances and permit the board to ascertain and certify the persons or organization favored by a majority of the employees to represent them in collective bargaining, when the question of that representation is in doubt or dispute. Beyond this the bill does not go. A crude illustration is this: The bill indicates the method and manner in which employees may organize, the method and manner of selecting their representatives or spokesmen, and leads them to the office door of their employer with the legal authority to negotiate for their fellow employees. The bill does not go beyond the office door. It leaves the discussion between the employer and the employee, and the agreements which they may or may not make, voluntary and with the sacredness and solemnity to a voluntary agreement with which both parties to an agreement should be enshrouded. . . . Let me emphasize again: When the employees have chosen their organization, when they have selected their representatives, all the bill proposes to do is to escort them to the door of their employer, and say, "Here they are, the legal representatives of your employees." What happens behind those doors is not inquired into, and the bill does not seek to inquire into it. It anticipates that the employer will deal reasonably with the employees, that he will be patient, but he is obliged to sign no agreements; he can say, "Gentlemen, we have heard you and considered your proposals. We cannot comply with your request; and that ends it." [112]

But the next time that Senator Walsh discussed the matter, he stated:

All the section does is to designate the agency to negotiate on behalf of the employees, with whom the employer must deal. He does not have to accept any particular contract with them, but he must bargain with them in a *bona fide effort* to reach a mutually satisfactory agreement. [Emphasis supplied.][113]

Again, a few minutes later, Walsh interpreted the bill:

All the bill does is, for the sake of peace and harmony, for the sake of bringing employers and employees together, to lay the foundation of machinery for getting a proper representation of employees at the door of the employer to discuss and argue out their difficulties. That is all it does. An agreement arrived at with the representatives chosen by a majority has the best chance of achieving general acceptance, and thus stabilizing employment relations and promoting peace.[114]

Finally, Senator Walsh stated, "We are requiring employers to negotiate with the properly designated representatives of their employees in the hope of having peace, in the hope of removing misunderstanding, not for the purpose of taking rights away from either party." [115]

83

On May 16, 1935, the Wagner Act passed the Senate by a vote of 63 to 12.

The House hearings on the Wagner-Connery Bill have been aptly characterized: ". . . only a pale reflection of those held by the Senate and the arguments were echoes."[116] The House report which accompanied the Connery bill emphasized the importance of the experience under Section 7(a). According to the committee report, "The bill was merely an amplification and further clarification of the principles enacted into law by the Railway Labor Act and by Section 7 (a) of the National Industrial Recovery Act with the addition of enforcement machinery of familiar pattern." [117]

The report discussed the principles of the National Labor Board, observing that an employer must deal with the chosen representatives of his employees even though such representative may be an "outside" union.[118] The report also commented that the "National Labor Relations Board, following the lead of its predecessor, the National Labor Board, has enriched the body of labor law by a notable series of decisions interpreting and applying to Section 7 (a)." [119]

The report's discussion of the bill began by asserting:

Section 7 (a), as it now appears in the National Industrial Recovery Act, is amplified by the specific prohibition of certain unfair-labor practices, which by fair interpretation would constitute infringements upon the substantive rights of employees declared in Section 7 (a).[120]

The only specific comment on Section 8(5) was: "The fifth unfair labor practice, regarding the refusal to bargain collectively, rounds out the essential purpose of the bill to encourage collective bargaining and the making of agreements." [121]

The major difference between the House bill and the

Senate bill was whether the National Labor Relations Board should be located in the Department of Labor or remain an independent agency, as contemplated by the Senate bill. The sketchiness of the House debates is revealed by the following statements, which appear to exhaust the discussion on the duty to bargain. In arguing for the bill, Congressman Griswold stated that it gave labor the right to go to the door of the employer and say:

We are ready to sit around the table and argue this matter out and reason it out with you. If we can reach an adjustment, all well and good; if we cannot we go back to the old system of dog eat dog which we have had before. This bill does not adjust labor disputes; it puts both sides in a position where they can adjust them.[122]

Congressman Greenwood also stated that the bill "recognizes not only the theory of collective bargaining, but it goes further and provides that where collective bargaining exists there shall also be collective responsibility." [123]

Congressman Connery summed up the bill by stating:

Two years ago, when we passed the National Industrial Recovery Act, we passed Section 7 (a) as a part of that bill. There was not any fight on Section 7 (a) either in the House or in the Senate. It passed by a great majority. Section 7 (a) set out the rights of labor to bargain collectively, through representatives of their own choosing. All the Wagner-Connery bill, which is before you today, does is to see that this Board which had the enforcing of Section 7 (a) is given the power to enforce what we wrote into that Section when we passed the NIRA bill in this house.[124]

Another congressman, Mr. Welch, stated:

It does not require an employer to sign any contract to make any agreement, to reach any understanding with any employee or group of employees. This board created in the bill is not empowered to settle labor disputes; nothing in the bill allows the Federal Government or any agency to fix wages, regulate rates of pay, limit hours of work, or to effect or govern any working condition in any establishment or place of employment. . . . This bill is designed to put into force and effect the principle of collective bargaining.[125]

On June 19, 1935, after approving an amendment to the committee report to set up the NLRB as an independent agency and not under the Department of Labor, the House passed the bill without a rollcall vote. Minor disagreements between the House and Senate bills resulted in a conference between the managers of the bills in both houses. The bill passed both houses on June 27 and on July 3, 1935, President Roosevelt signed it. He then issued a statement in which he said:

This act defines, as a part of our substantive law, the right of self-organization of employees in industry for the purpose of collective bargaining, and provides methods by which the Government can safeguard that legal right. It establishes a National Labor Relations Board to hear and determine cases in which it is charged that this legal right is abridged or denied, and to hold fair elections to ascertain who are the chosen representatives of employees. A better relationship between labor and management is the high purpose of this act. By assuring the employees the right of collective bargaining it fosters the development of the employment contract on a sound and equitable basis. By providing an orderly procedure for determining who is entitled to represent the employees, it aims to remove one of the chief causes of wasteful economic strife. By preventing practices which tend to destroy the independence of labor, it seeks, for every worker within its scope, that freedom of choice and action which is justly his.[126]

CHAPTER 4 · THE LEGISLATIVE INTENT
AND THE DUTY TO BARGAIN

A remarkable oddity that has characterized the attacks on the duty to bargain is the preoccupation with one of Senator Walsh's remarks during the legislative debates. In explaining his concept of the bill, Senator Walsh stated:

A crude illustration is this: The bill indicates the method and manner in which the employees may organize, the method and manner of selecting their representatives or spokesmen, and leads them to the office door of their employer with the legal authority to negotiate for their fellow employees. The bill does not go beyond the office door. It leaves the discussion between the employer and the employee, and the agreements which they may or may not make, voluntary and with the sacredness and solemnity to a voluntary agreement with which both parties to an agreement should be enshrouded. . . . Let me emphasize again: when the employees have chosen their organization, when they have selected their representatives, all the bill proposes to do is to escort them to the door of their employer and say, "Here they are, the legal representatives of your employees." What happens behind those doors is not inquired into, and the bill does not seek to inquire into it.[1]

This quotation from Senator Walsh runs like a red thread in the fabric of every condemnation of NLRB policy in this area. After citing Senator Walsh, the Smith Committee attacked the board's entire approach on good-faith bargaining as "certainly contrary to the Congressional intent, as demonstrated by statements repeatedly made by the sponsors of the measure on the floor of both houses when the bill was under consideration in 1935." [2] The committee report concluded:

The Congressional intent, as evidenced by the above excerpts from the debate, was clearly that the duty to bargain did not compel employers to enter into any agreement with their workers. Yet the Board's requirement of counterproposals as evidence of good faith on the part of employers has nullified this intent. Such a requirement means that if the union accepts the counterproposals thus forced from the employer by the Board's fiat, the employer is then made a party to a labor agreement.[3]

The Smith Committee also made a sweeping attack on the board's conduct and procedures which has been described as "not justified by any complete review of the available evidence." [4] The Smith Committee's criticism of the board was followed up by the introduction of numerous bills to amend the Wagner Act. One of them did not change the wording of Section 8(5), but added the following definition of collective bargaining:

The phrase "collective bargaining" for purposes of this act shall be understood to mean the meeting together of employer and his employees through accredited representatives voluntarily chosen by them, with the full and free opportunity for negotiating concerning the terms of conditions of employment.

The National Labor Relations Board made the following comment on the import of such a definition:

This provision reduces an employer's obligation to bargain collectively to an obligation merely to meet with the representatives of his employees. Historically the procedure of collective bargaining has involved far more than this. It is meant not only that the employer meet with the representatives of his employees but that he bargain with them in good faith in an honest attempt to achieve an understanding upon terms, and, if an understanding is reached, embody such understanding in a collective agreement.[5]

The use of Senator Walsh's statement as the basis for changing the law can be seen in the more recent comments of Professor Sylvester Petro, who pointed out that to do away with good-faith bargaining would mean that an employer satisfied the duty to bargain if he did no more than listen to the union representatives and unqualifiedly reject without discussion every suggestion or proposal. This conception of bargaining was, according to Professor Petro, the duty "which the Congress thought it was imposing in the original Wagner Act. . . ." [6]

SCHOLARS' ATTACKS ON THE DUTY TO BARGAIN

Partisan hostility to the purposes of the act was not the only occasion for the use of Senator Walsh's statement on the meaning of Section 8(5). In May, 1941, a legal article by Russell A. Smith on the evolution of the duty to bargain was published.[7] This article was to be a standard source for subsequent writing on the early meaning and development of the duty to bargain, and still stands as the most exhaustive appraisal of legislative intent. Professor Smith believed that the legislative intent was at best uncertain. His review of the legislative history of the Wagner Act on the meaning of the duty to bargain was summarized in his comment that "not only was singularly scant attention given to the matter, but such consideration as it did receive reveals anything but diaphanous clarity of thought." [8] Moreover, Professor Smith stated that the inclusion of the duty to bargain was "fortuitous," for it was not in the original Wagner Bill. In his discussion of the legislative history he emphasized Senator Walsh's statement, as well as several isolated statements by Congressmen Welch and Griswold, to support the conclusion that despite the standard of good-faith bargaining contained in the Senate committee report, the prevailing intention in Congress was "of a delimiting character." [9] Smith also indicated that the references to the principles established by the old labor boards were too "casual" to mean that the new law was intended to embody such views. He concluded that "in short, the Congress which made the duty to bargain explicit for most employers did not make a substantial contribution to its meaning." [10]

Subsequent writers made continual use of the Walsh quotation.[11] For example, in 1948 Professor Taylor, in his discussion of government intervention in collective bargaining, made innumerable references to his belief that the original intent of the duty to bargain was to attain minimal recognition.[12] In his subsequent work Professor Taylor continued to attack the duty to bargain.[13]

The most significant citation of Senator Walsh occurred in a very important article on the duty to bargain by Professors Cox and Dunlop.[14] The article itself was an attack upon the board doctrines concerning the duty to bargain, which, in the view of the authors, are an unfortunate encroachment of government on free collective bargaining. The starting point of the argument was that the legislative background of the Wagner Act "was concerned with organization for bargaining—not with the scope of the ensuing negotiation, nor with the procedures through which they are carried on." [15] The authors cited Senator Walsh's statement twice in developing this view and characterized his description of the purpose of the bill as very fair. The article went to the length of asserting: "There was not a world in the hearings, in the committee reports, or in the debates to suggest that the Act would define the subjects of collective bargaining and give the Board power to resolve the issue in disputed cases." [16]

The legislative history was treated at great length because of the authors' strong conviction that the board has no business to prescribe the subjects of collective bargaining. Indeed, they thought that Section 9(a)'s cataloguing of "rates of pay, wages, hours of employment, or other conditions of employment" was included in the act not to describe the subjects of collective bargaining, but for the curious and implausible purpose "of defining the area from which the union preferred by the minority should be excluded . . ."[17]

The reason given for discussing the legislative history at such great length was its alleged materiality to the criticism of board policy. Very reluctantly Professors Cox and Dunlop stated that as a practical matter the NLRB practice of defining the scope of collective bargaining could not be challenged. However, in their view, it was "historically sounder" to conclude that the duty to bargain dealt only with "the problem of recognition, not with the scope of collective bargaining."[18]

Notwithstanding the settled law on this subject, the authors considered that the board doctrine which requires the discussion of such matters as pensions, vacations, and sub-contracting

as substituting government decree for the process of "defining the scope of collective bargaining by collective bargaining" would, by substituting government regulation for private agreement, carry the administration of the Act into a field which its sponsors believed the government should not enter.[19]

The conclusion of the authors was: ". . . the N.L.R.B. should make it plain that it is not an unfair labor practice for an employer to bargain in good faith for an agreement assigning particular subjects of collective bargaining to management's exclusive control for the duration of the contract."[20]

It is unnecessary to dwell at any length on the substance of Cox and Dunlop's proposals. It has already been pointed out that board decisions had put their main suggestion into effect.[21] Clearly, employers and unions may make and explore any proposals that they see fit with the proviso that they act in good faith. Any discussion of the *Borg-Warner* doctrine would show that the impropriety of the employer's action lies in an adamant insistence upon subjects which are outside the scope of collective bargaining. There is nothing in the law which prohibits discussion of any subject, mandatory or not, or any agreement upon any lawful subject.

The logic of Cox and Dunlop's approach breaks down when the question is whether an employer should be found to have violated the duty to bargain if he refuses to discuss such subjects as wages, hours, seniority, or the establishment of a grievance procedure. Cox and Dunlop conceded that such a refusal should be a violation on the grounds that "tradition teaches us that every union which has received true recognition has bargained about those subjects." [22] However, they would draw the line at such questions as pensions, merit increases, or subcontracting, on the basis that these are "subjects which have long been handled in different ways in different industries." [23]

The whole point of the mandatory bargaining doctrine lies in the elimination of some sources of dispute by establishing certain minimum standards of bargaining. The method implicit in this approach can be seen if we consider the meaning of requiring employers to bargain about wages. However reluctant an employer may be to change wages, he must discuss the subject with the union. While he is under no obligation to raise wages, bargaining differences are centered on the issue of wage changes and not on whether wages are to be discussed. Economic force, of course, can be applied to the question of what wages should be, but not to whether they should be talked about. The requirement of bargaining about wages thus narrows the scope of possible conflict in exactly the same manner as does the statutory requirement that a majority union need not exercise economic force in order to receive recognition.

Plainly and simply, Cox and Dunlop's proposal would enlarge the battleground and subordinate the give and take of discussion to continual trials of force. While this may be an arguable position—despite its inconsistency with a major purpose of the statute—its relationship to the ideal of free collective bargaining is hard to see.

What is relevant for our purposes is Cox and Dunlop's use of Senator Walsh's argument to represent legislative intent. Other attacks on board policy in this area are also based upon Senator Walsh's statement. For example, Professor Fleming cited it to prove his point "that a good legal argument can be made that the sponsors of the Wagner Act never intended any such result" as requiring employers to bargain about insurance, retirement, rest or lunch periods, bonus payments, merit rating, employer-owned rental housing, bonuses, and stock-purchase plans.[24] In a later article Professor Fleming repeated this point of view, stating that "the legislative history of the subsection leaves considerable doubt as to what the Congress had in mind."[25] Again he adverted to Senator Walsh's statement as demonstrating the congressional purpose.

The significance of the legislative history was again demonstrated in a later article by Professor Cox, which was cited three times in one Supreme Court decision on the duty to bargain.[26] Professor Cox again used Senator Walsh's statement to show that the original function of the duty to bargain was merely to bring employer and employee into conference. Relying heavily upon Professor Smith's article, Cox asserted that

So far as the records show . . . no one attributed much significance to the imposition of a duty to bargain collectively . . . Neither the witnesses who testified in committee nor the senators and representatives who took the floor paid great heed to the section and none of them showed an appreciation of the difficulties of application.[27]

After reviewing cases decided by the board and the courts, Cox stated, "We are drawn to the conclusion, therefore, that the conventional definition of good faith bargaining as a sincere effort to reach an agreement goes beyond the statute."[28]

On the basis of his overall view of the propriety of board action in this area, Cox questioned whether the NLRB can effectively regulate the actual conduct of collective negotiations, particularly when the parties had bargained together and had signed "some kind of an agreement."[29] The import of Professor Cox's article was that the NLRB is imposing more and more government regulation on the processes of collective bargaining in order to develop objective standards of good bargaining practice. Cox is, of course, opposed to this development.

OTHER ATTACKS ON THE DUTY TO BARGAIN

The use of Senator Walsh's statement in attacks on board policy concerning the duty to bargain is also seen in the CED report on the national labor policy. After citing Senator Walsh, the committee commented:

Senator Walsh's objective was a sensible one, and an appealingly simple one, too. Unfortunately, as time has passed, the simplicity has been lost. It has been succeeded by a flood of litigation and an increasingly complex set of regulations stemming from amendments of the original provisions and from interpretations by the NLRB and the courts. The efficacy of the process in achieving a more ambitious objective—to compel the parties to bargain in good faith—is at best doubtful.[30]

The conclusion of the CED study group was that the effort to legislate bargaining in good faith should be abandoned and that the issues involved in the board's interpretation of the duty to bargain should be returned to "the door of the employer or union, where Senator Walsh wisely left them." [31]

On a number of occasions, the Supreme Court also utilized Senator Walsh's statement to illustrate congressional intent, in order to limit the jurisdiction of the board. For example, Justice Harlan's dissent in *Borg-Warner* stated:

. . . the legislative history behind the Wagner and Taft-Hartley Acts persuasively indicates that the Board was never intended to have power to prevent good faith bargaining as to any subject not violative of the provisions or policies of those acts. As a leading exponent for the Wagner Act explained . . .[32]

And then followed Senator Walsh's statement limiting the sweep of the duty to bargain in the original act.

However, Justice Brennan qualified Walsh's remark with the following observation:

The limitation implied by the last sentence ["What happens behind those doors is not inquired into, and the bill does not seek to inquire into it"] has not been in practice maintained—practically, it could hardly have been—but the underlying purpose of the remark has remained the most basic purpose of the statutory provision.[33]

Apparently Justice Brennan instinctively recognized that despite Walsh's language, and even assuming its relevance, the same considerations of historic expediency which led to the development of good-faith bargaining on the basis of the Transportation Act of 1920 and the vague language of Section 7(a) of the NIRA would have worked to the same effect in any statute intended to promote collective bargaining and eliminate industrial strife.

Another writer stated:

. . . the original idea of an advisory group of employees meeting with an employer to confer, which is what the act provided, was a good one. Every writer on the subject, and there had been many, [citing a number of articles] points out that the chairman of the Senate Committee in Education and Labor, Senator Walsh, indicated that that was the purpose of Section 8(5) of the original act.[34]

One textbook has stated that "Congress would have been surprised to know that pensions, for example, would fall within the statutory reference to 'wages' . . ." [35]

Without exception, every legal article which discusses the duty to bargain refers to the publications of Professor Smith and Professors Cox and Dunlop, particularly in treating of the history of the doctrine of good faith.[36]

CONGRESSIONAL INTENT IN THE WAGNER ACT

The discussion has shown that assumptions about the congressional intent in establishing the duty to bargain are the basis for the various criticisms of board doctrine as developed over the years. It would, therefore, appear necessary to analyze critically the charge that the board has somehow usurped the legislative function in the evolution of its principles of good-faith bargaining.

The repeated citation of Senator Walsh is no accident. His statement appears to support completely the notion that Congress had no intention of going beyond the door behind which negotiations were to take place. But a careful review of the entire legislative history discloses that this statement of Senator Walsh is the *only* basis for concluding that Congress intended to limit the scope of the duty to bargain. As a matter of fact, the quotation from Senator Walsh invariably stops short of his complete remarks. For example, after Senator Walsh stated that the bill does not seek to inquire into what happens behind the doors of the conference room, he further stated:

It anticipates that the employer will deal *reasonably* with the employees, that he will be patient, but he is obliged to sign no agreement; he can say "Gentlemen, we have heard you and considered your proposals. We cannot comply with your request" . . . All the section does is to designate the agency to negotiate on behalf of the employees with whom the employer must deal. He does not have to accept any particular contract with them, *but he must bargain with them in a bona fide effort to reach a mutually satisfactory agreement.* [Emphasis added.][37]

There is an obvious inconsistency between the assertion that the law did not intend to scrutinize what goes on in negotiation and the legal requirement that an employer must deal reasonably and make a bona fide effort to reach an agreement. However, despite the ambiguity in Senator Walsh's full comments, there exists far stronger—in my view, incontrovertible—evidence that the legislative intent was to incorporate in the duty to bargain exactly the criteria which the board later imposed.

To begin with, it must be emphatically stated that although Walsh was chairman of the Senate committee, S. 1938 was Wagner's bill. Senator Wagner drafted the bill, made numerous appearances before the Senate and House committees in support of it, and, most significantly, wrote the Senate report which recommended its passage. It must be repeated that Senator Walsh's role, unlike his performance during the consideration of his substitute bill in 1934, was a purely passive one. It will be recalled that the original Wagner bill introduced in 1934, S. 2926, contained a specific unfair labor practice which imposed the duty to bargain upon employers.[38] In introducing his bill to the Senate, Senator Wagner asserted that the requirement to bargain was of extreme importance, as evidenced by his experience as chairman of the National Labor Board. The duty to bargain in the original bill was based upon the successful experience of the Railway Labor Act which, as we have seen, contained such a duty.[39]

We have already reviewed the hearings on the original Wagner bill, with their lengthy discussions on its value. Witness after witness stressed the critical role of the duty to bargain, particularly the administrators of the NRA Labor Boards. It will also be recalled that representatives of employers speaking in opposition to this provision interpreted the duty to bargain as contained in Senator Wagner's bill in the light of existing decisions of the National Labor Board.

The substitution of the Walsh amendments for the Wagner bill, S. 2926, eliminated the duty to bargain. This was not accidental. In presenting his bill to the Senate, Senator Walsh described the bill in almost exactly the same manner as he used to describe S. 1958.[40]

We have already recounted the circumstances which led to the substitution of Public Resolution No. 44 for the Walsh bill. But it should be remembered that Senator La Follette substituted on the floor of the Senate certain amendments which Senator Wagner intended to introduce if the Walsh bill was to be voted upon. They included the provision that it should be an unfair labor practice for employers "to refuse to recognize and deal with such representatives for the purpose of collective bargaining." [41] Senator La Follette concluded his explanation of the Wagner amendments by stating:

What boots it, Mr. President, if representatives are chosen by the employees or if elections are held as provided by the joint resolution if after those representatives are chosen the employers refuse to meet with them? In instance after instance, after representatives were chosen by the wage earners, employers have contended that they have complied with their obligations as to collective bargaining when they permitted representatives to enter their offices but have declined to consult with them further.[42]

Much has been made of the omission of a specific duty to bargain in the Wagner Bill, S. 1958, introduced in 1935. The introduction of Section 8(5) has been characterized by Professor Smith as fortuitous, and other writers have repeatedly emphasized the accidental nature of its inclusion. But it is clear beyond doubt that the exclusion of a specific requirement of the duty to bargain was based solely upon considerations of statutory draftsmanship.[43]

The Senate debate was replete with additional evidence of the meaning attributed to the duty to bargain. This included several colloquies between Senator Walsh and Senator Wagner, in one of which Senator Walsh repeated his illustration of what could happen to an employer if he met with the representatives of his employees and did not agree with them. To this Senator Wagner responded: "Of course, he need not reach an agreement, but if he evidenced bad faith by not really attempting to bargain collectively, that would be an unfair labor practice, because it would be interference with the right of employees to bargain collectively."[44]

It seems unnecessary and superfluous here to repeat the entire legislative history of the duty to bargain which is recited in the preceding chapter. There was extensive debate on the meaning of Section 8(5) and lengthy explanations of this provision during committee hearings by numerous witnesses. All the witnesses who discussed this provision, and both the Senate and House committee reports, emphasized the significance of the duty to bargain.[45]

It should not be overlooked that the experience of the NRA labor boards played a prominent role in the congressional debates. There was continual reference to the decisions of the early labor boards on the nature of the duty to bargain, including the insertion of the boards' principles in the Congressional Record. This reference to NRA boards took place in the consideration of the 1934 bills as well as of the Wagner Bill itself in 1935.[46]

We can only conclude that the universally held assumption about the legislative intent concerning the duty to bargain is untenable. Furthermore, the statement by Cox and Dunlop that "there was not a word in the hearing, in the committee reports, or in the debates to suggest that the Act would define the subjects of collective bargaining and give the Board power to resolve the issues in disputed cases" is also not supported by the evidence.

As Senator Wagner put it, unionization "will prove of little value if it is to be used solely for Saturday night dances and Sunday afternoon picnics." The *Houde* decision, which was the leading NRA labor board holding on the duty to bargain, specifically condemned a company's practice of discussing with the union matters of secondary importance, such as toilet facilities, safety measures, coat racks, slippery stairs, etc. The board held, it will be remembered, that such discussion could not be considered collective bargaining since the employer refused to discuss "the recognized subjects of collective bargaining, namely, wages, hours and basic working conditions."

It will also be recalled that the early boards had made the mandatory subjects of collective bargaining both very explicit and very sweeping, including change of plant location, introduction of a new line of products, and even the failure of an employee to pay a union-imposed fine. It appears that "a good legal argument" cannot be made that the sponsors of the Wagner Act did not intend to have the Board define the scope of bargaining. It is also clear that Professor Smith's conclusion that "the Congress which made the duty to bargain explicit for most employers did not make a substantial contribution to its meaning" neglects the congressional concern with and ratification of the NRA labor boards' doctrines which were later reaffirmed and extended under the Wagner Act. It can only be concluded that in passing the duty to bargain Congress intended to provide legislative authority for the definition of good-faith bargaining which was to be adopted later by the NLRB.

On August 24, 1935, the Senate set the machinery of the law in motion by confirming the appointment of the first three board members. When the first formal meeting of the board took place on September 4, the first order of business was the creation of an organization and the adoption of procedural rules and regulations. The Wagner Act itself provided for the transfer of the staff of the old National Labor Relations Board to the new board, and on September 14, 1935, the new board promulgated rules and regulations governing its procedure. Not until early October was the board open for business and ready to entertain petitions and charges arising from the statute.[1]

THE STATUTORY BASIS FOR COLLECTIVE BARGAINING

The explicit statutory basis for the board's regulation of collective bargaining was Section 8(5) of the act, which stated that it was an unfair labor practice for an employer "to refuse to bargain collectively with the representatives of his employees, subject to the provisions of Section 9(a)." Section 9(a) of the act provided:

Representatives designated or selected for the purposes of collective bargaining by the majority of the employees in a unit appropriate for such purposes, shall be the exclusive representative of all the employees in such unit for the purposes of collective bargaining in respect to rates of pay, wages, hours of employment, or other conditions of employment: *Provided,* That any individual employee or a group of employees shall have the right at any time to present grievances to their employer.

In the enforcement of Section 8(5), the board had for its guidance the act's statement of "Findings and Policy" which condemned "the denial by employers to accept the procedure of collective bargaining." Furthermore, the statute decried the existence of an "inequality of bargaining power between employees who do not possess full freedom of association or actual liberty of contract, and employers who are organized in the corporate or other forms of ownership association."

The fundamental purpose of the act was set out as follows:

It is hereby declared to be the policy of the United States to eliminate the cause of certain obstructions to the free flow of commerce and to mitigate and eliminate these obstructions when they have occurred *by encouraging the practice and procedure of collective bargaining* and by protecting the exercise by workers of full freedom of association, self-organization, and *designation of representatives of their own choosing, for the purpose of negotiating the terms and conditions of their employment* or other mutual aid or protection. [Emphasis added.]

A general statement of the rights of employees was given in Section 7 of the act, which assured them the right "to bargain collectively through representatives of their own choosing, and to engage in concerted activities, for the purpose of collective bargaining." And Section 8(1) of the act made it an unfair labor practice "to interfere with, restrain, or coerce employees in the exercise of the rights guaranteed in Section 7."

The obvious purpose of the statute was to encourage the practice of collective bargaining and to redress the unequal bargaining power of unions and employers. But the full meaning and content of a law depend upon the decisions made in specific cases and often turn upon particular facts and circumstances. It is proposed to examine board decisions on the basis of the statutory mandate in order to ascertain the precise meaning of the duty to bargain.

THE EMPLOYER'S DUTY TO MEET WITH THE UNION

It was the explicit statutory duty of an employer not to decline to bargain collectively with the majority representative of his employees in an appropriate unit. Patently, the most elementary violation of the duty to bargain was a refusal to meet with the union. In a number of early cases, the board established the principle that to fail to reply to or accept communications requesting meetings for the purpose of collective bargaining, or to return them, was a violation of Section 8(5).[2] The union's request to bargain, however, must be clear and unequivocal.[3] Conduct tantamount to failure to meet and negotiate includes failure to arrange personal conferences at reasonable times and places, and failure to make available authorized representatives.[4]

In the *Lorillard Co.* cases, the board found that a company's refusal to meet with union representatives in the towns in which its plants were located, and its corresponding insistence that negotiations take place in its home offices, constituted a violation of Section 8(5). This holding of the board is of interest in demonstrating the rationale behind its construction of the statutory duty. In its analysis, the board cited its interpretation of Section 8(5) in the *Inland Steel Company* case[5] that the employer's obligation to bargain requires him "to accept in good faith the procedure of collective bargaining as historically practiced." Furthermore, the board cited an earlier case, *Matter of S. L. Allen & Company*,[6] on the nature of collective bargaining:

Interchange of ideas, communication of facts peculiarly within the knowledge of either party, personal persuasion and the opportunity to modify demands in accordance with the total situation thus revealed at the conference is of the essence of the bargaining process.

It followed that "bargaining in the field of labor relations is customarily carried on over the conference table at which the representatives of both parties confront each other and exercise that personal and oral persuasion of which they are capable."[7]

The board concluded that as a matter of law "the procedure of collective bargaining requires that the employer make his representatives available for conferences at reasonable times and places and in such a manner that personal negotiations are practicable." In the *Lorillard* case, the failure of the employer to do so meant that he had not fulfilled his obligation to bargain.

THE DUTY OF THE EMPLOYER TO NEGOTIATE

If an employer met with the duly designated representative of a majority of his employees in an appropriate unit, did this meeting fully satisfy the requirement to bargain? From the very earliest cases, the answer was no. Section 9(a) of the act makes the union the exclusive representative for all employees in an appropriate unit, so that an employer is guilty of an unfair labor practice if he offers to bargain only for members of the union.[8] Furthermore, the status of the union as the representative of all employees in the appropriate unit is not affected by the failure of the union to ask in writing for this recognition.[9] A violation also exists if the employer offers to bargain only for part of the unit found appropriate by the board in a prior representation proceeding.[10]

Inasmuch as the union is the exclusive statutory representative of the employees, it is refusal to bargain to negotiate directly with the employees rather than with the union,[11] to enter into contracts with individual employees through an independent bargaining committee,[12] and to induce individuals to execute contracts of employment.[13] It is also a violation to meet and negotiate with the duly designated representative of its employees but to refrain at the same time from according the union full recognition. The board stated its position as follows:

> To meet and negotiate with a committee of employees while deliberately withholding union recognition does not satisfy the requirements of the Act. The paramount importance of the fact of union recognition alone in securing collective bargaining has been asserted repeatedly in our decisions.[14]

In another case, the board said:

> It is plain from these facts that although the respondent met with the Union representatives and discussed terms with them, it neither recognized nor bargained with the Union as the representative of its employees. We have repeatedly held that to meet with the Union representatives and to discuss terms does not satisfy the requirements of the Act if Union recognition is withheld as it was in this case.[15]

THE SUBJECT MATTER OF COLLECTIVE BARGAINING

The statutory language imposed an additional requirement which can result in the sustaining of a refusal to bargain notwithstanding an employer's compliance with the other terms of the act. Section 9(a) of the act stated that the majority union is the exclusive spokesman of all employees in the appropriate unit "in respect to rates of pay, wages, hours of employment or other conditions of employment." Hence the test of legality was not met by an employer's meeting and negotiating with the statutory representative if the statutory subject matters were excluded by employer fiat.

This conception of the duty to bargain was expressed in an early case in response to the employer's defense that he ". . . at all times conferred with the Locals, the Employees' Representation Plan and individual employees on matters of alleged grievances and complaints and that such grievances have been happily adjusted." The board stated:

Collective bargaining means more than the discussion of individual problems and grievances with employees or groups of employees. It means that the employer is obligated to negotiate in good faith with his employees as a group, through their representatives, on matters of wages, hours and basic working conditions and to endeavor to reach an agreement for a fixed period of time. The respondent's conception of its duty is merely to consider any grievances its individual employees may care to present, discuss them and then act upon them as it may deem fit. It is evident that the grievances that the respondent discussed and was willing to discuss were the individual problems of its employees and matters of ordinary detail, and did not pertain to the employees as a group. The recognized subjects of collective bargaining are wages, hours and basic working conditions; therefore, the duty of an employer to bargain collectively is not at all exhausted when he considers individual grievances.[16]

The board had also found that the subject of grievances falls within the compass of Section 9(a) and is a mandatory issue for bargaining.[17] In one case the board decided that the interpretation of a contract was "plainly an issue of substance between the parties and a legitimate subject of collective bargaining within the contemplation of the Act." [18] The board held that there was no duty incumbent upon the employer to agree to the union's interpretation, but a duty did exist to discuss the issue. The board cited in support of its view the finding of the Supreme Court in the *Sands* case "that the Act imposes upon the employer the further obligation to meet and bargain with his employees' representatives respecting proposed changes of an existing contract and also to discuss with them its interpretation, if there is any doubt as to its meaning." [19]

Notwithstanding a history of unilateral control of merit increases unchallenged by the union, the board found that merit increases "are an integral part of the wage structure," and that an employer had an obligation to bargain about them. [20] Among other subjects found to be within the area of mandatory bargaining were sub-contracting, work rules, and working schedules. [21]

In one case, an employer insisted upon the retention of the right to discontinue payment for paid holidays, vacations, and bonuses. [22] In his brief, the employer argued:

In any event, we submit that an employer is perfectly justified in retaining something that he may give to his employees. It is not necessary that every gratuitous act of an employer benefiting employees be converted into a contractual obligation. An employer is entitled to give and to feel that he may give benefits aside and in addition to his legal obligations and upon occasions to have his employees know and appreciate that he is in his relations with them going beyond the strict letter of his legal obligations. Therefore, although vacations and bonuses are proper subjects of bargaining negotiations, it does not follow that the employer must accede to the request of the negotiators and embody his intentions in regard thereto into a legally binding instrument. He may say: "These I reserve from the contract for the very reason that I want the privilege of granting them, not under compulsion, but of my own free will." [23]

The board treated the employer's position as resting "upon a fundamental misconception" of its duty to bargain. "Paid holidays, vacations, and bonuses constitute an integral part of the earnings and working conditions of the employees . . . The Act plainly contemplates that the employees shall have the right, through representatives of their own choosing, to bargain collectively with respect to such conditions of employment, if they so desire." [24]

Apparently, in only one decision did the board remove a subject from the ambit of collective bargaining. In the *Times Publishing Company* case,[25] the employer was held to be under no obligation during and after an economic strike to negotiate with the union on the conditions of employment of strike replacements. While the employer's obligation to bargain with the union was not extinguished by the strike, the right of the employer to replace the strikers would be "nullified" if the terms of employment of the new employees were subject to joint negotiations.

THE DUTY TO BARGAIN IN GOOD FAITH

Assuming that the explicit, specific, formal statutory requirements of bargaining have been met—that an employer met in a convenient place with the majority representative of his employees, according them full recognition for the appropriate unit, and did not remove unilaterally from the area of discussion any subject included in "wages, hours and other conditions of employment"—circumstances may still arise which result in a refusal to bargain.

From the very first cases, the board was confronted with situations which led it to develop the test of good faith. In the *Allen* case,[26] the employer asserted that it had complied with the requirement to bargain because it had held many conferences with the union. Furthermore, the employer asserted that an impasse justified a refusal to meet with the union until a reasonable possibility of agreement was apparent. The board's analysis of the circumstances of the case led it to condemn the employer's position as based upon a misunderstanding of the import of the collective bargaining provision of the Act. To meet with the representatives of his employees, however frequently, does not necessarily fulfill an employer's obligations under this Section. A construction of the collective bargaining provision which overlooked the requirement that a bonafide attempt to come to terms must be made, would substitute for non-recognition of the employees' representatives the incentive simply to hamstring the union with endless and profitless "negotiations." In the absence of an attempt to bargain in good faith on the employer's part, it is obvious that such "negotiations" can do nothing to prevent resort to industrial warfare where a dispute of this nature arises.[27]

Under the circumstances, the refusal by the employer to renew meetings was due to its refusal to bargain and not to an impasse occasioned by irreconcilable differences in positions.

The key points in the decision were the requirements that an employer must make a "bonafide attempt to come to terms" with the union, and that meetings, no matter how frequent, are not equivalent to genuine bargaining in the absence of "good faith."[28] The concepts embodied in these words were to be applied time and again in subsequent cases.

The board repeatedly affirmed that meeting and discussion were insufficient by themselves to prove good faith. In the *St. Joseph Stockyards* case,[29] the board held that "genuine collective bargaining" did not follow from the employer's willingness to meet at all times with the representatives of his employees and to discuss all issues. While the employer had not refused unqualifiedly to negotiate with its employees, the board held that Congress had intended to protect more than "the barren right of discussion."

In deciding what constituted a failure to negotiate in good faith, the policy of the board was to examine in each case "the dealings between the parties and scrutinize the activities of the employer during the course of the negotiations in an effort to determine whether the employer has been bargaining in good faith." [30]

The board's annual report cited the following quotation from its decision in *Matter of Atlas Mills, Inc.*[31] as illustrative of its approach and method of analysis.

There is no doubt that the respondent negotiated with the representatives of Local 2269, meeting with them, receiving proposals, and putting forward counterproposals of its own. But there is equally little doubt that if the obligation of the Act is to produce more than a series of empty discussions, bargaining must mean more than mere negotiation. It must mean negotiation with a bonafide intent to reach an agreement if agreement is possible. Negotiations with an intent only to delay and postpone a settlement until a strike can be broken is not collective bargaining within the meaning of Section 8(5) of the act. The present record persuades us that the respondent did not bargain in good faith with Local 2269. The discharges which met the first request to bargain; the delays and postponements, always at the instance of the respondent's representative, that characterized the negotiations once they were begun; the refusal to sign a written agreement; the constant changes in the basis of negotiations, each time further away from the desires of Local 2269; the efforts made by one of the respondent's agents while the negotiations were still going on to win the higher paid leaders away from Local 2269, break the strike, and avoid the necessity to bargain at all: these are not indications of a bonafide effort to reach an agreement. Rather they suggest a design, facilitated by the youth and inexperience of the striking employees, to use the negotiating process as a strike-breaking device.[32]

The basis of the board's determination of good-faith bargaining, therefore, was its appraisal of an employer's "bonafide intent to reach an agreement if agreement is possible." The indications which the board found in this case were negative: discharges, delays, refusal to sign a written agreement, constant shifts in negotiation positions, and efforts to break the strike. In many subsequent cases, the board inferred the absence of good faith from such conduct by employers.

But the board has made an important distinction in the weight to be assigned to specific conduct. As a general rule, the board, particularly in the early years, took into consideration the history of the labor relations between the parties and the "totality of conduct" of the respondent. In a very early case, the board remarked:

The question of whether an employer has failed in his affirmative duty to bargain collectively with the representatives of his employees has meaning only when considered in connection with the facts of a particular case. The history of the relationships between the particular employer and its employees, the practice of the industry, the circumstances of the immediate issue between the employer and its employees are all relevant factors that must be given weight.[33]

Consequently, the condemnation of an employer's conduct in a negotiating session during which the union officers "were relegated to the position of bystanders and were permitted scant opportunity to present their demands" was a factor in a finding of bad-faith bargaining, but only one of many.[34] Other elements of bad faith were present, including the employer's announced intention of not recognizing the union and his activities designed to eliminate it.

The investigation of bad faith was not merely an inquiry into an employer's state of mind; it was an examination of employer behavior. The board itself has stated that the problem was often one of drawing inferences from the employer's conduct in order to determine whether or not the employer had "entered into negotiations in good faith in a bonafide attempt to reach a collective bargaining agreement." [35] The question of good faith was accordingly to be tested with reference to collective bargaining, which the board held was "a procedure looking forward toward the making of a collective agreement by the employer with the accredited representatives of its employees concerning wages, hours, and other conditions of employment." [36]

A test of good faith—perhaps a major test—lies in the employer's acceptance of the procedure of collective bargaining. The duty to bargain as construed by the board imposed upon an employer the objective of establishing such a contractual relationship. For reasons independent of the statutory language treated in the preceding section, it followed that the logic of collective bargaining required more than union recognition and negotiations of the terms and conditions of employment. In order for the procedure of collective bargaining to be adopted, there must be a duty "to enter into discussion and negotiation with an open and fair mind and with a sincere purpose to find a basis of agreement concerning the issues presented and to make contractually binding the understanding upon the terms that are reached." [37]

It followed that an "open and fair mind" and a "sincere purpose" were expressed by conduct designed for or consistent with the reaching of a collective bargaining agreement.[38] But the acceptance of the procedure of collective bargaining by an employer required more than good-faith negotiations. There must also be acceptance of the practice of collective bargaining, which required the employer "to make contractually binding the understanding upon terms that are reached, and, under ordinary circumstances, to reduce that obligation to the form of a signed written agreement if requested to do so by the employees' representatives." [39]

POSITIVE ACTION REQUIRED OF EMPLOYERS

We have already shown in general that a lack of good faith may be inferred from employer conduct. It is now necessary to consider what positive action, if any, was required of employers in the fulfillment of their duty to bargain. Again, the decisions in the earliest cases provided the lead in tracing the development of the employer's duty. In one such case, a refusal to bargain was found where the employer merely heard the union's representative read a proposed agreement and then turned down the proposal completely without offering counterproposals or "entering into an honest and sincere discussion of the proposals." [40]

The question soon arose whether an employer was required to offer counterproposals as part of his duty to bargain. In an early case the Fifth Circuit held that, while a counterproposal was not indispensable to bargaining where it was apparent that it would be unacceptable, "Still when a counter-proposal is directly asked for, it ought to be made, for the resistance in discussion may have been only strategy and not a fixed final intention." [41]

In another case, relying upon the *Globe* decision, the board based a refusal to bargain in part upon the failure of an employer to make an effort to submit to the union any plan or offer. The board concluded, "It is obvious that the respondent's failure in this respect made any productive negotiations impossible." [42]

But a close reading of the decisions does not support the view that the refusal to offer counterproposals was a per se violation of the act. In the *Wilson* case, the board's decision was influenced by and in part based upon other independent evidence of a refusal to bargain. The rationale for requiring positive action by an employer can best be studied by examining two contrasting cases, one in which a refusal to bargain was found and the other in which it was not.

In the former instance, an employer had met frequently with the representative of his employees and discussed in great detail the union's proposed contract. In the eyes of the board, this alone was insufficient to establish good-faith bargaining, for during the lengthy discussions the employer

did not agree to any portion of the agreement and refused to offer any counter-proposals of his own although asked to do so by the Union. Thus, while not agreeing to the proposals of the Union, Covington [the employer] at the same time avoided any affirmative indication of possible terms to which he might be willing to agree.[43]

But the employer's violation did not consist exclusively of the failure to offer counterproposals. The board considered the tactics of the employer at the bargaining table a "technique not calculated to make productive negotiations possible" and interpreted the technique in the light of the employer's concomitant anti-union activities, which included the discriminatory discharge of union members and unilateral changes in working conditions. The board's language was particularly significant in its stressing of the total evidence. For example, the decision concluded as follows:

We are satisfied from a consideration of all the evidence that the respondent was deliberately pursuing a policy designed to evade its duty to bargain and that it continued meeting with the Union for the purpose of giving the appearance of obedience to the Act without, as the Act requires, attempting in good faith to bargain collectively with the Union.[44]

On the other hand, in the *Easton* case,[45] the board overruled a trial examiner's finding of a refusal to bargain which was based solely on the employer's failure to make a counterproposal. During the negotiations, agreement was reached on a number of the union's proposals which were accepted without change by the employer. On a number of others, joint agreement was reached as a result of management's suggestions. Agreement was not reached, however, on wages or the closed-shop demand. The union made no effort to inspect the employer's books, although the employer consented to inspection and the discussion on wages hinged upon the firm's revenues. The employer was firm in its refusal to grant the closed shop. Although the employer was requested to offer a counterproposal on wages and never did so, the board found that the actual breakdown of negotiations was not precipitated by its refusal. Other factors, including the impasse on the closed shop, were evident. The board's conclusion therefore was that "the entire record does not support a finding that the respondent has failed to bargain collectively with the Union." [46]

The differences between the two cases are clear despite the fact that neither employer made any counterproposals. The conclusion is also clear that the failure to make a counterproposal may be evidence of bad-faith bargaining only in a particular factual context.

The board at all times was very careful not to equate good-faith bargaining with a surrender by the employer to the union's demands. In one case, the board stated

that the difference between the semblance and substance of collective bargaining may be tested by the extent to which the parties evidence a sincere purpose to explore the total situation and find a basis for agreement. The employer must in a very real sense undertake to discover with the union such common ground as may exist between the parties. On the other hand, satisfaction of the statutory obligation does not require an employer to capitulate to the demands addressed to him. [47]

The issues in this case, as stated by the board, were that the parties were irreconcilably opposed with respect to the preferential shop, seniority, and arbitration. But even though the employer stood its ground and refused to yield to the demands of the union, no inference of bad faith was made since there was agreement on many other subjects; a grievance procedure had been established and there had been frequent adjustment of grievances. And, significantly, there was a total absence of other conduct by the employer which would be inconsistent with its obligation to bargain in good faith.

REFUSAL TO SUPPLY RELEVANT INFORMATION
UPON REQUEST

From the first, the board has construed the collective bargaining process as requiring "the communication of facts peculiarly within the knowledge of either party." [48] For instance, the board held in one case that an employer had not engaged in collective bargaining when it told a union that its financial condition was poor but refused either to prove this or to permit independent verification. [49]

The link between the duty of an employer to furnish information and the obligation to bargain in good faith was clearly brought out in the *Singer Manufacturing Company* case. [50] Although the employer had met the union's organizational campaign by instituting two unilateral wage increases, it insisted that a first contract incorporate a wage reduction because of "business exigencies." In addition, the employer insisted upon reserving to itself the right to reduce wages further during the term of the agreement, again because of business necessities. The employer flatly refused to permit an accountant to examine its books or to submit the wage issue to arbitration, and proposed no alternative method which might satisfy the union of the economic justification for its position.

The employer also relied upon business exigencies to justify its refusal to continue its current practice on paid holidays and vacations and to include these points in a written contract with the union. What is more, the employer demanded that the union agree that the employees should work twelve hours per day and fifty-six hours per week without payment of overtime. Under the then existing Fair Labor Standards Act these hours would have been unlawful in the absence of a collective bargaining agreement.

Essentially, the employer demanded that the union accept the company's offer, giving only a bare statement of the reason and making no effort to convince the union of the rightness of its position. The board reasoned that the employer clearly had no desire to reach an agreement with the union and made no effort in good faith to do so.

In another case, an employer had unilaterally raised wages upon a basis of its classification of jobs. The union then requested a complete job classification list for all employees, giving their names, the nature of the jobs, and the wage rates. The employer declined to give this information on the grounds that it was confidential, and that the union could secure it directly from its members.

The background of this dispute was that the employer had agreed to reconsider its wage schedule under the grievance procedure. The board held that the information requested by the union was necessary to its understanding of the employer's wage action and that without this information it could not process grievances or discuss the issues intelligently. Furthermore, the prospect of the union's getting all the data promptly and accurately seemed remote, and involved a considerable loss of time and the imposition of inconvenience and difficulty on the bargaining process. Accordingly, the board held: "In this situation, an employer bargaining in good faith would not have withheld the information requested, nor would the employees be privileged against disclosure since the information is essential to the intelligent bargaining on their behalf required by the Act." [51]

But the refusal to grant the union all information available to the employer was never considered a per se violation of the duty to bargain. During negotiations, one employer announced that it had completed a survey of competitive wage rates, on the basis of which it was prepared to raise wages for certain categories of employees. The employer refused to divulge the wage rates in effect in all the concerns on the grounds that this information was given in confidence, but it did disclose the names of the firms covered in the survey. The board held that under the circumstances of the case, the refusal to give out all details of the survey was not intended to defeat the negotiations since the employer sincerely believed that the requested information was confidential, and since the union did not claim that it lacked sufficient knowledge of the competitive rates based upon its own experience. [52]

In another case, the board found a violation of 8(5) in the institution of a unilateral wage increase by an employer, but refused to find bad faith in the company's rejection of the union's request for certain wage information. The basis for the board's decision was that the employer had invited the union to conduct its own engineering studies at the plant and that considering all the circumstances of the case, including evidence of substantial counterproposals by the employer, there was no violation of Section 8(5) of the act. [53]

POSITIVE ACTS IN DEROGATION OF AN EMPLOYER'S DUTY TO BARGAIN

The board has found in many cases that a unilateral grant of wage increases or other benefits at a time when a union was seeking to negotiate was evidence of bad-faith bargaining. In a very early case, the issuance of a "statement of policy" announcing wage increases and other benefits was held by the board to be "a clear evasion" of the employer's duty to bargain with the employees, since the changes affected matters which were currently under negotiation with the union.[54]

The rationale of this decision was explicated in succeeding cases. In *Chicago Apparatus Company*,[55] the board stated that the company's conferring upon employees many of the benefits sought by the union

constituted a direct attack upon the union's efforts to bargain collectively. The publication of this statement dealt a severe blow to the union's prestige by demonstrating to the employees that so far as respondent was concerned collective bargaining was neither desirable nor necessary.[56]

The circumstances which led to the condemnation of a unilateral increase in wages were typified in one case, in which an employer persistently rejected all the union's proposed terms for a contract without making any counterproposal. Nevertheless, immediately after the end of the fruitless negotiations, the employer unilaterally put into effect a wage increase after rejecting one demanded by the majority union.[57] In affirming a board order in a similar case, a circuit court stated that the instituting of a vacation concession during negotiations showed "deliberate contempt for the whole plan of collective bargaining."[58]

However, circumstances alter cases. Situations may arise in which unilateral determination of the terms and conditions of employment is not evidence of bad faith. In one case, in which the employer continued to discuss and consider the proposals of the union after changing conditions unilaterally, no bad faith was found.[59]

A unilateral increase in benefits is a violation when the union is bypassed. Consequently, in one case where a union accepted an incentive wage plan, and the facts indicated that the employer was at all times willing to bargain about it, there was a finding of no violation of 8(5).[60]

BYPASSING OF THE UNION

Normally, unilateral changes in any working conditions that have been fixed by contract is an unfair labor practice. The board has said:

> To permit an employer to change the terms of an existing collective agreement without first notifying the bargaining agency and submitting the matter to negotiations, would nullify Section 8(5) of the Act, for what was made collectively could be promptly unmade unilaterally.[61]

But not every breach of contract is an unfair labor practice.[62] The violation stems from a breach without prior negotiation with the statutory bargaining agent about the proposed deviation from its terms. One commentator has stated in this connection:

> There is nothing in the Act to indicate that its framers intended that its force should be expended after it had once operated to cause an employer to bargain collectively with his employees. In our view, if Congress had intended that the duty to bargain collectively which it imposed should be limited in duration . . . it would have so provided in clear and specific terms.[63]

The board has extended this concept to mean that even prior to the commencement of bargaining, an employer must not make any changes in the terms and conditions of employment once a union has been selected as a majority representative of its employees.[64]

BYPASSING OF THE UNION—INDIVIDUAL BARGAINING

From the earliest cases, the board has condemned direct dealing by an employer with his employees when a majority union exists.[65] In all these cases, the board has characterized this direct dealing as an attempt to evade the responsibility to negotiate only with the exclusive majority representative. As one court said:

To permit the employer to go behind the chosen bargaining agent and negotiate with the employees individually, or with their committees, in spite of the fact that they had not revoked the agent's authority, would result in nothing but disarrangement of the mechanism for negotiation created by the Act, disparagement of the services of the union, whether good or bad, and acute, if not endless, friction which it is the avowed purpose of the Act to avoid or mitigate.[66]

The Supreme Court, in a series of decisions, has affirmed the board's rulings in this area. In one case, the court held that individual agreements, regardless of the legality of their origin, cannot be relied upon to nullify the principles of majority rule and of collective bargaining by delaying the initiation of the bargaining procedure for any employees in the unit, or by excluding the individual contracting parties from the unit, or by limiting or conditioning the terms of the agreement.[67]

In another case, the board made a very interesting application of its principle that to bargain directly with one's employees is not to bargain with their designated exclusive representative. Here, all the employees approached the employer and stated that they were ready to abandon the union if they were given wage increases. The board held that the employer was under a duty to refrain from any action which would influence the employees to abandon the union and found that the granting of the increases under these circumstances constituted interference with the self-organizational rights of its employees. This action was also a denial to the union of its statutory status and hence a refusal to bargain. The board held that it was immaterial that the direct dealing emanated from the employees rather than from the employer. The essence of the violation lies in the direct negotiations with the employees while there existed a majority bargaining representative.[68]

The board has also held that it is a violation of the duty to bargain for the employer to bypass the union and attempt to get individual strikers to return to work.[69]

ACTS DESIGNED TO DISSIPATE A UNION'S MAJORITY

When a union's request for negotiations was met by the discharge of its members, the board has found a refusal to bargain.[70] An employer's bad faith can be demonstrated by its refusal to reinstate large numbers of union employees following a plant shutdown.[71] In many cases, the board has found a violation of 8(5) of the act when the employer attempted to induce its employees to withdraw from the union, assisted and dominated a rival union, or imposed preference as between unions when in fact a majority union represented its employees.[72]

The granting of exclusive recognition to a company-dominated union prior to an election which the board had ordered was also held to be a refusal to bargain with the majority union.[73] The courts have upheld the board's finding of a violation of the duty to bargain where there was coercion and intimidation to destroy the union's majority,[74] where a bulletin board notice was derogatory to the union's purpose,[75] where there was a disparagement of the union,[76] and where the employer denounced the union in a newspaper interview.[77]

In another connection, the Supreme Court, in discussing the propriety of a broad board order restraining an employer from violating all provisions of the act, stated, "After an order to bargain collectively in good faith, for example, discriminatory discharge of union members may so affect the bargaining process as to establish a violation of the order." [78] Shutdowns and the threat of shutdowns during the course of bargaining have also been found to justify a finding of a violation of the act. [79] In other cases, however, the existence of unfair labor practices had no connection with the breakdown of negotiations and consequently there was no violation of the duty to bargain. [80]

THE EFFECT OF THE DESTRUCTION OF A UNION'S MAJORITY UPON THE EMPLOYER'S DUTY TO BARGAIN

If an employer has engaged in unfair labor practices in order to avoid its obligation to bargain collectively and has succeeded in destroying the majority status of the union by causing the employees to revoke their designation of that union as their bargaining agent, or to designate a company-dominated labor organization as their new agent, this revocation or change of designation has been given no effect by the board. [81] The board's view was that the purposes of the Wagner Act would otherwise be circumvented and the employer would be enabled to use the fruits of its unfair labor practices as a defense in its refusal to bargain. [82]

In the leading case, where the issue was whether the board could properly order bargaining even though during the interval between the filing of the charges and the issuance of a complaint the union lost its majority standing through personnel replacements incidental to the normal operations of the employer's business and not due to unfair labor practices, the Supreme Court upheld the order as a reasonable exercise of the board's discretion to determine how the effects of an unremedied unfair labor practice should be dissipated.

The court indicated that the reasonableness of such a

remedy lay in the recognition that the bargaining relationship, once rightly established, must be permitted to exist and function for a reasonable period in which it can be given a fair chance to succeed. Otherwise the policies of the act to promote collective bargaining would be frustrated, and a recalcitrant employer would be permitted to profit from his own wrongdoing if he were allowed to interpose the lack of majority as a defense to bargaining.[83]

THE TERMS OF A COLLECTIVE BARGAINING
AGREEMENT AND THE TEST OF GOOD FAITH

We have already discussed the various constraints imposed upon an employer's conduct by the board, and the courts' construction of the duty to bargain. It is appropriate now to discuss the impact of this duty on the terms of the collective bargaining agreement itself.

The earliest guideline was established in *Consumers Research Inc.*, in which the board stated: "By the Act, the terms of agreement are left to the parties themselves; the Board may decide where the collective bargaining negotiations took place but it may not decide what should or should not have been included in the union contract." [84]

The board has consistently adhered to this position.[85] If an employer was not required to agree to any proposal offered by a union, the question arose as to what test the board could employ in order to determine good faith. In an early case, the board discounted as "tactics" the employer's participation in discussion with the union because "its agents carefully avoided any semblance of agreement to proposed terms and offered no suggestions for changes acceptable to them . . ." [86] The board described the employer's conduct as merely giving an appearance of obedience to the Wagner Act without entering into genuine collective bargaining. In enforcing the board's order in this case, the court stated, "We believe there is a duty on both sides, though difficult of legal enforcement, to enter into discussion with an open and fair mind, and a sincere purpose to find a basis of agreement touching wages, hours, and conditions of labor . . ." [87]

Citing this decision, the board found a refusal to bargain when an employer flatly rejected a union's entire proposal and worded its rejection in a manner which avoided any "affirmative indication of possible terms upon which it would be willing to agree." [88] Here, the employer refused to change its position, refused to submit a counterproposal, and refused to discuss any of the particular provisions in the union's proposed contract. The board concluded that

clearly an employer is not required under the Act to agree to whatever proposals a labor organization submits to him. It is obvious, however, that the technique employed by the respondent in this case was calculated to and did make any productive negotiations impossible. [89]

The courts have also scrutinized the conduct of employers at the bargaining table. Board orders to bargain were affirmed because the employer's actions were "thinly disguised refusals," [90] because the employer "pretended" bargaining in order to avoid a direct collision with the act,[91] and because the employer's conduct revealed a "mind hermetically sealed against even the thought of entering into an agreement." [92] Other courts have found a refusal to bargain because an employer stood pat in negotiations,[93] and because in two years of negotiating the employer never receded from a position on any point.[94]

It is instructive to note that in one case, which the board described as a "borderline case," no refusal to bargain was found although no contract was signed, since agreement was reached on many items in negotiations.[95]

But some difficulty in the application of the above-cited principles may result from the need to determine an employer's good faith. The question immediately arises whether good faith is capable of any objective tests at all. The courts have disposed of this issue on a number of occasions. For example, a Circuit Court of Appeals has commented:

The greatest of rascals may solemnly affirm his honesty of purpose; that does not foreclose a jury from finding from the evidence submitted that he possesses no trace of such innocent quality. We find the Board has full authority to determine as a fact whether petitioner was acting in good faith or whether its actions amounted to a mere superficial pretense at bargaining—whether it had actually the intent to bargain, sincerely and earnestly—whether the negotiations were captious and accompanied by an active purpose and intent to defeat or wilfully obstruct real bargaining.[96]

This court also discussed the employer's defense to a finding of bad faith, which rested upon the argument that no law or administrative order can compel men to be "fair, just, honorable, generous, kind and humane." The argument continued that the requirement of good faith falls in the same category. The employer also argued, "Laws are made to govern action, not to control beliefs and opinions." [97]

The treatment of this question by the court requires little comment. The court stated:

We realize full well that Congress has provided only that certain acts shall be performed or omitted. The statute requires of the employer that he bargain collectively and whether he does so depends upon the character of acts he commits or omits. Collective bargaining is an act; pretended collective bargaining is an omission to perform the act, and no unusual difficulty arises because, in determining whether bargaining within the meaning of the Act has indeed occurred, the trier of the facts must determine whether the acts proved were rendered in good faith or were merely in pretended good faith and performed with the actual intent to achieve the very opposite of collective bargaining. Existence or non-existence of good faith, just as existence or non-existence of intent, involve only inquiry as to fact. Whether a crime has been committed not infrequently depends upon existence or non-existence of a felonious intent. Whether one is a bonafide purchaser for value of negotiable paper before maturity without notice puts in issue questions of fact. The neutrality required of an employer in his transactions with his employees is another intangible product of fact, the existence or non-existence of which usually depends upon the character of acts committed or omitted. The civil law furnishes repeated instances of application of the principle.[98]

DEFENSES TO THE DUTY OF GOOD-FAITH BARGAINING

Section 8(5) of the act imposes a duty on the employer to deal only with the majority representative of its employees. It is therefore not an unfair labor practice for an employer to refuse to discuss grievances with the representatives of a minority union.[99] As a condition for collective bargaining, the board has consistently required that there must be a demand for recognition by the union in an appropriate unit and that upon request, adequate proof of majority status must be presented.[100] However, an employer is not justified in dealing with a committee of striking employees who have no authorization from the majority to represent them.[101]

The board and the courts have evolved the rule that doubt as to majority status is not a defense if in fact the refusal was otherwise motivated. In one case, the refusal was due to "a positive rejection . . . of the principle of collective bargaining."[102] The general rule is that the duty to bargain is not excused by a doubt as to the union's majority representation which was not advanced in good faith.[103]

Upon request, a union must furnish proof of its majority status which does not have to be a board certification. But an employer is under a correlative obligation of co-operating with the union to a reasonable extent when the latter is attempting to prove its majority. In one instance, the employer insisted in bad faith on a certification.[104] In still another case, an employer could not claim as a defense its uncertainty as to the union's majority, having rejected a card check or a consent election.[105] An employer who refused to consent to an election but insisted that the union submit a list of members for its inspection was held to violate Section 8(5) of the act; in fact a majority of its employees had designated the union as their agent.[106] But in another case, an employer was held to have fulfilled his obligation to co-operate in proving a majority when he consented to an election but the union insisted upon a card check.[107]

In some circumstances, however, a union may insist upon not going to an election. This ordinarily occurs when the employer is, contemporaneously with the union's demand for recognition, undertaking acts to undermine and dissipate the union's majority. The board remarked:

. . . under ordinary circumstances, and particularly when the labor organization claiming to represent a majority of the employees is unwilling to disclose the names of its members in proof of such claim, an employer's request that the labor organization acquiesce in a consent election to demonstrate such proof is entitled to considerable weight in determining the attitude of the employer to the collective bargaining request of a labor organization. As fully described below, however, the respondent was then in the midst of a campaign to discredit the union among its employees. Its conduct had plainly placed in jeopardy the majority status of the union and indicated its bad faith in making such proposals. Under the circumstances, the refusal of the union to test its strength at that time without the full protection of the Act was not unreasonable.[108]

If an employer did not question a majority status at the time of its refusal to bargain, this silence has been held to indicate that the refusal was not motivated by a bona fide doubt of majority status.[109] However, the board has dismissed a charge because the charging union did not go far enough in pressing its demand for recognition or bringing its majority status to the attention of the employer.[110]

The board has consistently held that authorization cards designating a union as representative of the employees were sufficient to establish majority standing.[111] Application cards for membership and petitions expressly designating a union as a bargaining agent were also sufficient.[112] On occasion, other methods of proving union majority have been accepted by the board. In one case, the board accepted the uncontradicted testimony of a union representative that a majority of the employees had signed cards.[113] In some cases majority standing of the union has been inferred from participation of a majority of employees in a strike or other concerted action.[114] However, signed application cards were not rendered ineffective as proof by the fact that the signers did not participate in a strike or returned to work before the end of the strike.[115]

When an employer refuses to bargain with the union on the basis of a loss of majority standing, it must rebut a presumption that majority status continues in the absence of evidence to the contrary.[116] This presumption of majority status was held to continue for "a reasonable" time. What is reasonable, of course, varies with the circumstances, but the board has established the rule that majority standing based upon a certification is normally operative for one year in the absence of unusual circumstances.[117]

It has been settled law that the duration of majority standing is a question for the board to determine. The justification is that "a bargaining relationship once rightfully established must be permitted to exist and function for a reasonable period in which it can be given a chance to succeed." [118] Another court noted that some measure of permanence was necessary for a successful administration of Section 9 and that "Surely, Congress . . . could not have intended to defeat the administration of the Act by denying such measure of stability to a certification." [119]

But a court will sometimes scrutinize a board order requiring bargaining and refuse to enforce it. In one instance the court held the board's conclusion that the union had a majority to be incorrect as a matter of law, on the showing that some of the employees, sufficient in number to affect the majority, had not of their own free will authorized the union to represent them.[120]

REFUSAL TO BARGAIN ON
THE INAPPROPRIATENESS OF THE UNIT

By and large, the courts will not interfere with the methods adopted by the board for ascertaining the bargaining representative in an appropriate unit. In the leading case, a court sustained as proper the board's action in according finality to the rulings of its regional director on the conduct and results of a consent election, upon a finding by the board that such ruling was neither arbitrary nor capricious. Enforcing the board's order directing the employer to bargain with the union designated by the regional director, the court stated that the board has exclusive authority under the Wagner Act to select suitable methods for ascertaining the appropriateness of the unit and that the court will not set itself up as a judge of these methods.[121]

Accordingly, the board has usually been sustained in its holding that a certification remained effective notwithstanding a subsequent change of management and ownership, if there had been no substantial changes in the operation of the business or in its personnel.[122]

Where the refusal to bargain followed certification in a representation proceeding, the majority status of the union was not normally an issue unless the employer offered evidence which was not cumulative and was not available at the time of that representation hearing.[123] However, occasionally in an unfair labor practice case the board has reviewed its prior determination in a representation case where it had relied upon a misinterpretation of court decisions.[124]

A complaint alleging that an employer has refused to bargain with the representatives of his employees may be sustained only if such representatives were designated by employees in a unit appropriate for the purposes of collective bargaining, as determined by the board pursuant to Section 9(b) of the act.

An employer's doubt as to the appropriateness of the unit is not a defense if the refusal to bargain was otherwise motivated. One court commented that "an employer is in an unfortunate position in attempting to justify before the Board its refusal to bargain for a reason that apparently did not occur to the employer prior to the time of hearing." [125]

In general, a failure to object to the unit when the union requests bargaining is held to rebut any later claim of doubt as to its appropriateness. This has been true even though the union did not specify the unit it sought,[126] even though the unit requested was not the same as the unit later found appropriate,[127] and even though the unit requested was larger than the unit found appropriate.[128] Where an employer, however, reasonably and in good faith challenged the appropriateness of the unit requested by the union, the board held that there was no violation of the act.[129] The board has consistently held that any doubts an employer has concerning the appropriateness of a unit cannot excuse a failure to bargain with a union after the board has validly certified the union in a unit as the representative of its employees.[130]

In determining the appropriateness of a unit, the board has stated the general considerations which determine its actions:

In determining whether the employees of one, several, or all plants of an employer, or the employees in all or only part of a system of communications, transportation, or public utilities, constitute an appropriate unit for the purposes of collective bargaining, the Board has taken into consideration the following factors: (1) the history, extent, and type of organization of the employees; (2) the history of their collective bargaining, including any contracts; (3) history, extent and type of organization, and the collective bargaining, of employees of other employers in the same industry; (4) the relationship between any proposed unit or units and the employer's organization, management, and operation of his business, including the geographical location of the various plants or parts of the system; and (5) the skill, wages, working conditions, and work of the employees.[131]

Under the act a board determination of unit is not subject to direct review in the courts. However, an employer can challenge its ruling in an unfair labor practice proceeding, generally one which resulted as a consequence of the filing of a refusal-to-bargain charge.[132] The Supreme Court has consistently found that the statutory standards which the board applies in determining appropriate units are not capricious, arbitrary, or an unconstitutional delegation of legislative power. The court has held, "The Board must comply . . . with the requirement that the unit selected must be one to effectuate the policies of the Act, the policies of efficient collective bargaining." [133]

CHAPTER 6 · THE TAFT-HARTLEY ACT
AND THE DUTY TO BARGAIN

THE BACKGROUND OF THE TAFT-HARTLEY ACT

No sooner had the Wagner Act been signed into law than bills to repeal or amend it were introduced in Congress. It has been estimated that at least 282 separate legislative proposals of some consequence were introduced in Congress between 1937 and 1947.[1] The vast majority of these proposals consisted of attacks upon the principles and policies established by the NLRB. The House sponsors of the bulk of the proposals were by and large southern Democrats and eastern and midwestern Republicans.[2] Political changes had also increased the desire of Congress to restrict union activity, a tendency which led to the passage of the Smith-Connally Act[3] in 1943, the first anti-union legislation ever passed by Congress. It should also be noted that a bill sponsored by a hostile critic of the board, Congressman Smith of Virginia, passed a Democratic House in 1941, and another anti-union bill, sponsored by Congressman Case, was passed by a Democratic House and Senate in 1946, only to be vetoed by President Truman.

The Republican victory in the 1946 elections, coupled with the wave of strikes in 1945 and 1946, provided the historical background for the enactment of the Taft-Hartley Act.[4]

LEGISLATIVE HISTORY OF SECTION 8(a)(5) OF THE
TAFT-HARTLEY ACT

Both the Senate and House Labor Committees held hearings on the large number of labor bills that had been introduced in the late winter of 1947. There were considerable differences in the nature of the hearings. The House concentrated on an investigation of alleged union abuses along the lines of the later McClellan Committee hearings; the Senate committee, on the other hand, listened to a number of witnesses from unions, industry, universities, and the government, who testified on the various issues involved in the bills that had been referred to the committee.

There were very striking differences between H.R. 3020 which was reported out of the House and H.R. 3020 which was reported out of the Senate Committee to the Senate. Both bills passed in their respective chambers.

The substantive differences between the House and Senate bills were enormous. Perhaps as significant as any were the differences in the declaration of policy. The Senate bill carried over verbatim the findings and policies of the Wagner Act with two minor changes. The first change was the adding of the adjective "some" to qualify the finding that employers have denied the right of employees to organize and have refused to accept the procedure of collective bargaining. A new paragraph was also added to the Senate bill reciting a legislative finding that some unions had engaged in activities which burdened or obstructed commerce. This addition was presumably the foundation for the establishment of union unfair labor practices. But most important was the reaffirmation of the Wagner Act's policy to encourage the practice and procedure of collective bargaining. The Senate bill also contained a finding that there was an inequality of bargaining power between employees and employers, and restated the public policy of restoring the balance.

It is most significant that the House bill contained no public policy statement with respect to the promotion of collective bargaining. Instead, it was declared the purpose and policy of the bill

to prescribe the legitimate rights of both employees and employers in their relations affecting commerce, to provide orderly and peaceful procedures for preventing the interference by either with the legitimate rights of the other, to protect the rights of individual employees in their relations with labor organizations whose activities affect commerce, to encourage the peaceful settlement of labor disputes affecting commerce by giving the employees themselves a direct voice in the bargaining arrangements with their employers, to define and proscribe practices on the part of labor and management which affect commerce and are inimical to the general welfare, and to protect the rights of the public in connection with labor disputes affecting commerce.[5]

Another contrast between the two bills was in the changes made in Section 7 of the Wagner Act. The Senate bill contained the same language as the unamended section with only one very minor change, and added that employees had the right to refrain from any of the protected activities.[6]

The proposed Section 7(a) of the House bill, while stating that employees had the right to organize and to bargain collectively, qualified this statement in a number of ways. To begin with, the rights guaranteed were withdrawn if there was a violation of any part of Section 8(b),[7] which provided, *inter alia,* that it was an unfair labor practice for a union to strike with the object of compelling an employer to agree to the inclusion in a collective bargaining agreement of any subject which was not specifically included as a proper subject of collective bargaining in the proposed Section 2(11). Section 2(11) listed as the proper subjects for bargaining wage rates, hours of employment, and work requirements; procedures and practices relating to a specified number of issues, including discharge, suspension, safety, sanitation, and health; vacations; and administrative and procedural provisions relating to the foregoing subjects.[8] It is to be noted that this would exclude from a contract such subjects as welfare funds, vacation funds, hiring halls, union security provisions, apprenticeship qualifications, assignment of work, checkoff, subcontracting of work, and many other items.

The rights affirmed in the House-proposed Section 7 also were not applicable if there had been a violation of a collective bargaining contract or if there had been a commission of any "unlawful concerted activities" enumerated under the proposed Section 12. These unlawful concerted activities included the use of force or violence, or the threat of such use, during strikes, picketing an employer in more strength "than is reasonably required to give notice of existence of a labor dispute," [9] picketing under the guise of a labor dispute when there is no labor dispute as defined in the proposed act, and engaging in sympathy strikes, jurisdictional strikes, monopolistic strikes, illegal boycotts, sit-downs, or a number of other prohibited activities.

The House bill also made it an unfair labor practice for a union to refuse to bargain collectively with an employer. Section 2(11) of the House bill defined collective bargaining as requiring compliance with the procedure in a contract which provided for the adjustment or settling of disputes. In the event that there was no agreement in effect, the following procedure was required: receiving proposals or counterproposals of the other party; discussing such proposals; continuing to discuss the matters in dispute "at not less than four separate additional conferences with the other party held within the thirty-day period following the initial conference, unless agreement is sooner reached";[10] and if agreement was reached, executing the agreement. If an agreement was not reached, certain procedural requirements had to be complied with before a lawful strike or lockout could take place. These requirements, in effect, provided that the new administrator of a new labor board should hold a strike vote on the employer's last offer and that no strike or lockout should be lawful unless a "majority of the employees in the bargaining unit concerned voted to reject the employer's last offer of settlement, and to strike." [11]

The proposed House bill also outlawed industry-wide bargaining in Section 9(f)(1)[12] and, in addition, modified an employer's duty to bargain in Section 8(a)(5) by imposing the duty to bargain only for unions currently recognized by the employer or certified under Section 9.

The House bill also defined supervisors and removed them from the category of employees within the meaning of the proposed act. In addition, a proviso to Section 9(a) was inserted which permitted employees to settle grievances without the participation of a union.

THE HOUSE BILL ON THE DUTY TO BARGAIN

Since the House bill represented the greatest departure from the established rules of collective bargaining as developed during the administration of the Wagner Act, it deserves some comment. The House report which accompanied the bill[13] stated that the definition of the procedure and subjects of collective bargaining was for the purpose of "limiting bargaining to matters of interest to the employer and to the individual man at work." [14] The ban on industry-wide bargaining was designed to enable "the workers to keep closer control of the bargaining in their behalf." [15]

The basis for changing the preamble was a finding that the encouragement of the practice and procedure of collective bargaining reflected a "highly prejudiced approach to the problems with which the Act attempted to deal." [16] and that the NLRB had taken this language "as a mandate to it to force employees to bargain collectively, even against their will." The exclusion of supervisors from the status of employees was based upon a conclusion that most of the organization of supervisors was done by rank and file unions and that management must have faithful agents.

The explanation for defining narrowly "bargain collectively" and "collective bargaining" was the absence of such a definition in the Wagner Act which led, in the view of the writers of the report, to "some of the most glaring injustices of decisions of the present Board . . ." [17]

The committee cited with approval the language of the Supreme Court in *Jones and Laughlin,* 301 U.S. 1, which stated in part, "The Act does not compel agreements between employers and employees." In the view of the authors of the report,

the present Board has gone very far, in the guise of determining whether or not employers had bargained in good faith, in setting itself up as the judge of what concessions an employer must make and of the proposals and counter-proposals that he may or may not make.[18]

The committee cited a number of cases and quoted with approval two books on the act.[19] Five NLRB cases were cited in support of the allegation that the refusal of an employer to yield to a union's demand for a closed-shop contract had been held to be evidence of bad-faith bargaining. The same assertion had been made by Iserman[20] and Metz.[21] An examination of the board's decisions would seem to be in order.

In the first case, *Matter of International Filter Company,* 1 NLRB 489, the respondent employer refused to meet with the union representing a majority of its employees on the grounds that the employees had no problems or grievances to discuss, that recognition of the union in meeting with union representatives would require entering into a closed-shop contract, and that the Wagner Act was unconstitutional. The board disposed of the closed-shop defense as follows:

The respondent's position that meeting with union representatives ipso facto draws it into a closed shop agreement is too specious to merit consideration. Our experience has been that the cry of "closed shop" is constantly being raised by employers who seek an excuse to evade their duty to bargain collectively under the Act and to obstruct and deny the rights of employees to do so. There is not an iota of evidence that the union representatives in this case proposed a closed shop as part of an agreement. The respondent never permitted the chosen representatives of its machinist employees an opportunity to propose anything. The Act requires that the employer bargain collectively with the representatives of his employees by entering into negotiations with them in good faith with a bona fide purpose of making an agreement concerning rates of pay, wages, hours of employment, and other conditions of employment. An unfounded apprehension that employees may demand a closed shop is no excuse for a flat refusal to bargain collectively.[22]

The background of the second case, *Matter of Columbian Enameling and Stamping Company,* 1 NLRB 181, was a strike in which martial law had been declared and picketing enjoined. The employer had publicly announced for some time that it would neither recognize the union nor make any contract with it. Furthermore, throughout the strike, the employer solicited individual strikers to return to work and told them that it would not deal with the union. The basis for the finding of a refusal to bargain was the employer's refusal to meet with the union during the strike after it had agreed to do so. The company's defense was that the union was trying to force it to accept a closed-shop contract. The board made a finding of fact that although the union had previously clung to its closed-shop demand,

it was improbable it would do so any longer; the union sought to approach the respondent through conciliators, through persons primarily interested in composing differences; ostensibly its move was conciliatory, its principal interest in settling the strike. Under all these circumstances, the respondent could not have reasonably believed that collective bargaining would necessarily have been futile . . . That the respondent was under a duty to meet with the committee, if settlement were possible, seems clear. The Act requires the employer to bargain collectively with its employees. Employees do not cease to be such because they have struck. Collective bargaining is an instrument of industrial peace. The need for its use is as imperative during a strike as before a strike. By means of it, a settlement of the strike may be secured.[23]

The third case cited as evidence that the board required an employer to accept a closed-shop contract or risk a finding of unfair labor practice was *Matter of Jackson Daily News,* 9 NLRB 120. The board's decision on this point was as follows:

While the Act does not compel an employer to enter into a closed-shop agreement, or to agree upon any particular terms, it does require him to accept the procedure of collective bargaining, that is, to negotiate with the honest intent to reach a collective agreement. In his interview with Wilson [union representative], Johnson [business manager of the employer] not only refused to consider the proposed closed-shop provision but also failed to indicate that he might consider a contract which did not contain such a provision or to offer any counterproposal. The evidence clearly establishes that the respondent's attitude goes beyond an unwillingness to sign a closed-shop agreement. The respondent's action throughout the negotiations, particularly the refusal to meet with a committee of the employees, and the refusal even to discuss a closed-shop contract, do not evidence a serious attempt upon the part of the respondent to come to an agreement with the union.[24]

Contemporaneously with the refusal to bargain, the employer had also engaged in other unfair labor practices which included a threat to fire all employees "whenever a union contract was placed" on the employer's desk, and the granting of wage increases for an admitted purpose of discouraging employees from pressing for a union contract.

In *Matter of Uhlich and Company,* 26 NLRB 679, the board found that the employer, immediately after the union requested bargaining, promised its employees benefits if they abandoned the union in favor of a company union, and while ostensibly bargaining with the union "continued its attempts to secure employee adherence" to the company union. At the bargaining table, the company replied to the union's proposals that it would never sign a contract, that it would never give the union a closed shop, and finally that it did not want to consult with the union on the hiring and firing of employees. The trial examiner and the board found that negotiations broke down on the refusal of the employer to execute a written contract. The board also found no merit in the contention that the union insisted upon a closed shop as a condition for a contract. On the contrary, the board made a specific finding that the union was willing to compromise on the subject.[25]

The final case cited was *Matter of J. I. Case Company,* 71 NLRB 182. Here the employer refused to discuss a closed-shop and checkoff demand made by the union on the basis that eight years before, the union had written the employer a letter agreeing that all the employees had an unquestioned right to join or to refrain from joining the union. The employer contended that this letter constituted a valid and continuing written collective bargaining agreement which was still binding and would be binding in perpetuity upon the union, and which would forever foreclose union security in its plant. The board's decision concluded:

Our finding, as well as the Trial Examiner's, that the respondent refused to bargain collectively as to the closed-shop and checkoff proposals, is grounded not on its failure to grant them, but rather on its repeated refusal even to consider or discuss them as a proper subject for collective bargaining, which of necessity foreclosed any possibility for agreement.[26]

It seems too clear for dispute that the cases relied upon by the House report and by Iserman and Metz by no means support the propositions advanced.

The House report, moreover, stated that the board had held it an unfair labor practice "for an employer to insist that he and the union settle their differences by collective bargaining, instead of submitting them to some form of 'collective litigation' like arbitration." Two cases were cited in support of this;[27] the first was *Matter of Dallas Cartage Company*, 14 NLRB 411. We have already discussed at some length the basis for the board's finding of refusal to bargain in this case. It is extraordinarily difficult to see even a slight connection between the House report's point and the board's decision. It is sufficient to repeat here the board's finding in this case:

No concession or modification offered by the union to meet the respondent's objections served to provide a common basis of understanding, for new grounds of criticism were offered on each occasion. On the other hand, every apparent concession made by the respondent was retracted and dissipated on being taken seriously.[28]

Likewise, in the second case cited, *Matter of Register Publishing Company*, 44 NLRB 834, the board's decision stated specifically that an employer was not required under the act to agree to any particular terms and that the failure to reach an agreement did not in itself establish a violation of the duty to bargain. However, it added:

Such matters may be relevant in conjunction with the entire course of conduct, in evaluating the intent of the parties. In view of the past relationship between the parties, including the closed shop, apprentice control, and the payment of prevailing rates, the respondent's insistence, without any justification shown, that the union surrender benefits it had gained, is the very antithesis of any desire to reach a mutually acceptable agreement. The respondent's refusal to arbitrate the matters and disputes, establishes that it was not concerned with the merits of the substantive issues but was determined rather to deny to the union the benefits of a collective agreement. That this was its motive was established by the respondent's anticipatory refusal to reduce to writing and make contractually binding any agreement which might be reached.[29]

In addition, the board cited statements by the respondent that a contract would never be signed with the union, and the respondent's refusal to discuss reinstatement of the strikers except on an individual basis.

The House report also criticized the board for decisions based upon a demand by an employer that a union "take steps making it legally responsible for its contract violations." [30] The first case cited substantiating this view was *Matter of Jasper Blackburn Products Company*, 21 NLRB 1240. A reading of the board's decision reveals that the employer had violated the act in many respects. It had engaged in interrogations of employees on their union activities, disparaged the union, told employees that it would never sign a contract with the union, threatened to move the plant and discharge all employees to avoid signing a contract, created a company-dominated bargaining committee, made wage and other concessions through this committee to head off the union, refused to recognize the union as the exclusive bargaining agent, and refused to execute a contract unless the union posted a bond. The board's decision said in part:

> The respondent, in refusing to execute a signed agreement, binding upon both the parties, unless the union posted a bond, sought to prefix the fulfillment of its statutory obligation with a condition not within the provisions, and manifestly inconsistent with the policy of the Act. Even assuming a bond of the kind requested to be obtainable, the employer cannot lay down the blanket requirement that the union pay a tax to a surety company before the result contemplated by the Act, a signed bilateral agreement, can come to pass. Since the respondent had in 1937 stated its intention not to sign any agreement, and since neither proposals advanced either by the respondent, or by the union, called for any performance whatsoever on the union's part, it would seem clear that the primary purpose of the respondent's demand for a bond was to avoid the required fundamentals of collective bargaining.[31]

The other cases cited by the House report likewise fail to support the accusation of "unfairness" by the board.

The House report also severely criticized the board for having held that an employer was guilty of an unfair labor practice if it asked the union to agree to a no-strike clause, and in support of this charge cited a number of cases. The first case cited was *Matter of Metal Mouldings Corporation,* 39 NLRB 107, 119. Again, it is extremely difficult to see any relationship between the House report's criticism and the case it relied upon. Here the charge was not refusal to bargain, but that the employer had violated Section 8(2) of the act by establishing and dominating a local "independent" union. The evidence indicated that the employer had contributed financial and other support to the independent union, furnished office services and facilities, meeting place, and other aid, permitted solicitation of members and collection of dues during working hours, and undertaken many other activities in support of the union. There were many other signs of company domination, including the presence of supervisors on the independent union's bargaining committee, compensation of employees for time spent in handling internal affairs of the independent union, and donation of money to the union. One of the very many factors cited by the board in its finding that the independent union was company-dominated was the fact that this union

in its initial contract with the respondent surrendered for the term of the agreement the employees' right to strike, labor's most powerful economic weapon, without obtaining under the contract any concessions with respect to wages, hours, or other terms or conditions of employment. The conduct of such character, rare if not unheard of in negotiations involving legitimate labor organizations, furnishes striking evidence of the subserviency of the M.T.U. [the independent union] to the will of the respondent.[32]

The citation of cases by the report, as well as by Iserman and Metz, shows an utter disregard for the board's holdings and for the basis for its decisions.[33] Nevertheless, on the basis of its evaluation of the board's rulings on the duty to bargain, the House committee thought it necessary to correct the situation by defining collective bargaining. The usefulness of the definition was described in the report:

. . . it sets up objective standards by which the Board can determine whether or not a party has refused to bargain. In opposing the suggestion that unions, as well as employers, be required to bargain collectively, the Chairman of the Board has stated that whether or not a person is bargaining "in good faith" requires appraising his "state of mind." The possibility of error and injustice when three Board Members, none of whom are psychiatrists, undertake to do this is very great as can be seen from decisions of the Board itself. The committee therefore takes the question out of the realm of speculation, guess work, and, too often, bias and prejudice, and provide that "free opportunity for negotiations" that the Supreme Court said the act should bring about. Since the bill requires unions as well as employers to bargain, the committee's doing this is as important to them as to employers.[34]

THE SENATE MAJORITY REPORT

The Senate majority report was prepared by two staff lawyers, Thomas B. Shroyer and Gerald Reilly.[35] The final bill which became the Taft-Hartley Act was almost identical to the bill that was reported out by the Senate. The Senate report stated that the bill was based upon the belief

that a fair and equitable labor policy can best be achieved by equalizing existing laws in a manner which will encourage free collective bargaining. Government decisions should not be substituted for free agreement but both sides—management and organized labor—must recognize that the rights of the general public are paramount.[36]

In furtherance of this aim, the findings and policies of the amended act were to contain a reaffirmation of public policy in support of the promotion of collective bargaining. It should be noted that the proposed Senate bill made it an unfair labor practice for an employer under Section 8(a)(6) and for a union under Section 8(b)(5) to violate the terms of a collective bargaining agreement or the terms of an agreement to submit a dispute to arbitration. In its report, the committee took pains to state that it did not intend that the National Labor Relations Board should adjudicate all disputes alleging a breach of contract. It hoped that the board would develop a policy of handling only those cases which could not be disposed of by the machinery established by the contract, by arbitration, or by litigation in court.

In its explanation of Section 8(d), which defined the duty to bargain, the report stated that this definition "makes it clear that the duty to bargain collectively does not require either party to agree to a particular demand or to make a concession." It should be noted that the word "concession" was used rather than "counterproposal" to meet an objection raised by the chairman of the NLRB to a corresponding provision in one of the earlier drafts of the bill.[37]

According to one report, the final bill which came out of conference was made within the framework of the Senate bill because of the close division in the Senate on a number of controversial provisions and the prospect of a presidential veto.[38] However, in deference to the wishes of the House conferees there was an elimination of Sections 8(a)(6) and 8(b)(5), which provided that the board should enforce contracts. The explanation for this was given in the House conference report: "Once parties have made a collective bargaining contract the enforcement of that contract should be left to the usual processes of the law and not to the National Labor Relations Board." [39]

The House, however, accepted the Senate definition of collective bargaining in Section 8(d), which

while it did not prescribe a purely objective test of what constituted collective bargaining, as did the House bill, had to a very substantial extent the same effect as the House bill in this regard, since it rejected, as a factor in determining good faith, the test of making a concession and thus prevented the Board from determining the merits of the positions of the parties.[40]

In summary, it seems clear that the Senate view of the duty to bargain prevailed. It must likewise be noted that the duty to bargain did not suffer any change because of the amendment of the Wagner Act. In defending his bill after the presidential veto, Senator Taft stated:

. . . we have drafted this bill and it is based on the theory of the Wagner Act, if you please. It is based on the theory that the solution of the labor problem in the United States is free, collective bargaining—a contract between one employer and all of his men acting as one man. That is the theory of the Wagner Act, that they shall be free to make the contract they wish to make . . . We have not made unlawful a single act on the part of employees which was not made unlawful on the part of employers in the original bill.

Otherwise we have left those provisions alone and untouched, except perhaps for the provision of freedom of speech. In the United States there is a demand that we restore complete freedom of speech to both sides, and that we have done. Otherwise there is no modification. No employer can beat down a union; no employer can discriminate; no employer can refuse to deal with the union which is duly certified to him.[41]

On June 23, 1947, the Senate joined the House in overriding the veto of President Truman, and the Taft-Hartley Bill was enacted into law.[42]

THE TAFT-HARTLEY ACT AND THE EMPLOYER'S DUTY TO BARGAIN

In a very large measure, the passage of the Taft-Hartley amendments did not materially affect the huge body of case law established by the board in the interpretation of Section 8(5) of the Wagner Act. Indeed, the amendments to the act, particularly the language of Section 8(d),[43] merely codified board precedents in most respects. In its first annual report after the passage of Taft-Hartley, the board stated:

Except, however, for other limitations on the duty to bargain collectively which the Board has not had an opportunity to construe during the fiscal year, the basic elements of a finding of unlawful refusal to bargain appear to have remained unchanged by this definition.[44]

The following year, the board stated with respect to Section 8(d) that "generally speaking, this portion of the definition merely codified the decisional standards existing prior to 1947 amendments; consequently, its application to cases decided during the fiscal year did not materially affect the holding in any given case."[45]

However, the new act did result in a number of significant substantive changes in the area of collective bargaining. Without question, the most important change was the act's definition of the lawful subject matter of collective bargaining. The new Section 8(a)(3) prohibits management and unions from incorporating a closed-shop clause in their contracts and also narrowly circumscribes all other union security agreements. Section 14(b) also permits states to ban all union security agreements. In addition, checkoff procedures are made a crime in the absence of compliance with the specific terms of the proviso to Section 302 of the act. The legal right of unions and management to agree on health and welfare plans is also made conditional upon compliance with Section 302, which spells out, subject to criminal enforcement, the objectives of all such plans along with certain administrative requirements, the most important of which is dual administration of the funds.

THE DEVELOPMENT OF BOARD DOCTRINE ON THE DUTY TO BARGAIN— DURATION OF DESIGNATION OF UNION

In general, the board's certification of a union is an absolute bar to a redetermination of representatives for one calendar year. Section 9(c)(3) of the Taft-Hartley Act reinforces this long-standing board policy by prohibiting the holding of a representation election within twelve months after a prior valid election. The purpose of this policy is to permit a newly certified union to establish bargaining relationships by giving it a year free of rival claims or decertification proceedings in which to negotiate a contract.[46]

An employer's duty to bargain with a certified union exists during the one-year period despite the union's loss of majority status. In a number of cases the board has held that even raising the question of a union's majority status during the certification year amounts to a violation of Section 8(a)(5) of the act.[47]

The duty to bargain remains despite significant changes in personnel,[48] repudiation of the union by employees,[49] and a bona fide transfer of the employer's plant.[50] In the *Krantz* case the board affirmed the finding of the trial examiner, who said, "The certification is not limited merely to the particular employer operating the business at the time of its issuance but runs with the 'employing industry.'"

However, in unusual circumstances the presumption of majority status during the certification year may be challenged. The board has indicated that these circumstances include the dissolution of the certified union, doubt as to the union's identity following a change in affiliation, and a substantial increase in the number of employees in the bargaining unit during the certification year.[51]

No similar calendar-year immunity from rival union intrusions or from decertification proceedings is conferred upon a union which has been recognized by an employer on the basis of a card check or a settlement agreement.[52] If a certification has run longer than a year, or if a union has never been certified, an employer may refuse to bargain only on the basis of a good-faith doubt of the union's majority status.

The board has stated:

After the first year of the certification has elapsed, though the certificate still creates a presumption as to the fact of majority status by the union, the presumption is at that point rebuttable even in the absence of unusual circumstances. Competent evidence may be introduced to demonstrate that, in fact, the union did not represent a majority of the employees at the time of the alleged refusal to bargain.[53]

In cases involving uncertified unions, the board would find no violation of the duty to bargain if the employer had bargained in good faith to an impasse and had reasonable grounds for thinking that the union had lost its majority status during an economic strike when more than half of the strikers had been replaced.[54] On the other hand, a violation was found when an employer refused to accept the unconditional offer of economic strikers to return to their jobs prior to the hiring of replacements, since this offer fixed their status as employees and consequently gave the union a majority.[55]

The general rule is that a certification is valid until rescinded or superseded.[56] In one case a violation was found where an employer withdrew recognition from the union upon receipt of the revocation of checkoff authorization from a majority of the employees, at a time when the union's contract had one year to run although the certification year had expired.[57]

APPROPRIATENESS OF UNIT

A request for bargaining in a unit which is clearly inappropriate need not be honored.[58] In one case the board stated, "However, as in the cases involving the question of the bargaining agent's majority status, the employer cannot legally refuse to bargain in the absence of a good faith doubt regarding the appropriateness of a unit specified in the union's bargaining request."[59]

The general rule established during the administration of the Wagner Act that the board's determination of unit is conclusive unless arbitrary or capricious has been continued under the Taft-Hartley Act.[60] The board has wide discretion in selecting the unit appropriate for purposes of collective bargaining[61] and consistency in board decisions on units is not required.[62] The basic standard for the board's determination of questions of unit is the effectuation of the policy of the act.[63]

INDIVIDUAL BARGAINING AND UNILATERAL ACTION

In a reaffirmation of its findings under the Wagner Act, the board has stated:

Once a union has been designated as the statutory representative and an employer is put on notice of the union's majority status, the Act not only imposes on him the affirmative duty to bargain collectively upon request but requires him to abstain from subverting the designated representative by direct dealings with individual employees.[64]

However, direct negotiations with employees are not unlawful "where the employer's action was clearly not motivated by a desire to circumvent the union and to undermine its authority." [65]

Consequently, in one case the board dismissed a charge based upon an employer's unilateral change in the contract rate because the employer's conduct was not

part of a conscious campaign . . . to undermine the authority and prestige of the union . . . or to evade the employer's obligation to recognize and deal with the union . . . the employer discussed the matter with the union immediately after it protested; in the past similar isolated disputes were amicably settled between the employer and the union. Moreover, the union filed charges without having made an attempt to utilize the contractual grievance and arbitration procedures which were available for the handling of matters involving interpretation and administration of the union's contract . . . indeed, the Board has frequently stated that the stability of labor relations which the statute seeks to accomplish through the encouragement of the collective bargaining process ultimately depends upon the channelization of collective bargaining relationship within the procedures of a collective bargaining agreement. By encouraging the utilization of such procedures in this case, we believe the statutory policy will best be effectuated. Affirmative Board action would on the other hand put the Board in the position of policing collective bargaining agreements, a role we are unwilling to assume.[66]

THE DUTY TO BARGAIN AS AFFECTED BY SECTION 8(d)

Section 8(d) states that the duty to bargain

shall not be construed as requiring either party to discuss or agree to any modification of the terms or conditions contained in a contract for a fixed period, if such modification is to become effective before such terms and conditions can be reopened under the provisions of the contract.

The board has held that this is applicable only to those subjects covered by the contract

and that as to matters not so covered, in the absence of an effective waiver, the continuing duty to bargain is unaffected. It thus held the employer under a duty to bargain in respect of "pension program" during the term of a contract, even though the issue had been discussed during negotiations. In this case the union had not waived its right to raise the issue, but expressly reserved the right to do so by verbal notice to the employer during contract negotiations.[67]

However, the waiver by the union must be explicit.[68] The omission of any matter which is subject to collective bargaining does not constitute a waiver by the union.[69] Consequently, the board has refused to find that the union had waived its right to obtain data necessary to the effective administration of the contract where the contract clause stated, ". . . this agreement contains the entire agreement between the parties and no matters shall be considered which are covered by the written provision stated herein." [70]

THE DUTY TO BARGAIN AS AFFECTED BY UNLAWFUL
OR UNPROTECTED CONDUCT OF EMPLOYEES

In one case, when employees went out on strike in violation of a no-strike clause in a valid existing contract, the
union requested the employer to bargain in order to settle
the strike. Upon his refusal, the employees abandoned the
strike and offered to return to work unconditionally. At
this point, the union again sought to bargain about grievances of some employees. The refusal of the employer to
bargain about these grievances was held to be a violation
of Section 8(a)(5). The board stated:

> Under the holding in the *Reed Case* [76 NLRB 548], we agree with
> the Respondent that it was *then* [during the period of the strike]
> under no obligation to bargain with the Union concerning the settle-
> ment or cause of the wrongful strike. However, this does not mean
> that wrongful strike action by employees extinguished permanently
> the employer's statutory obligation to bargain, but rather that such
> obligation to bargain, at least with respect to the settlement or
> causes of the strike itself, was merely suspended during the life of
> the wrongful strike. In our opinion, the policies of the Act impel
> the conclusion that the obligation to bargain may again become
> operative as soon as the employees correct their wrongful action.[71]

REFUSAL TO FURNISH INFORMATION

In its traditional practice of requiring the employer to
supply relevant information when reasonably requested,[72]
the board has consistently applied certain principles. In
one case, the board held that where the information
sought is for the purposes of collective bargaining, it is
sufficient that the requested information "is related to the
issues involving collective bargaining, and . . . no specific
need as to a particular issue must be shown." [73]

However, information need not be given in the exact
form requested,[74] and the relevance of the information is

not affected by the subsequent execution of a contract without receipt of it.[75] The union is entitled to specific individual wage data and the confidential nature of the information is not a valid ground for refusal.[76]

When an employer claimed that it could not afford to pay high wages and refused to produce supporting information, a refusal to bargain has been found.[77] In enforcing this decision, the Supreme Court said in part:

> Good faith bargaining necessarily requires that claims made by either bargainer should be honest claims. This is true about an asserted inability to pay an increase in wages. If such an argument is important enough to present in the give and take of bargaining, it is important enough to require some sort of proof of its accuracy and it would certainly not be farfetched for a trier of fact to reach the conclusion that bargaining lacks good faith when an employer mechanically repeats a claim of inability to pay without making the slightest effort to substantiate the claim.[78]

However, a waiver of the right to the information may be a valid defense if it is clear and unmistakable.[79]

MANDATORY SUBJECT MATTER FOR
COLLECTIVE BARGAINING

The statutory subjects of collective bargaining have been held to include Christmas bonuses,[80] company housing and rental,[81] stock bonuses,[82] re-employment of employees displaced by the discontinuance of a department,[83] and contract provisions for checkoff of union dues.[84] Other mandatory subjects for collective bargaining have included the refusal of an employer to negotiate with the union about the transfer of employees to a new location,[85] and the failure to inform the union of a projected plant removal and to bargain on the effect of the removal on the tenure of employees.[86]

The board has considered it proper for an employer to bargain with the union for a no-strike clause, even though this would require the union to give up for the duration of the contract a right expressly provided by Section 7 of the act. The basis for the board's decision was that insistence of the employer on the union's waiver of its right to strike was a "salutary objective" in line with the purpose and policy of the act.[87]

However, in an important case, the board found a violation of the duty to bargain when management insisted to the point of impasse upon the inclusion of a very wide management prerogative clause which would reserve to the company the exclusive right to determine unilaterally such conditions of employment as work rules, work schedules, establishment of extra shifts, layoff policy, lunch periods, granting of leaves of absence, and distribution of overtime.[88] The board's theory was that these subjects were proper issues for collective bargaining and that the employer's ". . . insistence on excluding these subjects from the area of collective bargaining, as a condition precedent for a contract, was inconsistent with good faith bargaining." Moreover, the board held that this action was a per se violation of Section 8(a)(5).

However, the Supreme Court reversed the board on the per se approach.[89] The court rejected

the Board's holding that bargaining for the management functions clause proposed by Respondent was, *per se*, an unfair labor practice. Any fears the Board may entertain that use of management functions clauses will lead to evasion of an employer's duty to bargain collectively as to "rates of pay, wages, hours and conditions of employment," do not justify condemning all bargaining for management functions clauses covering any "condition of employment" as *per se* violations of the Act. The duty to bargain collectively is to be enforced by application of the good faith bargaining standards of Section 8(d) to the facts of each case rather than by prohibiting all employers in every industry from bargaining for management functions clauses altogether.[90]

The *American National Insurance Co.* case represents in some respects a major break with past board doctrine as enforced by the courts. The court's statement of the policy of the act contained nothing new, holding that the statutory intention was to promote collective bargaining. The court acknowledged past board decisions as well as its own prior holdings that the duty to bargain does not require any agreement, nor does the act regulate the substantive terms of wages, hours, and working conditions. The court did not take the duty to bargain lightly. It said:

Enforcement of the obligation to bargain collectively is crucial to the statutory scheme. And, as has long been recognized, performance of the duty to bargain requires more than a willingness to enter upon a sterile discussion of union-management differences . . . the Act does not encourage a party to engage in fruitless marathon discussions at the expense of frank statement and support of his position. And it is equally clear that the Board may not, either directly or indirectly, compel concessions or otherwise sit in judgment upon the substantive terms of collective bargaining agreements.[91]

The court nevertheless rejected outright the board's finding that the bargaining for a management functions clause was a per se violation. In the court's view, the board's argument was a technical one inasmuch as there was nothing unlawful in the proposal by management of the broad prerogative clause. On the basis that similar management functions clauses have appeared in many contracts, the court held that the board's finding would prevent employers from bargaining for more flexible treatment" . . . even though the result may be contrary to common collective bargaining practice in industry. The Board was not empowered so to disrupt collective bargaining practices." [92]

In a strongly worded dissent, Justice Minton asserted that the majority had misapplied the facts. Justice Minton stated:

> . . . this case is one where the employer came into the bargaining room with a demand that certain topics upon which it had a duty to bargain were to be removed from the agenda—that was the price the union had to pay to gain a contract. . . . No one suggests that an employer is guilty of an unfair labor practice when it proposes that it be given unilateral control over certain working conditions and the union accepts the proposal in return for various other benefits. But where, as here, the employer tells the union that the only way to obtain a contract as to wages is to agree not to bargain about certain other working conditions, the employer has refused to bargain about those other working conditions. . . . Where there is a refusal to bargain, the Act does not require an inquiry as to whether that refusal was in good faith or bad faith. The duty to bargain about certain subjects is made absolute by the Act.[93]

The *American National Insurance Co.* case received a great deal of attention, not only from scholars but from the circuit courts. The seeming rejection of the per se approach implied that a violation could be found only by application of the good-faith test.

The question soon arose of how to judge traditionally illicit employer behavior, such as unilateral action, in cases where the negotiations themselves did not support a finding of bad faith. Additional support for the rejection of the per se approach appeared in a subsequent Supreme Court case involving a refusal to bargain charge against a union. Here the court held that economic sanctions such as slowdowns employed by a union while unprotected were not necessarily unlawful and, in any case, did not constitute per se violations of the union's duty to bargain. Interestingly enough, the court also held that Congress had incorporated Section 8(d) into the act in an effort to restrain the board's control of the terms and conditions of a collective bargaining agreement.[94]

On the basis of these two cases, a circuit court rejected the board's finding that an employer's unilateral action constituted a per se violation of the duty to bargain.[95] In a unanimous decision, the Supreme Court reversed the decision on the grounds that a unilateral change is equivalent to a refusal to meet, in that the issue of subjective good faith is irrelevant to a determination of a violation of Section 8(a)(5). In other words, good faith in the sense that an employer has every desire to reach an agreement and bargains to that end does not immunize activity which is tantamount to a refusal to negotiate. The court went on to state, "Unilateral action by an employer without prior discussion with the union does amount to a refusal to negotiate about the affected conditions of employment under negotiations, and must of necessity obstruct bargaining, contrary to the congressional policy."[96]

Although the court distinguished the *Insurance Agents Union* case and left the possibility that some unilateral employer action might be lawful, the decision apparently ratified the past practice of the board in permitting a condemnation of specific conduct without reference to the totality of behavior or an inquiry into a subjective intent.

GOOD-FAITH BARGAINING IN GENERAL

In general, good faith is determined by "a fair appraisal of the circumstances and particular facts of a case."[97] The usual criteria for bad faith as worked out by the board during the administration of the Wagner Act have remained substantially unchanged. Indications of bad faith include changes of position, such as a substitution of terms previously rejected,[98] and the reopening of subject matters which had previously been settled.[99] Other criteria include dilatory and evasive behavior in negotiations, failure to give reasons for rejection of proposals, and intransigence without any willingness to seek compromise or make concessions. As one circuit court stated, referring to the *American National Insurance Co.* case,

it seems clear that if the Board is not to be blinded by empty talk and by the mere surface motions of collective bargaining, it must take some cognizance of the reasonableness of the positions taken by an employer in the course of bargaining negotiations. Thus if an employer can find nothing whatever to agree to in an ordinary current-day contract submitted to him, or in some of the union's related minor requests, and if the employer makes not a single serious proposal meeting the union at least partway, then certainly the Board must be able to conclude that this is at least some evidence of bad faith, that is, of a desire not to reach an agreement with the union. In other words, while the Board cannot force an employer to make a "concession" on any specific issue or to adopt any particular position, the employer is obliged to make *some* reasonable effort in *some* direction to compose his differences with the union, if Section 8(a)(5) is to be read as imposing any substantial obligation at all.[100]

Further application of the good-faith test, and the standards imposed by the board, are reflected in one case where an employer made a clause-by-clause counterproposal to a union's proposed contract. This company's counterproposal refused to grant any measure of union security, prohibited union stewards from being on company premises, and denied employees the right to discuss union business at any time on company grounds; refused to establish any grievance system and reserved to the company complete and unilateral authority to make all work rules; refused to establish any seniority system, retained for the employer the right to change wages up or down at any time it saw fit, and denied the employees the right to recognize picket lines.

The board commented upon this company offer as follows:

It can be seen therefore that the Respondent proposed shackles for the Union, while reserving unrestrained freedom for itself. Such a contract, if entered into, would have amounted to a formal negation of the collective bargaining principle. The Respondent's president, the principal negotiator herein and one familiar with contemporary bargaining contracts, must have known that no union, let alone the certified bargaining representative, could possibly have agreed to such a contract.[101]

In finding a violation of the duty to bargain, the board did not resort to a per se theory. It stated in its decision:

The stigma of bad faith introduced by the submission of this counterproposal could have been removed by engaging in the "give and take" of collective bargaining. Thereafter, however, the respondent showed no inclination to modify its proposal. The record is quite clear that throughout the three bargaining conferences it steadfastly refused to make a single change.[102]

In enforcing the board order in this case, the Fifth Circuit Court of Appeals applied the test of good faith as enunciated in the *American National Insurance* case. The court took note of the possible danger that the parties' freedom to contract as to substance might be affected by the good-faith test, but concluded that "we think the circumstances of this case support the Board's finding that the employer, while freely conferring, did not approach the bargaining table with an open mind and purpose to reach an agreement consistent with the respective rights of parties." [103]

Another outstanding example of the board's approach to good-faith bargaining occurred during a case involving a contract reopening between the union and employer.

Numerous meetings were held and the board found a failure to bargain on the basis of a speech by the plant manager to all the employees, telling them that the employer was unilaterally changing wage rates and existing practices on vacations, sick benefits, rest periods, seniority, and other matters; and a speech by the company president to the striking employees in which strikers were told that they did not need a contract to work in the plant—all they needed was a Bible and belief in the Bible and in the company president. Other evidence of a violation was the company's unwillingness

to accept or consider any contract other than its proposed contract . . . which constituted such a radical departure from the previous contract in eliminating approximately twenty-six existing benefits—such as, the right to process as a grievance discharges based on the failure of any employee to perform his duties, notice of layoffs, seniority rights, and prohibition against discharge without cause—as to be predictably unacceptable to the union.[104]

In enforcing this court order, the Fifth Circuit Court of Appeals again addressed itself to the impact—possible or probable—of the good-faith requirement upon the substance of the contract. The court stated that the

government, through the Board, may not subject the parties to direction either by compulsory arbitration or the more subtle means of determining that the position is inherently unreasonable or unfair or impractical or unsound. The obligation of the employer to bargain in good faith does not require the yielding of positions fairly maintained. It does not permit the Board under the guise of finding of bad faith to require the employer to contract in a way the Board might deem proper.[105]

The application of the good-faith test to the facts of this case did not at all trouble the court. Notwithstanding the limitation imposed by the statute on the board's regulation of the subject matter of collective bargaining, the court stated that while the employer is assured these valuable rights, he may not use them as a cloak. In approaching it from this vantage, one must recognize as well that bad faith is prohibited though done with sophistication and finesse. Consequently, to sit at a bargaining table, or to sit almost forever, or to make concessions here and there, could be the very means by which to conceal a purposeful strategy to make bargaining futile or fail. Hence, we have said in more colorful language it takes more than mere "surface bargaining" or "shadow boxing to a draw," or "giving the union a runaround while purporting to be meeting with the union for purposes of collective bargaining." [106]

THE DUTY TO BARGAIN IN GOOD FAITH AS AFFECTED
BY THE IMPOSITION OF CONDITIONS ON BARGAINING

A request that the union withdraw a pending unfair labor practice charge as a condition for the signing of a contract has been held to be a violation of the act.[107] However, the board has held that a proposal during bargaining that litigation be terminated was not a violation in the absence of a showing that the employer later insisted to an impasse that the pending charges be withdrawn.[108]

The board has consistently held that Section 8(a)(5) is violated when the employer insists as a condition of further bargaining upon a surrender by the union of its rights guaranteed by the act. Thus, in one case, the board found an unlawful refusal to bargain where the employer declined to execute a contract except upon the condition that the union agree to a clause permitting a union steward to be present at the initial adjustment of grievances only if the aggrieved employee so elected. The board pointed out that under Section 9(a) of the act, the bargaining representative has an unqualified right to be present in the adjustment of grievances regardless of which managerial representative hears the grievance. The board further observed:

163

Grievances are usually more than mere personal dissatisfactions or complaints of employees and their adjustment frequently involves the interpretation and application of the terms of a contract or otherwise affects the terms and conditions of employment not covered by a contract. For this reason, these matters are unquestionably the concern of the bargaining representative.[109]

The courts have consistently enforced the board doctrine that certain conditions lie outside the area of compulsory bargaining. In one case, where the employer made bargaining conditional upon the union's registration under a state licensing law, the court enforced a board order finding a violation.[110] In another case, where the employer attempted to qualify the recognition clause as a condition of bargaining, the court enforced a board order finding a violation of Section 8(a)(5).[111]

It has also been held to be a violation of the statutory duty to bargain if the employer insists as a condition of bargaining that the union forego some right guaranteed by the act. Such violations have included demanding that the union abandon a strike,[112] requiring the union to post a performance bond, and insisting that the employer would only deal with a union representative if he were accompanied by a local committee composed of the firm's employees.[113]

The leading case of the present law with respect to imposing conditions is *Borg-Warner*.[114] Here, the employer insisted that the contract include two provisions found objectionable by the board. The first was a recognition clause which excluded the certified international union as a party to the contract and substituted an uncertified local union. The second was a ballot clause which required that prior to a strike, a secret ballot on the company's last offer must be taken among all employees in the unit, including non-union employees as well as union members.

The board held, on the basis of the record, that the employer was not merely proposing its recognition and ballot clauses as subjects which the union could voluntarily accept or not. On the facts of this case, the employer insisted adamantly on the inclusion of these two clauses as a condition for the execution of a contract. The board therefore based the employer's liability under Section 8(a)(5) not on its bad faith,

but rather upon the legal question of whether the proposals are obligatory subjects of collective bargaining. For, if the proposals are permissible statutory demands, the Respondent was privileged to adamantly insist upon bargaining as to them and the Union could not refuse to so bargain; on the other hand, if they were not, the converse is true. . . . we do not hold that the respondent "had no right to put these proposals on the bargaining table." On the contrary, we recognize that the respondent could make these proposals or any other proposal not in conflict with the provisions of the Act. However, we are here concerned not with what the parties might do by mutual consent beyond the obligatory mandate of the statute, but with what the obligation to bargain under the Act requires the parties to do. Of course, that obligation encompasses good-faith bargaining, but only with respect to wages, hours, and conditions of employment, as enumerated in the Act. Thus, a union might propose that an employer reduce the salaries of its officers as a means of obtaining wage increases for employees, and the employer may *voluntarily* agree, but it does not follow that the employer is *required* to bargain about such a matter. . . . To hold . . . that good faith is the only basis for determining whether or not the union or employer has fulfilled its obligation to bargain under Section 8(a) (5) of the Act, means, in effect, an amendment to the Act's statement of the required subject of collective bargaining and that they are required under the Act to bargain about matters wholly unrelated to wages, hours, and other conditions of employment.[115]

Even assuming, as the board did here, that the employer was not acting in bad faith, the board found a violation in the employer's insisting upon the ballot clause, which it held to be a purely internal union matter unrelated to any condition of employment. The employer, in essence, was insisting upon a procedure which was considered to bypass the union and thus to violate the exclusive representation concept of the statute. The board stated that: "Indeed, insistence on a strike ballot clause means only that the union must dilute its authority, diffuse its responsibility, and ultimately dissipate its strength." [116] Such company action constituted "a subversion of the collective-bargaining process" and is violative of the duty to bargain.

Similarly, on the basis of precedents established under the Wagner Act, the qualification of the right of the union to be recognized was considered an additional violation of Section 8(a)(5). The board stated in this regard: "What has been won through the Board's election processes need not be rewon at the bargaining table." [117]

In his dissent, Chairman Farmer was unable to discover a violation since there was no allegation of bad faith on the part of the respondent employer. The dissent noted with alarm the expansion of the mandatory subjects for bargaining, citing specifically the *Inland Steel* case and the *Richfield Oil* cases. These cases established that pensions and stock purchase plans for employees were required subjects for bargaining. In language which borrowed heavily from two critics of NLRB policy,[118] the dissent asserted:

Any attempt to codify the issues which are bargainable and those which are not would bring about a premature and artificial crystalization of labor-management relations, and moreover, would inject the Government into the collective bargaining process to a degree which would be disruptive of labor-management relationships.[119]

The dissent concluded by maintaining that the only test which Congress intended to apply was that of good faith, although "the adoption of this view does not mean that either party to contract negotiations could disrupt bargaining and forestall agreement by making and adamantly pressing outrageous demands." [120]

In a 5 to 4 decision, the Supreme Court enforced the

board order in this case. The court agreed with the board's finding that the company's obligation to good faith had been met as to the subjects of mandatory bargaining. However, the court went on to say that

good faith does not license the employer to refuse to enter into agreements on the ground that they do not include some proposal which is not a mandatory subject of bargaining. We agree with the Board that such conduct is, in substance, a refusal to bargain about the subjects that are within the scope of mandatory bargaining. This does not mean that bargaining is to be confined to the statutory subjects. Each of the two controversial clauses is lawful in itself. Each would be enforceable if agreed to by the unions. But it does not follow that, because the company may propose these clauses, it can lawfully insist upon them as a condition to any agreement.[121]

On the basis that the two clauses did not come within the definition of mandatory bargaining, it was held that the employer had violated Section 8(a)(5) of the act.

Justice Harlan, in a sharply worded dissent, feared that the majority decision "may open the door to an intrusion by the Board into the substantive aspects of the bargaining process which goes beyond anything contemplated by the National Labor Relations Act or suggested in this Court's prior decisions under it." [122] The dissent stated, "The legislative history behind the Wagner and Taft-Hartley Acts persuasively indicates that the Board was never intended to have power to prevent good-faith bargaining as to any subject not violative of the provisions or policies of these Acts." In support of this, the dissent quoted Senator Walsh's statement on the duty to bargain during the legislative consideration of the Wagner Act. Also cited was the House report accompanying the Hartley Bill which asserted that the board had gone very far in setting itself up as the judge on the substantive terms of collective bargaining.

The dissent also relied upon the court's decision in the *American National Insurance Co.* case, which it considered as rejecting the per se approach entirely in favor of the application of a uniform test of good faith. On the basis of the lawfulness of the employer's proposal and the fact that the employer did bargain in good faith over its proposals, the minority would find no violation. The dissent did agree that the qualification of recognition contained in the employer's proposal violated the duty to bargain. This was distinguished from the ballot clause proposal on the basis that Section 8(d) did not require the good-faith test with respect to the execution of a written contract. Thus, good faith or not, the failure of an employer to execute a contract would be a violation of Section 8(a)(5) of the act.

The distinction between mandatory and non-mandatory subjects for bargaining enunciated in *Borg-Warner* has served as a lightning rod in attracting the major contemporary condemnations of the duty to bargain. The dire implications of the *Borg-Warner* doctrine can be summarized in the widely accepted view that it would lead to a governmentally imposed "rigidification of the collective bargaining process.[123] This fear has been strongly presented by a number of writers. The authors of one recent textbook decry the *Borg-Warner* decision as putting collective bargaining "in a straight jacket" which would cripple the bargaining process by preventing the parties from bargaining about such new issues as automation. Why this should come about is not explained, except that the argument is tied into the fallacious notion that the Wagner Act was not concerned with the subject matter of bargaining.[124]

The importance of *Borg-Warner* lies in the fact that it is controversial and not in the predicted consequences. We can quickly pass over the objections based upon the legislative intent, merely noting the persistence and constant application of the erroneous view of the legislative genesis of the duty to bargain. Perhaps the easiest way to dispose of the objections to the concept of mandatory bargaining is to analyze the consequences of its abandonment. No one seriously advances the proposal that an employer who refuses to bargain about wages would be innocent of a violation, and the same would presumably hold for hours, grievances, and a number of other subjects. But the finding of a violation would have to be based on the grounds of bad faith. The critics of *Borg-Warner* are constrained to argue that if the negotiations themselves were conducted in good faith, no violation under Section 8(a)(5) could be found.

But let us assume that an employer had conducted his contract negotiations with a union in the utmost good faith and was ready to conclude an agreement which the union conceded was a good one. But the employer during negotiations raised the issue of the union's participation in community or political affairs in support of policies which he considered objectionable. Suppose further that the employer insisted that the union withdraw, let us say, from a Community Chest drive as a condition of agreement, and an impasse developed. Or suppose that the employer insisted that the union support political candidates of the employer's choosing. It is difficult to think that our society would permit employers to exercise their economic strength in this manner; but it would be impossible to find a violation under these circumstances except by the use of the mandatory subject matter doctrine.

While it may be argued that these examples are strained and unlikely, the same objection can be made of the facts in the *Borg-Warner* case itself. The value of the distinction between mandatory and non-mandatory subject matters lies in the definition and delimitation of extreme behavior. The history of the development of the duty to bargain suggests that its application will be very limited and that the forebodings about its consequences miss the point.

CHAPTER 7 · THE IMPACT OF THE DUTY TO BARGAIN

INTRODUCTION

The foregoing discussion of the development and growth of an immense body of case law on an employer's duty to bargain leads naturally to the question of its consequences. It is safe to say that the requirement to bargain in good faith imposes innumerable restraints upon employers' freedom of action, but it is much more difficult to evaluate, without investigation, the operational meaning of these constraints. After all, the NLRB does not possess any punitive powers, its orders are not self-enforcing, and the ultimate sanction imposed upon any defiant employer is a court decree which merely enjoins the employer to bargain in good faith. As we have already seen, no board order or court decree can require the inclusion of any particular term in a collective bargaining agreement. Furthermore, the delays inherent in any formal proceeding are such that only in exceptional circumstances will a court decree enforcing a board order issue in less than two years from the filing of the charge.[1]

As a matter of fact, the actual time in most litigated cases is longer than two years. The Textile Workers Union calculated that in the southern textile industry just after the war the time interval between filing of charge and compliance subsequent to a court decree was close to four years.[2] On an average, a contested unfair labor practice charge consumes 475 days from filing to a board decision, and an additional 396 days elapses for a typical case to reach the stage of a judicial decree, giving a total of nearly two and a half years.[3]

It must also be noted that the entry of a court decree does not inevitably conclude the matter. Violation of the decree, of course, constitutes contempt of court. But contempt proceedings ordinarily involve a protracted hearing before a master appointed by a court, with all the investigation and trial preparation which precede any litigated case. These procedures include briefs to the master, exceptions to his report, and oral argument before the court. A union lawyer has stated that any general counsel is reluctant to press contempt proceedings because it is difficult to win contempt cases.[4]

One contempt case, which may be atypical in its length but which illustrates the legal complexities, is that involving the Weirton Steel Co. in the Third Circuit Court of Appeals. On May 18, 1943, an enforcement decree was entered by the court, concluding a very lengthy board proceeding which started in 1937. The chronology of subsequent events was:

August 12, 1944: Contempt petition filed.

October 16, 1944: Argument before the court.

December 22, 1944: Court issued decision that special master be appointed.

January 17, 1945: Court entered order appointing special master.

March, 1945, to August, 1947: Hearings conducted before special master, with a number of recesses during hearings.

February 1, 1950: Special master issued report.

February 21, 1950: Court entered order directing that report to special master stand confirmed unless exceptions thereto were filed. Subsequently exceptions were filed.

June 12, 15, and 16, 1950: Argument before court.

July 28, 1950: Court entered order adjudging respondent in contempt.[5]

THE EXISTING EVIDENCE ON THE EFFECTIVENESS
OF THE DUTY TO BARGAIN

By and large, the only direct evidence on the effectiveness of the duty to bargain, or for that matter of any section of the national labor law, is contained in testimony before congressional committees. Typically, these hearings consist of statements and arguments by employers and unions attacking or defending some provision of the act, on the basis of experience in a case or a limited number of cases.

Very frequently, NLRB officials answer or rebut this testimony and assemble statistics on various subjects as the occasion demands. Such investigations include an investigation of the NLRB by a Senate subcommittee in 1938 to determine whether a full-scale senatorial investigation was needed,[6] a lengthy Senate hearing in 1939 on proposed amendments to the NLRA,[7] the Smith Committee investigation of the NLRB,[8] the House committee hearings on proposed amendments to the NLRA,[9] the congressional hearings that preceded the passage of the Taft-Hartley Act,[10] the hearings of the joint committee (Ball Committee) set up by Section 401 of the Taft-Hartley Act,[11] the Senate subcommittee hearings on the southern textile industry already referred to, the 1949, 1953, and 1959 hearings on proposed amendments to the Taft-Hartley Act, and the Pucinski Committee hearings of 1961.[12]

In general, the reports issued by the various committees offer a tendentious selection of the testimony in order to support a politically preconceived notion on the desirability of particular provisions of the act. For example, the majority report of the Ball Committee concluded that the Taft-Hartley Act was "working well, without undue hardship upon labor organizations, employers or employees." [13] However, on the basis of the same evidence, a minority report concluded that the act "had a substantial and disturbing impact upon collective bargaining" and should be repealed.[14]

A year later, when a new Democratic majority was in control of both houses, new hearings resulted in a Senate majority report which reached "the conclusion that the welfare of the country requires the repeal of the Taft-Hartley Act and the readoption of the national labor policy underlying the Wagner Act . . ." [15] Needless to say, a Republican minority expressed the view that such action

would have the effect of encouraging, fostering, and nurturing uncontrolled union monopolies in the United States, and of conferring upon labor union officials unbridled and unconfined monopolistic power over the lives and destinies of every American and even over the operations of Government itself.[16]

Apart from the congressional hearings, the only source of information on board operations is contained in its annual reports. Unfortunately, however, the format of these reports was worked out in the late 1930's and has remained rigidly unchanged. The bulk of each annual report consists of a hornbook of labor law with a very short statistical appendix. For fiscal year 1963 there were twenty tables of statistics in the appendix with the following information: total cases received, closed, and pending; types of unfair labor practices alleged; formal action taken; remedial action for cases closed; industrial distribution of unfair labor practice and representation cases docketed, and their geographic distribution; breakdown of the stages of disposition of cases closed; types of elections conducted; results of elections held; a breakdown of elections held according to industrial and geographical distribution and size of unit; and a record of injunction litigation.

With respect to charges alleging a violation of 8(a)(5) of the act, all we are told is the number of cases making this allegation which were filed in any fiscal year; presumably we can guess the number of meritorious cases by examining the table listing remedial action, which has a column headed "collective bargaining begun." For example, for fiscal year 1961, the number of 8(a)(5) charges filed was 1,676, or 20.6 per cent of all unfair labor practices filed against employers.[17] In this same year, a remedy of resumption of collective bargaining was established in 319 cases, 87 following board orders and 232 by agreement of the parties.[18] The report does not indicate whether a contract was ever entered into as a result of board action.

Despite the paucity of information in the annual reports, they have been an important basis of scholarly discussion on the significance of the act. Professor Slichter, for one, relied almost entirely upon the reports as the factual basis for his examination of the operations of the act, its effectiveness, and its consequences.[19]

In a Senate hearing held in 1950 on labor-management relations in the southern textile industry, the TWU bitterly criticized the ineffectiveness of the board. The union's attorney testified that southern textile employers have "complete contempt" for the requirements of the law and submitted evidence of the employers' methods

in which they carry on the completely frustrating process that they call collective bargaining. We have documented the strategy of delay and I have listed several cases just giving you the chronology of them. You will find cases running for 10 years, and no contract has been consummated, even though a circuit order has been handed down, because in the South the chances of getting a contempt proceeding against the employer are extremely slim, in my opinion.[20]

The union placed in evidence case histories of many mills in which after certification no contract ever resulted. Collective bargaining was depicted as follows: "The distinguishing characteristics of collective bargaining in southern textiles are the high degree of legal formalism, the studied strategy of delay and the employer demands in negotiations which, if granted, spell swift deterioration of the union." [21] Moreover, certification of a union subsequent to an election "merely means that a new campaign of attrition shall commence." [22]

The TWU presented the Senate committee with tables and other information showing the disposition of charges filed by it in the South from September 1, 1945 through August 31, 1949. The union gave the following summary of its experience:

Of the 56 charges filed: (a) 22 were withdrawn, but only four of them as a result of signing agreements. (b) Thirteen were dismissed without a hearing. No agreements resulted. (c) Two charges are still pending. (d) Five charges were adjusted by the parties but only two agreements resulted. (e) Only one charge was dismissed at the hearing by the NLRB. (f) Thirteen charges were sustained by the NLRB; eight Board Orders went to a Court of Appeals for enforcement actions; five Board Orders were enforced by a Court of Appeals and three were denied enforcement; two of the denials of enforcement were on the grounds that the C.I.O. had not complied with the filing requirements of the Taft-Hartley Act, despite the fact that the T.W.A. was in compliance; the third denial of enforcement was reversed by the United States Supreme Court which decreed enforcement of the Board Order.[23]

There were many other attacks on the efficacy of the duty to bargain. For example, Arthur J. Goldberg, then

General Counsel of the CIO, testified in a Senate hearing in 1953 on the weakness of the duty to bargain, which he thought stemmed from the definition of collective bargaining contained in Section 8(d) of the act. Mr. Goldberg observed that "The provision that the obligation to bargain collectively" does not compel either party to agree to a proposal or require the making of a concession "is a technically correct codification of Board Doctrine under the Wagner Act. But it serves no useful purpose and has done harm." [24]

Mr. Goldberg criticized the Supreme Court's decision in the *American National Insurance Co.* case, which relied on that part of Section 8(d) which does not compel an agreement as a condition of bargaining in good faith. Mr. Goldberg referred to the Senate hearings on the southern textile industry as evidence that this section of 8(d) "tended to encourage employers to conform to the definition only superficially. The psychological effect of this restatement has been unfortunate. . . ." [25]

Mr. Goldberg went on to state that the duty to bargain was being construed

both by the Courts, the Board, and the Employers, to permit an employer to refuse really to bargain in good faith with the Union. The essence of the collective bargaining process is and should be a complete, candid exchange on the part of both sides, and their willingness to attempt to make reasonable proposals and counter-proposals in the effort to arrive at a mutual agreement. While it is true that, under the collective bargaining process, neither party is compelled to make proposals that it does not believe in, or to agree to concessions that it does not feel are warranted, nevertheless this provision, having been written into the law, has encouraged a great concert of action on the part of employers, again particularly in the South, to refuse really to bargain in good faith and to refuse really to arrive at an agreement. This is one of the situations where, by writing into the law language which was unnecessary, language which only purported to codify what was in the law psychologically, encouragement has been given to intransigent employers not to arrive at an agreement.[26]

The Senate Subcommittee on Labor and Labor-Management Relations, headed by Senator Hubert Humphrey, issued a report which stated that Section 8(d) was harmful inasmuch as "the new section approximates a series of instructions on how to stay within the boundaries of the law by concentration on mechanical conduct to the detriment of meaningful efforts to achieve understanding."[27]

Other criticisms of the effectiveness of the duty to bargain include a statement by the Cox Panel, which asserted:

. . . a major weakness in the Labor-Management Relations Law is the long delay in contested NLRB proceedings . . . in Labor-Management Relations justice delayed is often justice denied. A remedy granted more than two years after the event will bear little relation to the human situation which gave rise to the need of government intervention.[28]

The report went on to state that

ordinarily a charge that an employer refused to bargain in good faith involves subtle factual inquiries which would make an interlocutory order inappropriate but the case would be entirely different if the Union had recently been certified and the Employer simply refused to begin negotiating a contract. Under present law, neither the General Counsel, the Union, nor the employees can do anything during the year or longer which it takes to prosecute the case through the Board and the Courts. During this period the Union may disintegrate from ineffectiveness.[29]

The chorus of complaints against the weakness of the 8(a)(5) mandate reached a crescendo during the testimony before the Pucinski Committee hearing. The attack on the effectiveness of the 8(a)(5) remedy was based upon the implications of its slow action as well as upon the administrative enforcement of this section. David McDonald, President of United Steelworkers Union of America, stated in his comment upon the administration of the NLRB:

If a union, rather than filing a petition with the Board, exercises its choice of filing a refusal to bargain charge against the Employer for refusal to recognize the majority union, its strength will be completely sapped by the time a decision is rendered even if the charge is ultimately upheld. The employees who join the union not only have been discouraged but may have been induced in the interim to desert the union. Accordingly, if the Order is issued to bargain, the union is now obliged, however impossibly, to bargain effectively.[30]

President Pollock of the Textile Workers Union stated in his testimony that before the passage of the Taft-Hartley Act, his union had won 58 per cent of all elections held in the South, while since 1947 it had won only 33 per cent of the elections held. He further testified that in practice his union never petitioned for an election unless it had 65 per cent of the workers signed up. President Pollock further stated that before 1947, 84 per cent of all union victories in the South resulted in the signing of a collective bargaining contract. Subsequent to the passage of Taft-Hartley, the percentage had fallen to 61 and, furthermore, in 17 per cent there was no renewal of the initial agreement.[31]

The General Counsel of the Textile Workers Union, Benjamin Wyle, also attacked the weakness of the 8(a)(5) remedy:

If the union does manage to win an occasional election, then the employer falls back on his next delaying device. He simply refuses to bargain in good faith with the representative chosen by his employees. Usually, he will meet with the union and negotiate with it after extensive evasions and delays. However, the meetings are mere superficial maneuvers to satisfy the law's requirement of good faith bargaining.[32]

Mr. Wyle also pointed out that a decision by the United

States Court of Appeals for the Second Circuit commented with approval on an observation about the impact of delay on board cases:

The one and one-half years it takes the National Labor Relations Board to reach a decision in an unfair labor practice case is said by one with long experience in that field to mean that apart from the cases being conducted under the shelter of a preliminary injunction, the ultimate decision almost never makes any practical difference to the labor relations between the parties.[33]

THE IMPACT OF THE DUTY TO BARGAIN—
THE EMPIRICAL EVIDENCE

It is clear that to a large extent the judgments and evaluations we have cited on the effectiveness of the duty to bargain are based on the board's formal decisions. However, from the beginning, the vast majority of board cases have been closed before reaching a hearing where formal action is taken.

The board reported with pride in its early years that approximately 85 per cent of all cases were closed informally.[34] In this report, the board placed great emphasis on this performance. It quoted the final report of the Attorney General's Committee on Administrative Procedure, which pointed out that administrative agencies generally perform the bulk of the work in cases which never reach the formal stage. The committee stated:

Examples could be multiplied from nearly every agency in the Federal Government. Enough have been given, however, to make clear that even where formal proceedings are fully available, informal procedures constitute the vast bulk of administrative adjudication and are truly the life-blood of the administrative process. No study of administrative procedure can be adequate if it fails to recognize this fact and focus attention upon improvement at these stages.[35]

A general counsel of the National Labor Relations Board has testified:

The real nature and consequences of a public interest statute like the National Labor Relations Act as amended, is not to be found just in law in the books but in law in action. Such words as "administrative due process" and "justice" have little meaning in themselves and take on clearer definition only by observing an administration in action under the statute. If you want to understand something about a law like the National Labor Relations Act, you have to ask, "How does it work?" [36]

Additional support of the significance of the informal disposition of cases is given by the analysis of the stages of disposition of unfair labor practice cases closed in the NLRB's annual reports. For example, in the fiscal year 1961, a total of 12,116 unfair labor practice charges were closed. Of this number, only 4.6 per cent reached the board in Washington for a decision.[37] Adding to this number the 1.1 per cent of cases which were closed after compliance with an intermediate report, we have a grand total of 94.3 per cent of all cases closed before a formal decision by either a trial examiner or a board order and/or court decree.[38] The number of cases going to the courts for enforcement constitutes about 1½ per cent of the total cases filed. It is therefore imperative that whatever method is used in obtaining and evaluating the empirical evidence, appropriate attention must be paid to those cases closed before a formal decision.

DR. BROWN'S STUDY

The only empirical study yet made on board activities, though restricted in scope, does employ this approach. During the war years, a limited study was made of the effectiveness of the act in cases where violations were found.[39] The results of Section 8(5) violations were analyzed for cases adjusted prior to hearing or board order and closed as in compliance, and for formal cases which were also closed in compliance with a board order, a court decree, or both.

The test used in judging the success of the board was the extent to which collective bargaining followed the closing of a case on compliance. Collective bargaining was considered in effect "where there was a contract, negotiations were under way for a contract, or a dispute as to contract provisions was before the War Labor Board . . ."[40]

For the years 1941 and 1942 in six regions of the NLRB, of the 228 adjusted cases closed before a formal hearing involving a violation of 8(5), collective bargaining as defined above was entered into in 188 or 82.4 per cent.

Of the thirty-eight formal cases, collective bargaining was in effect in 1943 for twenty-four, or 63.1 per cent of the total cases in this category.[41]

However, it should be noted that the significance of the statistics is considerably vitiated by the definition of collective bargaining. The fact that negotiations are under way for a contract may not always mean that an agreement between the parties resulted, and neither does a submission of a dispute before the War Labor Board establish such a relationship. Perhaps more than any other single factor, the time period covered limits the usefulness of this study. The war and the scarcity of labor may have had results which are completely unrepresentative of other periods, as indicated by the experience during World War I when the introduction to collective bargaining which was supported by the government did not in most instances take root to survive in the postwar period.

Despite these strictures, the results do have some significance. In particular, attention must be paid to the study of the results of enforcement of orders to bargain despite claims of union's loss of majority. These cases arise when a respondent employer has resisted the enforcement of an 8(5) order on the basis that the union no longer represents a majority of the employees. Dr. Brown studied forty-five such cases in which the circuit courts enforced board orders and discovered that contracts were secured in thirty-nine of the forty-six units involved. In two cases the bargaining was inconclusive. In addition, of the twenty-six contracts which had completed their original term, two had been renewed four times, one had been renewed three times, seven had been renewed twice, eleven had been renewed once, and five expired without renewal.[42]

AN EMPIRICAL ANALYSIS OF THE DUTY TO BARGAIN

Because of the limitations of the legislative testimony, the unanswered questions in the Brown study, and the lack of empirical evidence, an investigation was undertaken by the writer. Simply put, the question to be answered is, "What is the practical meaning of the duty to bargain?" It is abundantly clear that the prevailing belief in the ineffectiveness of the 8(a)(5) remedy is based upon experience usually gained from knowledge of particular cases. But surely as a first step it is necessary to discover the consequences of meritorious charges filed with the National Labor Relations Board alleging violations of the duty to bargain.

The first question concerns the test to be used as the measure of NLRB effectiveness. The obvious test, measuring success by whether a contract is signed following an order to bargain, appears to be a valid one. It is simple, objective, and meaningful in its own right. It is noteworthy that Dr. Brown used a similar though less rigorous test and that the Textile Workers Union also employed the same test in its criticism of the effectiveness of this sanction.

Since the vast majority of violations of the Taft-Hartley Act are remedied before formal hearing and court review, the study concentrated on this area of non-litigated cases. Six regional offices of the National Labor Relations Board were selected; the choice of regions was dictated solely by the desire to get as representative a selection as possible. Accordingly, the following regions were covered: Boston, Pittsburgh, Atlanta, Kansas City, Los Angeles, and San Francisco.

The writer examined all meritorious cases involving allegations of Section 8(a)(5) which were filed in the six regions during the calendar year 1960. Case summaries were prepared on the basis of a personal examination of the files, and subsequent bargaining histories were obtained by inquiries directed to the charging unions. A summary of the findings is given in Table 2.

It is to be noted that the cases are classified both by past collective bargaining history and by the nature of the major issue involved in the refusal to bargain. The overall results indicate that in only thirteen or 19.3 per cent of the total sixty-seven cases was a collective bargaining relationship not established or resumed.

Impressive as the percentage of contracts executed is, any meaningful interpretation of the statistics requires an understanding of the forces at work. For this purpose, it will be necessary to examine selected case histories.

However, before inspecting the individual case histories covered in Table 2, it appears desirable to examine the collective bargaining consequences of the formal cases, that is, those charges of refusal to bargain which required board orders for enforcement. The facts in these cases were obtained from the printed board decisions, and the follow-up information was secured from the parties involved.

MERITORIOUS FORMAL CASES WHICH RESULTED IN CONTRACTS OR OTHER COMPLIANCE

The first case involves a firm in the Los Angeles region of the board and a union which was newly organized. The facts are as follows:

The charge was filed by the Painters Union and a local of

TABLE 2

MERIT 8(a)(5) CASES (NOT GOING TO HEARING)
MAJOR ISSUES INVOLVED AND DISPOSITION BY ISSUES

Calendar Year 1960

Total Merit Cases, 67

a. Major Issue Involved

Major issue involved		Collective bargaining history		
	No prior contract	3 years or less of collective bargaining	More than 3 years of collective bargaining	Successor corporation
Recognition	11	0	9	2
Refusal to sign contract	3	0	1	0
Unilateral action	5	4	7	0
Bad-faith bargaining	8	3	3	0
Mandatory subject matter	0	0	0	0
Unit contested	0	0	2	0
Bypassing union	0	0	1	1
Refusal to supply information	1	1	5	0
TOTALS	28	8	28	3

184

Other allegations

Independent 8(a)(1)	11	1	8	3
Strike	12	1	4	0
DISPOSITION Withdrawn	16	5	19	0
OF CASES Settled	12	3	9	3

b. Disposition by Issues

Issue	Contract Signed	Agreement in effect	Collective bargaining resumed Agreement not in effect Contract eventually signed	Contract not signed	TOTALS
Recognition	6	1	11	4	22
Refusal to sign contract	2	1	0	1	4
Unilateral action	6	4	2	4	16
Bad-faith bargaining	3	2	6	3	14
Mandatory subject matter	0	0	0	0	0
Unit contested	1	0	1	0	2
Bypassing union	1	0	1	0	2
Refusal to supply information	2	1	3	1	7
TOTALS	21	9	24	13	67

the Teamsters Union on July 25, 1960, alleging a violation of 8(a)(3) and 8(a)(5) of the act. The company maintains a paint factory in California, and has forty employees. Early in July, 1960, an employee of the company contacted the charging unions and in a one-man organizational campaign signed up sixteen out of the twenty-seven employees

185

in the unit. On July 19, the charging unions requested recognition but were told by the president of the employer that before he would sign a contract he would fire all employees and close down the plant. On the same day, the unions filed an RC (election) petition. On the next day, the employee who organized the plant was fired and immediately fifteen other employees walked off the job. Within a week, the company hired fourteen replacements.

On July 20, wage increases ranging up to thirty cents per hour were given to several employees. On July 22, the employee who had organized the plant and who rented a house from the president of the company was served with an eviction notice for using the house as a campaign headquarters for the union. On July 27, the company president told the strikers on the picket line that the firm would close down rather than employ any of the strikers again.

On July 25, the employer filed an 8(b)7(C) charge against the charging unions, on August 8 a secondary boycott charge, and on August 10 an RM (or employer-sponsored election) petition. All these were dismissed. A complaint issued and on February 28, 1961, a trial examiner found a violation of 8(a)(3) and (5) of the act. The board confirmed this in its order dated July 12, 1961. On January 8, 1962, the Circuit Court of Appeals enforced the board order.

During compliance action with the court decree, the region estimated that the fifteen back-pay claimants were owed $32,562. On June 1, the employer offered to pay $20,000 to the discriminatees over a five-year period with 10 per cent down. He based this plea upon poverty. The region agreed that respondent employer was not in sound economic condition and recommended the time payment of a total sum in the neighborhood of $23,000–25,000. In the meantime, the employer had signed a contract with the charging unions.

The significance of the case lies in the consequences of board action. Here we have an employer who met the organization of his employees with hostility. The employee responsible for the unionization of the plant was fired and a strike was precipitated. In a very short time, practically all the employees were replaced and the plant was back in operation.

The consequences of a violation of the duty to bargain operated in the following manner. Since a majority of the employees had indicated a desire for union representation, the employer was under an obligation to bargain with the union even in the absence of a certification. Consequently, his charge alleging a violation of Section 8(b)7(C) of the act in that the unions were picketing for recognition when they did not represent a majority of the employees was dismissed. The same fate befell his efforts to force an election by filing an RM petition. The employer's desire for an election was tantamount to raising the question of representation. Since the facts of the case show that the employer did not have a good-faith doubt about the union's status, his petition was dismissed. Furthermore, his discharge of the strikers was unlawful since they were unfair labor practice strikers and consequently were entitled to their jobs upon request.

The employer's failure to reinstate the strikers and discharge the strike replacements resulted in the tolling of back pay which, in this case, was a considerable amount. Despite the fact that eighteen months passed from the filing of the charge to the enforcement of the board order by a Circuit Court of Appeals, the union survived the strike, and a contract was eventually signed.

A second case involved a long-established collective bargaining relationship. The facts in this case were as follows:

The charge was filed by the UAW on December 5, 1960, alleging violation of 8(a)(5) of the act. The employer is a factory making chucks, with 250 employees, and is located in Connecticut.

The union had represented the production and maintenance employees for about twenty-five years and the last contract expired on September 15, 1960.

The first meeting to negotiate a new contract was held on July 22, 1960. The company submitted to the union on this date a forty-page proposed contract which withdrew many of the benefits which the union had enjoyed under the existing contract. After the meeting on September 15, a strike began in which all employees participated. The next meeting was held on September 22, 1960, at the end of which the employer announced its plans to continue production. On that date it started to recruit replacements through newspaper and radio announcements. The plant reopened on September 26. By November 9, 1960, all but thirty-five strikers had been replaced. However, bargaining sessions were held on November 9 and 21, and December 19 and 22. From December 22 through April, 1961 there were twelve additional meetings. On June 18, 1961, the union abandoned the strike and virtually all the strikers made an unconditional offer to go back to work.

The hearing took about twenty-eight days between May 1 and July 18, 1961, and on July 12, during the hearing, the general counsel amended the complaint by alleging that the refusal of the company to reinstate the strikers, with the exception of ten or twelve employees, was a violation of 8(a)(3) of the act. During all conferences subsequent to September 15, 1960, the employer notified the union that the strike replacements were permanent employees.

The intermediate report stated, "Among the principal facts upon which the allegation of bad faith bargaining rests are the nature and extent of the contract change proposals presented to the Union by the Company."

On January 24, 1962, an intermediate report issued finding a violation of 8(a)(5). There was no finding that any specific proposal of the company was per se unlawful prior to the strike. However, the trial examiner stated that all the company's demands must be viewed in the context of the relations between the parties.

For the past contract year, there were over 200 grievances still pending while only two were brought to arbitration and decided, and those two were decided on the last day of the contract year. The company's position throughout negotiations that no decision from past or pending grievances would apply in the future as precedent did not lend itself to making negotiations easier. It follows that a new contract with a one-year term providing for a more stringent and complex grievance procedure could not solve many issues.

The trial examiner made a finding that the employer's underlying motives in negotiations had "as an objective to remove the Union as an effective representative of the employees" and that the company had no intention that there should be an agreement or a contract. The trial examiner cited *NLRB v. Reed and Prince,* 285 F. 2d 131, 139 (C.A. 1):

It is difficult to believe the Company with a straight face and a good faith could have supposed that this proposal had the slightest chance of acceptance by a self-respecting Union, or even that it might advance negotiations by affording a basis of discussion; rather it looks more like a stalling tactic by a party bent upon maintaining a pretense of bargaining.

The intermediate report concluded:

In sum, the Respondent was asking the Union to sign the contract which in reality was not a contract; it engaged in lengthy discussions over the details and fairness of the many precise numerical aspects of its proposed wage incentive system, and argued without end about the new system's impact upon the revised grievance procedure, while at the same time insisting that all of this would not necessarily be binding upon the Company at all.

This was viewed "as direct evidence that the company had no intention of reaching an agreement." In addition, the insistence that the union agree in writing that strikers be permanent employees was held to be a disruptive proposal and one not made in good faith. In the trial examiner's view, the employer's insistence upon superseniority for strike replacements was not a per se violation but part and parcel of the employer's determination not to bargain in good faith. There was also a finding that the strike from its inception was an unfair labor practice strike and that the strikers were 8(a)(3)'s on June 18, 1961, at the time of their offer to go back to work.

After the issuance of the intermediate report, the employer began rehiring strikers, and at the time of the board order in August, 1962, had rehired all the strikers and agreed to comply with the order. The employer has agreed to pay $250,000 in back pay to the strikers and has signed a new contract with the union.

The importance of this case lies not only in its demonstration of the sanctions imposed by the duty to bargain, but in its proof that a long collective bargaining history is no guarantee of permanent good-faith dealing. This case shows that there is no a priori reason for concluding that the standards of bargaining fixed by the board have no meaning in long-established collective bargaining relationships. Relative economic strength of the parties is always subject to change. The requirement to bargain in good faith is not only applicable to first bargaining relationships; it imposes obligations and sets standards which are enduring. The growth of government-aided unions during the period of World War I and their falling away when government controls were abandoned underscores the significance for established bargaining relationships of a permanent public policy in favor of collective bargaining.

In this case, twenty-five years of collective bargaining did not prevent the employer from attempting to break the union or to reduce its influence to a nullity. Significantly, all the conventional procedures of collective bargaining were followed by the employer. There were many meetings, no independent violations comprising unfair labor practices, and no deliberate bypassing of the union; institution of unilateral changes was avoided, and there were even some minor concessions to the union. Moreover, the employer continued to bargain, in the sense of meeting with the union, after the strike.

The only issue was whether the employer was in violation of Section 8(a)(5), and the survival of the union depended on the determination of this question. The union had done all its strength permitted. All employees went out on strike and stayed out on the picket line for nine months until the strike was abandoned. Within a week after the beginning of the strike operations were resumed, and within several months nearly all strikers had been replaced. Clearly, the employer had won the economic battle.

The status of strikers during a strike is well settled. A striker who is engaged in an economic strike for a lawful purpose and not in violation of an existing no-strike clause or of the procedural requirements of Section 8(d), and who has not engaged in tortious or criminal conduct during the course of the strike, may not be discharged or otherwise discriminated against for his concerted activity, but he can be permanently replaced.[43] While at first glance the distinction between an employee's being permanently replaced and discharged may appear minimal or even non-existent, in fact on occasion the distinction is critical. For example, the economic striker must be individually re-placed, and if he requests his job back, the employer is required to rehire him without any adverse conditions such as the surrendering of seniority and other rights. And, of course, economic strikers, although they may have been permanently replaced, have the statutory right to vote in a representation election within a year after the beginning of the strike. In this case, however, if the strike had been an economic one, the vast majority of strikers would have lost all their reinstatement rights.

On the other hand, the status of an unfair practice striker is entirely different. If the striker has been replaced in a strike caused or prolonged by an employer's unfair labor practice, the striker is entitled to reinstatement to his job, even if this requires the displacement or discharge of the employee hired to replace him.[44] In our case, the question of whether the employer had refused to bargain with the union determined the rights of the strikers to be reinstated. And where, as here, the strikers requested reinstatement and were denied on the basis of their per-manent replacement, a finding of a refusal to bargain meant that the strikers were entitled to back pay in addi-tion to reinstatement dating from the abandonment of the strike. The enforcement of the duty to bargain resulted in the restoration of the union; the discharge of strike re-placements who had been promised permanent jobs; a heavy financial loss for the employer in back-pay pay-ments, expenses incidental to the retraining of a new labor force, and litigation costs; and the execution of a new contract with the union. It seems hardly necessary to make additional comment on the efficacy of the remedy in this particular case.

A third example of the impact of formal board decisions involves an unaffiliated union and a large national corporation. The facts in this case are:

The charge was filed by the Salaried Employees Association of this corporation, unaffiliated, on September 27, 1960, alleging a violation of $8(a)(5)$ of the act. The employer is a manufacturer of electrical products, is located in California, and has about 1,700 employees.

Until May 31, 1960, the charging union was an affiliate of the Federation of Independent Salaried Employees Union and represented a unit of clerical and technical employees and a unit of professional employees at the employer's plant. On May 31, the union president notified the employer that the union had terminated its affiliation with the federation. On June 1, 1960, the employer filed RM petitions which resulted in elections being held on August 10, 1960. In the professional unit, the vote was 63 for the charging union, 18 for the federation, 152 votes for neither; in the clerical unit, the charging union received 424 votes, the federation got 169 votes, and there were 65 votes for neither. The president of the charging union was a professional employee and, as president, was an ex-officio member of the negotiating committee for both units. He submitted his resignation as president on August 23, but the membership voted to retain him despite the loss of the professional unit. The employer, however, refused to permit him to take time off during working hours for the purpose of negotiation, while insisting that meetings with the union could only take place during working hours. The company did offer to transfer the president, who was an engineer, to the technical and clerical unit, where it would then meet with him. The company's attitude was that professional employees had no business belonging to the clerical and technical union.

A complaint issued on October 31, 1960, and the allegations were sustained in an intermediate report which came out on February 13, 1961, and in a board order which issued on July 1, 1961. The board order required the employer to meet with the union without regard to whether the union's representatives were employees in the certified unit. The union's president resigned his office in February, 1961, but subsequent to the board order was appointed to the negotiation committee of the union and the meetings were held after working hours so that he could be present. The case was closed on October 19, 1961.

This case illustrates the influence of the board on matters not directly related to a contract. The act guarantees to both unions and employers the right to select representatives of their own choosing for the purposes of collective bargaining. In this case, the employer had a contractual relationship with a local union which was affiliated with a national independent union. Apparently the national independent union existed for the purpose of representing clerical and professional employees of the employer. The facts indicate a company resentment of the local's disaffiliation which took the form of preventing the union from designating its own representatives.

Aside from the pettiness of the employer's action, the case has several implications. In the first place, it is an example of the effectiveness of board policy in areas where the signing of a contract is inappropriate as a criterion. Second, it demonstrates the legal constraints on the relations between an employer and an unaffiliated or company union. Of necessity, an employer cannot push its economic advantages too hard because of the risk of legal consequences which would be inimical to the maintenance of the original relationship.

Like the preceding cases, this history, with its result of employer compliance with the board order, makes one ask what the outcome would have been in the absence of a duty to bargain as a legal mandate for bargaining behavior. Here it is not difficult to see a completely different result.

MERITORIOUS FORMAL CASES WHICH DID NOT RESULT IN CONTRACTS

Of course, not all cases resulted in the establishment of collective bargaining, and understanding of NLRB procedures requires consideration of this category of cases. The two case histories which follow have in common a board order succeeded by fruitless bargaining. The first example is *the apparel factory case:*

The charge was filed by the Industrial Workers Federation of Labor, Local 886 (Independent) on March 8, 1960, alleging a violation of 8(a)(3) and (5) of the act. The employer is an apparel factory located in California, and has 250 employees. In December, 1959, during the charging union's organizational campaign, the employer discriminated against an active union member by cutting down his working hours and a board order issued in December, 1960.

The union won an election held on October 14, 1959, by a vote of 139 to 89 and was certified on October 22. The 8(a)(5) complaint was based on bad faith expressed in four categories of conduct. (1) Dilatory tactics: The employer hired a labor relations consultant, Mrs. Edwin Selvin, who in six months succeeded, despite constant union effort, in meeting only five times with the union; the last two meetings occurred after the charge had been filed. At the end of each meeting, Mrs. Selvin would refuse to set a date for the next meeting on the pretext that she did not have her appointment book, or for some other such reason. On one occasion, the union representative asked her to call her office and have someone look up her appointment book but was told that it was not available to anyone in her office—it was locked up in a safe. She always declined to bring her book with her to meetings despite repeated requests. On March 15, 1960, the union wrote to her proposing meetings and suggested three alternative dates but Mrs. Selvin declined to meet on the ground that she would be busy. The intermediate report said, in part:

> One cannot review the bargaining history in this case without receiving the impression that Selvin has formulated a bargaining technique designed to postpone indefinitely any agreement or to make an impasse inevitable. This technique appears to consist of avoidance of frequent meetings, never setting a definite date for the next meeting at the close of any bargaining session, "letting sleeping dogs lie"; that is, never prompting a meeting but leaving the initiative always with the Union, never yielding to any demands of the Union on any matter that would alter her principal's present practice or policy on wages, hours, and working conditions or that would require her principal to make decisions other than unilaterally in any such matters, never volunteering unrequested information, and if requested, giving as little information as possible and then only when the law had settled the Union's right to such information, consuming as much time in bargaining meetings on trivial matters as circumstances permitted, and offering contract terms which cannot be legally insisted upon in order to be able to modify such proposals later to give an appearance of compromise. (Intermediate report, pp. 19–20.)

(2) Delay and failure to give information: The union was completely frustrated by the company's delay and failure to give requested information relating to the proper subjects of collective bargaining. (3) Unilateral wage in-

creases. (4) Surface bargaining: The employer's negotiations consisted of Mrs. Selvin's rejection of the union's proposed contract in its entirety and the making of a counteroffer which merely reduced to writing the existing conditions in the plant when it did not propose more onerous conditions; for example, it provided longer hours for piece workers, that is, time and a half after forty hours, when the current practice was time and a half after thirty-seven and a half hours. With respect to grievances, the employer agreed to discuss them but made the condition that its decision was final, and refused to have arbitration. The company also insisted that no contract could be signed without a no-strike clause. The employer furthermore rejected a union bulletin board and insisted upon a management prerogative clause which gave the employer unilateral control over all terms and conditions of employment. The intermediate report found a refusal to bargain.

No exceptions were filed to the intermediate report and the board order issued on January 16, 1961. The employer stated that it would comply with the board order. Subsequent to the order, seven meetings took place up to June 13, 1961. During these meetings, the employer supplied all requested information. However, the region, in examining the course of bargaining through the transcripts paid for by the company, found no fundamental change in the surface bargaining, pointing to Mrs. Selvin's position on the union's request for specific language on grievances as an example. The company refused to make any such specific provisions in the contract. There was also no change in the company's insistence that it should maintain unilateral control of the terms and conditions of employment, with a grievance procedure which would give the employer final authority to decide grievances, subject only to the union's right to strike.

Despite the protest of the employer, the region went to enforcement and got a court order on August 7, 1961. Four meetings were held after the issuance of the decree. At the last meeting on October 5, the union said that it would not request further meetings until the board acted on its contention that the company should be cited for contempt. At all meetings, the employer had a court reporter to take down the proceedings of each session. The only agreement reached was on a recognition clause and a grievance procedure; but after the issuance of the decree there was no new evidence of 8(a)(5) conduct. There was a complete impasse on wages, although the union had accepted the company's position that minimum wages be set in the contract with deviations subject to the grievance procedure. On the basis that an impasse had been reached and that the company had accepted the union's proposal on the grievance procedure, the case was closed on December 21, 1961. On December 28, 1961, an RD (decertification) petition was filed by some employees. An election was held on March 6, 1962, with the union losing by a vote of 89 to 11.

The retail furniture store case:

The charge was filed by the Retail Clerks Union on December 20, 1960, alleging a violation of 8(a)(3) and (5) of the act. The employer operates a retail furniture store located in California, and has five employees. The employer normally employs four men plus two office girls and a store manager.

All the men joined the union during an organizational campaign on November 16, 1960, and on November 28, the union representative informed the employer that it represented a majority of the employees and wanted recognition. That same day, the employer told one of the men that he would close down the store if the union came in, and on the following day, two men were fired for their "general attitude."

The union immediately started to picket. One of the remaining men quit his job because his wife, the office girl, informed him that she would "kick him out of the house" if he joined the union. The other male employee kept on working and crossed the picket line daily, although shortly after the start of the strike he began to wear a union button at work. Eventually he too joined the picket line. The union, which had filed an RC petition on November 30, 1960, withdrew it after filing the subject charge.

A complaint was issued alleging 8(a)(3) and (5) on January 13, 1961. On May 25, 1961, a stipulation was made which provided for 8(a)(1), (3), and (5) remedies to be enforced by a consent decree. The 8(a)(3)'s (the discriminatees) were to be put on a preferential hiring list and given back pay, since a marked decrease in business prevented their immediate rehiring. The decree was entered into on January 2, 1962, enforcing a board order of October 30, 1961.

The company has met subsequently with the union on a number of occasions but no contract was ever negotiated. The union began picketing on March 28, 1961, and the employer filed an 8(b)7(C) charge and an 8(b)(3) (refusal-to-bargain) charge on April 5, 1961. The refusal-to-bargain charge filed by the employer was based upon an allegation that the union walked out on a negotiation meeting held on March 28, 1961. The 8(b)(7) charge was dismissed as being inconsistent with the 8(b)(3) charge, and the latter was dismissed for lack of evidence.

On January 23, 1962, the union filed a new 8(a)(5) charge alleging that the employer had agreed upon the union health and welfare plan and then reneged. There was no evidence for this and it was dismissed on February

13, 1962, with no appeal by the union. By this time the union had no members working for the store. Subsequently the union did not show up at a scheduled bargaining meeting and it appeared that it would make no further efforts to bargain. The case was closed without union objection on March 9, 1962, as being in compliance "under the circumstances."

There are a number of common elements in the two cases. To begin with, it must be recognized that all meritorious unfair labor practices other than the violation of Section 8(a)(5) had been remedied; that is, the standard notices had been posted for violations of Section 8(a)(1), and there had been full compliance with the 8(a)(3) orders including reinstatement and back pay. The quantity of evidence needed to enforce such orders is such that ordinarily no difficulty can be expected from most respondents.

A second characteristic in these cases was the clearness, almost the ingenuousness of the violation of the duty to bargain. These cases did not demand close questions of fact or subtle considerations of legal doctrine. The refusal to bargain consisted of refusals to meet, undermining and bypassing the union, widespread threats, and discriminatory discharges. In the apparel company case, the negotiations which preceded the board's order were a caricature of bargaining which bordered on the ludicrous. And yet, despite the board order and the court decree, both companies succeeded in avoiding collective bargaining contracts.

The pattern in these cases is similar to the examples adduced by the Textile Workers Union during the legislative hearings previously discussed. This pattern consists of widespread violations of many sections of the act before the entrance of a board order and court decree, after which the employer's obduracy is masked by action which taken by itself constitutes formal compliance. If we compare the employer's conduct before and after the issuance of a court decree, perhaps we will be able to get some insights into the method by which the public policy can be thwarted.

First of all, the consequences of the employer's initial hostility to unionism, which was expressed in threats and discharges, cannot be considered entirely expunged by the posting of notices and the reinstatement of discriminatees. This is particularly true where the employer elects, despite the clarity of the violation, to litigate the issue to the end. Due process entitles the employer to be heard, to appeal, to have his day in court; and the passage of time ordinarily works to reinforce the employer's position and to weaken the union's hold among its members. It is difficult to imagine that, during the years required to obtain a board order and court decree, a union—any union—can build a viable organization in the teeth of employer hostility and the utter standstill of collective bargaining.

Under these circumstances, what can be the effect of a court decree enforcing an order to bargain if an employer still wishes to resist unionization? No one, of course, lightly defies a court order; but the affirmative portions of an order can be met without a contract's ensuing. In other words, an employer, as in each of our two cases, ends his unilateral action, meets with the union, ceases uttering threats and discharging union adherents, and no longer insists upon clearly unlawful contract terms. But despite the fears of its critics, the public policy in bargaining does not regulate, or even attempt to regulate, the substantive terms of a contract. As we have seen in our consideration of board doctrine, no board order can lawfully dictate the terms and conditions of a contract, nor can it compel agreement. All that the law requires is good-faith bargaining. And while a lack of good faith is a matter of fact and by and large easily ascertainable in the proceedings which lead up to an order, there remains the much harder question of establishing good faith *after* the entrance of a court decree.

If we examine the conduct of the employers subsequent to the enforcement of the board order, we notice an absence of the usual signs of bad-faith bargaining. The employer's conduct has changed as a consequence of the formal proceedings, even if his subjective opposition to the union has not. Moreover, he has been bargaining. It is precisely here that the difficulty of enforcement arises. Since the employer is not enjoined to agree with the union, he does not. He has been required to pay a certain price in litigation costs to reach this stage, and bargaining under a court order imposes certain constraints on his behavior, but he has also achieved a weaker union.

The conclusion appears inescapable that the ultimate sanction of the duty to bargain rests upon its acceptance by the employer. The evidence indicates that employers who wish to pay the price of not dealing with a union can do so. The most important part of the price is the risk of an unfair labor practice strike. An employer who violates the duty to bargain may be confronted by strikers who are entitled to retain their jobs. This considerably reduces the employer's economic strength. It little matters how weak the union may be, or how many strike replacements may be available; the employer's freedom of action is limited. He cannot recruit permanent replacements, and training new employees can be expensive, particularly if their employment is to be of short duration. The employer's future plans must always be conditioned by the fact that he must take back the unfair labor practice strikers at their request or else be liable for their back pay. The bite of the law lies precisely here.

How does an employer escape the duty to bargain and avoid permanent union relations? An examination of our cases leads to the belief that unions can be so weak that no strike—unfair labor practice strike or not—is possible. Of what value is a strike when only a small fraction of the employees go out? Furthermore, intelligent employer action can minimize the risk of an unfair labor practice strike by ending the violations when legal wisdom so dictates. It is important to note that most employer counsel realize the implications of an unfair labor practice strike; this fact accounts for employers' compliance with the law in those cases which are settled prior to formal action. These will be examined shortly.

We have examined formal board orders and court decrees, first, because a formal case establishes the legal requirements of good-faith bargaining; and, second, because examination of the consequences of formal orders enables us to evaluate the ultimate results of recalcitrance. The import of these formal cases will be further emphasized as we proceed to discuss and analyze the disposition of cases which do not reach the board.

CASES CLOSED IN COMPLIANCE WITH AN INTERMEDIATE REPORT

Time is the most important difference between cases closed upon compliance with an intermediate report and cases which have to be enforced following a board order or court decree. Although the delay between filing of the charge and closing of the case averages around a year for cases closed in compliance with an intermediate report, it is still considerably less than the time required for board orders. In every other respect, these cases are comparable to board order cases; that is, there has been a formal hearing with the issuance of a recommended order by a trial examiner.

MERITORIOUS 8(a)(5) CASES, CLOSED UPON COMPLIANCE WITH AN INTERMEDIATE REPORT, IN WHICH CONTRACTS WERE SIGNED

The Connecticut factory case:

The charge was filed by the IAM on June 1, 1960, alleging a violation of 8(a)(5). The employer has a factory which uses thirty-five employees, and is located in Connecticut. The union was certified on March 1, 1960. On March 10, the owner of the company told the employees that there would be no union contract in his plant and that he would never sign a contract. The first and only bargaining meeting was held on May 10, during which the employer harangued the union representatives and stated that the only law that he would observe was the overtime provisions of the Fair Labor Standards Act. In response to the union's request for another meeting, he replied that there was no necessity for it and that he would continue to give unilateral wage increases as had been his practice in the past. Subsequently a complaint issued and on November 22, 1960, an intermediate report sustained the finding of an 8(a)(5). On November 27, 1960, the employer signed an informal settlement agreement and on March 21, 1961, the case was closed upon the resumption of collective bargaining. A contract was eventually signed.

The poultry processing case:

The charge was filed by the IAM on August 15, 1960,

alleging a violation of 8(a)(5) of the act. The company is engaged in the manufacture of poultry processing machinery and is located in Missouri. There had previously been long contractual relationships between the parties, with the last contract expiring on March 29, 1960. Negotiations for a new contract had begun prior to this expiration date but were unsuccessful. On March 30, 1960, the union went out on strike. On May 17, 1960, the company sent all striking employees a letter which stated: "Acts of violence are unlawful and retribution in full will be the first matter to be settled in further negotiation with the Union, if any further negotiation takes place." Three more negotiating meetings were held from May to August 3, 1960. On August 3, company counsel stated: ". . . before any negotiating could be done in regard to wages and a new contract that the Union would have to come up with some $1700 or $1800 in damages that occurred through violence at their plant." Negotiations ceased at this point. Following the filing of the charge, counsel for the company repeated its position in a statement to the regional director that it would refuse to bargain any further with the union unless and until the union agreed to reimburse the employer for damages. However, on September 6, 1960, the company notified the union that it was willing to meet for negotiation.

On November 28, 1960, an intermediate report issued which found that the question of damages was not a mandatory subject for collective bargaining since it does not relate to "wages, hours and other conditions of employment." The intermediate report continued:

It follows that an Employer may not decline to negotiate regarding mandatory subjects unless or until nonmandatory subjects are negotiated. To hold otherwise would permit an Employer to avoid his obligations indefinitely by raising and insisting upon settlement of any subject which might occur to him.

In the meantime, since the change of company position in early September, meetings had taken place. On January 12, 1961, the charging party informed the region that on January 9, 1951, the parties had entered into a contract which achieved the original remedy sought, and therefore requested permission to withdraw the charge. On January 17, 1961, the respondent company filed a motion to dismiss the complaint. On January 18, 1961, the board granted the motion to dismiss the complaint which had issued on September 30, 1960.

The grocery store case:

The charge was filed by the Retail Clerks on October 24, 1960, alleging a violation of 8(a)(5) of the act. The company is a partnership which operates two grocery stores in Kansas. The charging union in this case was certified in 1957 for all regular employees with the usual exclusions. Since the certification, two succeeding contracts had been entered into with the 1958 contract terminating by its terms on September 3, 1960.

The union, pursuant to the notification clause in the latest contract, reopened the contract for the purpose of negotiating a new one. The company failed to respond to the union's written proposals. Shortly before the expiration of the last contract, company supervisors undertook a series of 8(a)(1) activities for the purpose of destroying the union's majority status and discrediting it as the employees' bargaining agent. The activities included promising benefits if the union was out, telling employees that there would not be a new contract, and threatening employees with the loss of their jobs if the union stayed in. The company also refused to give the union a list of the names of its employees upon its request in early August, 1960. Although the employer attended the negotiating meeting with representatives of other grocery stores in the area on September 12, 1960, and agreed at this time to meet again on October 4, the employer did not show up at the October 4 meeting. On September 30, 1960, the company filed an RM (election) petition with the board without indicating in any way that it doubted the union's majority before this action. On October 7, 1961, an intermediate report was issued upholding the 8(a)(5) allegation. On April 17, 1961, a contract was signed between the parties. The case was closed as being in compliance with the intermediate report.

The furniture factory case:

The charge was filed by the Upholsterers Union on January 21, 1960, alleging a violation of 8(a)(5) of the act. The employer has a furniture factory in southern California, and has thirty employees. The employer became a member of an association in 1955 as the result of a recognitional dispute with the charging union. The association, which has as its main purpose collective bargaining with the union, settled that dispute, and negotiated the initial contract between the parties in 1955. Thereafter, the employer joined with other members of the association (which has fifty members) in executing a series of agreements which had been negotiated by the association. The employer never participated in the negotiations and as a matter of routine signed the contracts presented to it. The union reopened the association contract in March, 1959, and ten meetings took place between May and August 13, 1959, at which time a new agreement was reached and was ratified by the union membership. Although the employer put into effect the appropriate wage increases, it was unhappy about some other of the contractual terms. It secured a labor relations consultant, Mrs. Edwin Selvin, who told the union that the company was not obligated to sign the contract. On October 27, 1959, the employer resigned from the association. A complaint subsequently issued, and an intermediate report, dated June 2, 1960, found that the resignation was "an untimely attempt to place its employees beyond the scope of the duly-established bargaining unit." On June 29, 1960, the employer signed a contract with the union which was identical with the association contract. The case was closed on September 6, 1960.

Each of these cases demonstrates a remarkable change in company behavior as a consequence of a finding of a refusal to bargain. In the Connecticut factory case, the adamant opposition of the employer to bargaining with a newly certified union was carried only to the point at which an intermediate report found a refusal to bargain. There seems to be little question that the resumption of negotiations which ended in a new contract was due to the board's action. The grocery store case also exemplifies the efficacy of NLRB standards. The apparent decision of the employer to break the union ended with the issuance of an intermediate report finding a violation of the duty to bargain. The other cases also demonstrate the operational impact of board decisions with respect to long-established collective bargaining relationships. In each of these cases, the change in employer behavior resulted in a resumption of bargaining and the execution of a new contract.

It is not without significance that in each of these cases the employer could have carried the case further. A decision to comply with an intermediate report may be taken to imply a greater readiness to conform to the statutory requirement of bargaining than does the decision to litigate to the end.

The same considerations which result in a failure to sign a contract appear to operate in cases closed at this stage. For example, consider the following case history:

The charge was filed by the IAM and a local of the Teamsters Union on February 10, 1960, alleging a violation of 8(a)(5) of the act. The employer is engaged in the sale of auto parts, is located in southern California, and has twenty employees. On November 3, 1959, the charging unions won an election which was held by the California Conciliation Department by a vote of 8 to 6. The first meeting between the parties was held on November 27, at which time the employer stated that it would not give any wage increases because it could not afford them. On December 3, wage increases were given unilaterally to four employees. At the next meeting, which was held on December 10, there was no progress whatsoever, with the employer absolutely refusing every suggestion made by the union. The employer's representative was a labor relations consultant. On January 2, 1960, she spoke to all the employees on company time and made a lengthy anti-union speech. In this address she stated that the employer could not afford to pay union wages, that it had tried to negotiate with the union, and that strikes do not work out for the employees since a company always manages to stay open and hire replacements. A final meeting between the parties was held on January 27, 1960, with no progress being made. The company at this point declined the services of a mediator. A complaint subsequently issued and an intermediate report dated July 7, 1960, sustained the allegations and found a violation of 8(a)(5). One bargaining session was held on September 1, 1960, and was completely unsuccessful. The union did not request another meeting and did not object to the closing of the case on compliance on October 11, 1960.

This case seems to be very similar to those board cases which did not result in a contract. Here there was widespread violation of the act, and apparently a very weak union. It may be surmised that the abandonment of the situation by the unions has some relationship to the prior unfair labor practices.

MERITORIOUS REFUSAL-TO-BARGAIN CHARGES WHICH DID NOT PROCEED TO A FORMAL HEARING

These cases fall into two groups: those in which there was a settlement or adjustment of the meritorious refusal-to-bargain allegation before a hearing but after the issuance of a complaint, and those which were adjusted before the issuance of a complaint and, of course, before a formal hearing.

The major distinction between settlements before and after the issuance of a complaint is one of time. Of course, all the informally adjusted cases require far less time than those cases which go to formal hearing, and it is these informal cases which are summarized in Table 2.

In order to examine the forces at work in resolving these cases, let us break down the meritorious charges by major issue involved and then examine the case histories.[45]

INFORMALLY ADJUSTED MERITORIOUS CASES, INVOLVING RECOGNITION AS A MAJOR ISSUE, IN WHICH CONTRACTS WERE EXECUTED

Case I:

The charge was filed on January 22, 1960, by the Retail, Wholesale and Department Store Union, alleging a violation of 8(a)(2), (3), and (5) of the act. The employer is a distributor of beverages with sixteen employees located in Massachusetts.

The union was certified in 1952 and has enjoyed contracts with the company since then. On December 1, 1959, a new owner took over the plant and did not assume or accept the old contract. However, he never questioned the majority status of the union until January 20, 1960, when he set up a shop committee, negotiated with it and the men individually, and unilaterally put into effect wage increases. All this occurred subsequent to a discussion of wage increases with the union on January 15, 1960.

A complaint was issued on March 25 and a settlement agreement was entered into on April 20, 1960, providing for the reinstatement of an 8(a)(3), disestablishment of the shop committee, and recognition of the union. A new contract was eventually signed and the case was closed on June 20, 1960.

Case II:

The charge was filed by the UE on November 7, 1960, alleging a violation of 8(a)(5) of the act. The employer is a manufacturer of phonograph records, is located in California, and has seventy-five employees. On October 24, 1960, the charging union was certified after the region issued a report overruling the employer's objections to the election. The employer then filed exceptions to the board and refused to recognize the union. On November 20, 1960, the board informed the employer that the regional director's decision was final since it was a consent election. On December 8, 1960, the employer told the union that it would recognize and bargain with it, and the first bargaining meeting was held on December 12. A withdrawal was solicited and approved on December 16, 1960. A contract was later executed.

Case III:

The charge was filed by the Building Service Employees Union on March 30, 1960, alleging a violation of 8(a)(5) of the act. The employer has an office building located in a California city, with thirty employees in the appropriate unit. The day after the union requested recognition, the employer gave raises to all employees and refused to meet or recognize the union. A strike took place on March 30, 1960, with twenty-five employees on a picket line. Subsequently, the employer hired fifteen replacements. On April 11, before completion of the investigation, the union submitted a withdrawal request since the employer recognized it and was currently bargaining. A contract was later executed.

Case IV:

The charge was filed by the UE on November 7, 1960, alleging a violation of 8(a)(5) of the act. The employer is a manufacturer of phonograph records who is located in southern California, and has thirty-two employees. The union won an election on September 8, 1960, by a vote of 18 to 11. Although the election was conducted under a consent agreement, the employer, after its objections to the election had been overruled by the regional director, filed exceptions to the board. The employer also refused to meet with the union unless the union agreed to another election. The union threatened to strike on December 9, and on December 8, the employer informed the union that it would recognize it and bargain. First bargaining session was held on December 12, 1960, and a withdrawal request was submitted to the region on December 16, 1960. A contract was subsequently executed.

Case V:

The charge was filed by the Operating Engineers on

February 9, 1960, alleging a violation of 8(a)(2), (3), and (5) of the act. The employer operates dairies in California.

The charges alleged that the employer had required its boiler room and maintenance employees to join the Teamsters Union and refused to bargain with the charging union. For many years, prior to December, 1959, the company was represented by an association which had contracts with various locals of the Teamsters and the charging union on a multi-employer basis. Having received notice that the employer had left the association on January 11, the union on that date and on February 8 requested bargaining on an individual unit basis. The company replied on February 10, 1960, stating that due to changes in boiler equipment, there was no need to bargain with the union.

Investigation revealed that in both locals, the company's general manager had called in all employees and told them that there was no longer a unit to be represented by the Engineers, and, thereafter, all employees had to join the Teamsters. He also at this time introduced a business agent of the Teamsters who immediately signed up all employees. Dues and initiation fees were paid to the Teamsters Union.

After the filing of the charge, the employer agreed to bargain and signed a contract with the charging union on March 25, 1960. The employer also agreed to refund the initiation fees and dues paid to the Teamsters if they were not refunded by the union. A withdrawal was approved on March 25, 1960.

Case VI:

The charge was filed by the Amalgamated Butchers Union on April 11, 1961, alleging a violation of 8(a)(5) of the act. The employer maintains a retail grocery store in eastern Kansas, and has three employees in the unit in question. The union has represented the meat department employees for a number of years and the last contract expired on January 2, 1960. On December 14, 1959, the employer replied to the union's reopening letter by stating that the business was going to be closed on January 1, and that therefore there was no necessity for negotiating a new contract. However, the store was merely being moved to a new location and the company admitted that the reason for the letter was that its competition was not organized and that union wages were too high.

After the company had moved to its new location, it threatened its employees that it would close the store if the union remained as the collective bargaining agent, gave wage increases in an effort to eliminate the union, and filed an RM (election) petition on April 7, 1960. On April 12, the union picketed the store and by May 12, a contract was signed and the withdrawal requests in both the 8(a)(5) charge and the RM petition were approved.

All these cases are characterized by a pure and simple failure of the employer to recognize the union representing a majority of its employees. Some of them concern unions with no prior collective bargaining relationships with the employer, while others involve unions with long-established relationships which were broken off by the employer. Noteworthy in each case is the simplicity of the issues, the very quick change in employer behavior as a result of the filing of the charge, and the execution of a contract. It is difficult not to be impressed with the efficacy of the act in these cases.

INFORMALLY ADJUSTED MERITORIOUS REFUSAL-TO-BARGAIN CHARGES INVOLVING RECOGNITION WHICH DID NOT RESULT IN A CONTRACT

While the majority of informally adjusted cases resulted

in the execution of a contract, attention must also be paid to those cases which did not. The following two case histories are in point.

Case VII:

The charge was filed by a local of the Teamsters Union on June 20, 1960, alleging a violation of 8(a)(3) and 8(a)(5) of the act. The employer is a trucking concern in Georgia. There were six drivers in the unit involved. During an organizational campaign, the employer fired employees and changed its method of operation to that of independent cartage. The issues in the case involved the 8(a)(3)'s and refusal to recognize the union. A complaint was issued on July 18, 1960. However, a settlement agreement was executed on August 8, 1960, which provided for reinstatement with back pay of the 8(a)(3)'s and recognition of the union. The case was closed on compliance on November 8, 1960. While the union did not object to the closing of the case, it brought to the region's attention the fact that the employer was not bargaining. However, the facts indicated that the employees, including the discriminatees, had quit the charging union and joined an independent union. There was no indication of employer sponsorship of the independent union and no 8(a)(1) conduct.

Case VIII:

The charge was filed by the Office Employees Union on October 14, 1960, alleging a violation of 8(a)(5) of the act. The company operates a wholesale laundry located in California, and has 100 employees. On September 26, 1960, the employer recognized the union on the basis of a card check, signed a recognition agreement giving the union a union shop for the office clerical unit, and also agreed to start contract negotiations not later than October 3, 1960. Meetings were held on October 3 and 12, and proposals were exchanged. On October 13, there was near-agreement on a new contract but the employer insisted that two employees be outside the unit. The employees refused to work that day but went back to work on October 14, when informed that they would be permanently replaced. The union received on October 14 a company letter dated October 13 which stated that the employer no longer recognized the union. On October 17, subsequent to the filing of the charge, a newly retained company counsel got in touch with the union and requested a meeting. The withdrawal was submitted on October 20, and was approved October 24, 1960. No contract was ever executed.

We must note once again the almost identical reaction of employers in meritorious cases involving refusal to bargain which do not result in a contract. There is always a change in behavior, resulting in meetings and conferences and a cessation of unfair labor practices. The employer is always careful to remedy its prior offenses, but, as the transport company case indicates, if the employer does not wish to establish a continuing relationship with the union, it may very easily take advantage of its past practices.

The case involving the office employees is an interesting one. While we do not have information other than that given in the case history, it seems that the union may have been unaware of its legal advantages. Moreover, the quick change in company attitude in this case, as shown by the employer's meeting with the union and recognizing it, may have sufficiently corrected its past refusal to bargain to permit it at this stage to bargain the union to defeat.

INFORMALLY ADJUSTED MERITORIOUS REFUSAL-TO-
BARGAIN CASES, INVOLVING UNILATERAL ACTION,
WHICH RESULTED IN A CONTRACT

The following three case histories describe a typical sequence of events and change in employer behavior after the adjustment of a meritorious charge involving unilateral action.

Case IX:

The charge was filed by the ILGWU on March 2, 1960, alleging a violation of 8(a)(3) and 8(a)(5) of the act. The company is an apparel manufacturer with thirty employees and is now located in Georgia. After twenty-five years of collective-bargaining relationship between the charging union and the employer, the company moved from its plant without notice. A complaint issued on April 4, 1960, but a withdrawal request followed on April 5, on the basis that a contract had been executed "settling all issues." The case was closed April 21, 1960.

Case X:

The charge was filed by the IAM on May 17, 1960, alleging a violation of 8(a)(5) of the act. The employer is a factory with 246 employees and is located in Tennessee. The union was certified in 1957. Contract negotiations bogged down and a strike ensued which resulted in a contract's being signed for a four-year term in 1958. The basis of this charge was the denial to the union of the right to participate in a conference on a grievance of an employee whose wages were involved. Although a complaint would have issued, a withdrawal request was submitted by the charging union on May 27, 1960, on the basis that the employer had changed its plant manager and adopted a new co-operative attitude.

Case XI:

The charge was filed by the United Packinghouse Workers of America on March 8, 1960, alleging a violation of 8(a)(3) and (5) of the act. The employer is a beef packing plant located in Kansas and has eighteen employees. The union was certified on November 13, 1959, and the first meeting to negotiate a new contract was held in early December. At this meeting, the union submitted a proposed contract to the employer. A second meeting was held on January 9, 1960, at which time the employer gave its counterproposals to the union. The next meeting was held on January 16 but for the following five weeks the company failed to keep the scheduled meeting dates. Finally, a meeting was held on March 12 after much urging by the union. However, at this meeting there was again disagreement on nearly everything. The basis for the charge was that three days after the election, the employer issued a set of safety instructions and plant rules and regulations unilaterally. There was no 8(a)(1) conduct. The alleged 8(a)(3), who was discharged on February 29, 1960, because of a garnishment levied against him, was also the union's observer at the election. Investigation disclosed that the company had a policy of discharge for repeated garnishments. This portion of the charge was dismissed. A settlement agreement was approved on April 6, 1960, containing standard 8(a)(5) language. The case was closed on June 27; by then the union had a two-year contract.

It seems unnecessary to make any further comment on the manner in which employer behavior is shaped by the filing of a meritorious charge.

Again, additional insight into the influence of the law

on employer conduct can be gained by examining a case in which no contract was ever signed. The case history follows:

Case XII:

A charge was filed by the UE on March 2, 1960, alleging a violation of Section 8(a)(5) of the act. The employer is a manufacturer of aircraft engines with about 100 employees and is located in eastern Connecticut. The union had been certified after winning an election on August 31, 1959. On September 11, 1959, a union member was discharged and thirty employees went out on strike to protest the discharge. The strike lasted until October 9, 1959, but during this period the plant operated with a reduced force. At the end of the strike, very few of the strikers came back to work. At the time of the discharges, a charge was filed by the union and since the employer had refused to reinstate the strikers upon request, an eventual board order resulted at the end of November, 1961, in which the employer agreed to pay $15,000 in back pay. The basis of the 8(a)(5) charge was unilateral wage increases given by the employer shortly after the end of the strike. During negotiations themselves, the employer had supplied wage data and job classification information, and had met other requests of the union. However, since the union had very few if any members left in the plant, it made no effort to bargain with the company even after the settlement of the 8(a)(5) charge. The employer, mindful of its obligations under the act, notified the union that it intended to put into effect certain wage increases and requested a meeting. Negotiations then were resumed, but an individual had filed a request for an election apparently motivated by hostility toward the union. When a direction of election was issued, the union filed a disclaimer of interest in the plant, and there have been no subsequent relations between the union and the employer.

I believe that this case, like those already cited, illustrates the choice available to the employer if it does not desire to have permanent collective bargaining. An employer can be required to end specific unfair labor practices such as discrimination, but, if it so chooses and if it is willing to pay the price, it can resist to the end the signing of a contract.

INFORMALLY ADJUSTED MERITORIOUS REFUSAL-TO-BARGAIN CHARGES ON THE MAJOR ISSUE OF BAD-FAITH BARGAINING

The following histories describe informally adjusted cases in which the issue was bad faith during negotiations, and in which contracts were eventually executed.

Case XIII:

The charge was filed by the ILGWU on January 15, 1960, alleging a violation of 8(a)(5) of the act. The employer manufactures apparel, has 300 employees, and is located in Georgia. An initial contract, valid for a three-year term, was signed in 1956. During negotiations for a new contract, the employer constantly shifted position, used different negotiators, thus impeding the progress of the negotiations, and made many independent 8(a)(1) statements which included threats to employees and promises of benefits in the event that the union was no longer in. Also, the company supervisors sponsored a decertification petition. A strike started on February 3, 1960, but immediately thereafter a contract was executed, and the strike was settled with a withdrawal request submitted to the region on February 26.

Case XIV:

The charge was filed by the IAM on May 16, 1960, alleging a violation of 8(a)(5) of the act. The company is a machine shop with eleven employees and is located in an Alabama town. The union was certified on November 6, 1959. The issue in this case was that the president of the company refused to meet with the union. Prior to issuance of the complaint, a withdrawal request was submitted by the charging union on June 8, since the president was by then meeting with them. The withdrawal request was approved on June 9, 1960. A contract was entered into after the case was closed.

Case XV:

An 8(a)(3) and 8(a)(5) charge was filed on January 6, 1960, by District 50, United Mine Workers of America. The employer is engaged in a lumber and construction business located in western Pennsylvania.

The employer recognized the union some time in January, 1957, and contracts were executed with the last contract expiring on January 6, 1960. Preliminary negotiations began in December, 1959. On December 24, 1959, the employer posted the names of three employees as being laid off. A few days later, the laid-off employees were called into the office individually, interrogated on their union sympathies, and ordered to sign a petition for decertification of the union. Later that same day, all the employees were called in and told to sign a decertification petition in order to retain their jobs. Most men signed.

Negotiation meetings took place on January 4 and 6, 1960, during which time the union was told that the company refused to negotiate for a new contract since it could not meet competition under the terms of the present contract. At the close of the last meeting, the company refused to meet any further. Before investigation was completed, a withdrawal was submitted on the basis that the company had signed a contract and reinstated all alleged 8(a)(3)'s. The case was closed on January 25, 1960.

Case XVI:

The charge was filed by the IAM on February 9, 1960, alleging a violation of 8(a)(5) of the act. The employer is engaged in the business of auto sales and services, is located in California, and has twenty-six employees. The union was certified on February 19, 1959, having won an election by a vote of 16 to 8.

The first bargaining meeting was held on March 13, 1959, and was spent in discussing the union's contract proposals. On March 24, the employer submitted its counterproposals, which would have given the employer the unlimited right to discharge employees for any one of thirty-seven enumerated reasons in addition to "any other act of dishonesty, gross misconduct or neglect." The proposed management prerogative clause also gave the employer absolute control over virtually every aspect of working conditions, including the setting of piece rates, the provision that the grievance procedure could only be invoked by the employee and not by the union, and an insistence that arbitration was not applicable to matters which the company considered to be covered by the management prerogative clause. Furthermore, either party could request the other to submit to a lie detector test in the proposed grievance procedure, and a refusal by a grievant to submit to this test would result in an automatic adverse disposition of the case.

The employer's counterproposals were submitted to the union membership, which authorized a strike. Before calling the strike, the union contacted the Federal Mediation and Conciliation Service, which arranged three meetings. The first meeting was held on March 27, but the employer refused to offer any more counterproposals. On May 5, the federal mediator told the union that the employer would not agree to any further meetings.

In July, when the mediator again told the union that the employer refused to meet, a strike took place. Twenty out of the twenty-six employees participated in the strike. On August 14, the employer wrote the union stating that it was willing to recognize the union until May 1, 1960, and offered to reinstate strikers without reducing their seniority but mentioned no other working conditions. The union rejected this and on September 30, the employer wrote another letter in which he offered to sign a contract establishing the same working conditions that existed prior to certification, and containing provision for what was described only as "usual discharge for just cause," grievance and arbitration clauses, and a maintenance-of-membership clause.

The federal mediators arranged a meeting on October 23, 1959, in which the employer stated that the above letter would constitute the complete agreement and refused to clarify the meaning of any of the terms in the letter. Negotiations were broken off by the union and no other meeting took place thereafter. An RM petition was filed four days after the end of the certification year with the employer's claim that the union no longer represented a majority. During the strike, the strikers were told by management that the employer would never sign a union contract and were threatened with discharge for striking or picketing.

A complaint was issued and a hearing was scheduled for August 9, 1960, but on August 8, the union requested a withdrawal of the charge on the basis of a signed contract and a strike settlement which provided for the return of all strikers to their jobs. A withdrawal was approved and the complaint withdrawn on August 10, 1960.

Case XVII:

The charge was filed on October 3, 1960, by the Laborers Union, alleging violation of 8(a)(3) and 8(a)(5). The employer is a manufacturer of charcoal briquets with 129 employees, and the plant is located in West Virginia.

The employer began operation in the spring of 1959 and enjoyed a promise by the local community that it could expect to have a two-year period free from unions. After several months, District 50 made an unsuccessful attempt to organize. In April, 1960, the Laborers began an organizational campaign; an election was set for July 12, 1960, pursuant to a stipulation for certification.

On June 27, the employer promulgated a new vacation plan for its employees replacing the previous plan of no vacations. On July 9, 10, and 11, the vice president of the company made speeches recounting the employer's experience with unions at other locations of the company. He stated that in its Missouri plant, the employees had voted for a union but had gained absolutely nothing, and had had to pay $9 dues; the company had given no raises until after the union was decertified. Following the decertification, all employees had received higher wages and improved working conditions. He further stated that the company expected a strike if the union won but that the plant would continue to operate and anyone who went on strike would be immediately and permanently replaced.

The election was held as scheduled and the union won

by a vote of 74 to 39. The day after the election, the employer posted twenty-one new rules for disciplinary action which included "No union activities of any description on Company time or property." Also, immediately after the election, there was a great increase in discipline, production was speeded up, permission to smoke was revoked, and foremen were instructed to bear down on employees because "the company was expecting union trouble." Numerous changes were made in working conditions and in the method of compensation of some employees, all resulting in a reduction of benefits for employees.

On August 3, an employee was appointed by the union business agent as a committeeman to request the company to reduce its pressure until negotiations between the company and the union took place. The foreman refused to talk with the employee, citing the rule of no discussion of union activities on company time and property, and fired the committeeman. Other employees were fired on the same day and a strike developed with picketing of about thirty-five to forty employees at the plant gate. That evening, violence occurred when a truck attempted to enter the plant. During the strike that followed, there were threats to strike replacements, car windows were broken, rocks and marbles were thrown by strikers, and caravans of strikers visited company kilns located at some distance from the main plant and made threats against replacements.

Between August 3 and 18, the union representatives experienced great difficulty in locating the company's labor relations consultant, who had, on August 3, set up August 19 as the very earliest date he would be available for a meeting. On August 18, the company's consultant cancelled the August 19 meeting and on the same day wrote the union that the company would not bargain while acts of violence were taking place. However, on August 23 the company wrote the union supplying certain wage information previously requested. Correspondence on contract proposals took place during the last week of August. On September 10, the union made an unconditional offer to return all employees to work and on September 13 the company's consultant replied that he did not think that this was an unconditional offer. On August 10, an injunction was received by the company against violence.

The region concluded that there was an 8(b)(1)(A) violation on the basis of the picket line violence, that an 8(a)(5) violation also existed, and that the strike from its inception was an unfair labor practice strike; also that it was a violation of 8(a)(3) for the employer to discharge its employees for engaging in the strike. The region also found many violations of 8(a)(1), including surveillance of union meetings, interrogation, speedup, and stricter enforcement of rules and disciplining of employees.

On October 27, a settlement agreement was entered into providing for 75 per cent of back pay for all strikers and reinstatement of all strikers except for one individual involved in picket line violence. There was also an informal settlement agreement of the 8(b)(1)(A) charge against the union. The settlement agreement provided that the reinstatements would be immediate for all workers when work was available, and that there would be preferential hiring for all strikers for whom no work was available.

The order was a standard bargaining order providing that the company would not make unilateral changes and giving a standard 8(a)(1) notice. The notice was posted in November, 1960, and after one week of posting, the plant shut down in conformance to its seasonal pattern. Hence the notice was posted until April 3. Back pay of $5,800 was paid and parties were meeting but no contract had resulted as of April 3 when the case was closed. However, a contract was later executed.

The preceding cases show that bad-faith bargaining is ordinarily not a difficult matter to prove, especially in the two cases involving unions which had just been certified. In both cases the employers showed marked hostility, and both companies operated during the strike. Attention should also be paid to the sequence of events in the auto sales case, where a strike of long duration was settled and a contract was executed just before the beginning of a hearing on the refusal-to-bargain charges.

MERITORIOUS CASES IN WHICH NO CONTRACT WAS SIGNED

Again, it may be useful to examine a meritorious case in this area in which no contract was signed. The following case history is in point:

The charge was filed by the Retail, Wholesale and Department Store Union on December 21, 1960, alleging a violation of 8(a)(5). The employer is a plastic factory with six employees, located in western Pennsylvania.

The union was certified in April, 1960, for all production and maintenance employees and meetings took place on June 30, July 7 and 21, August 2 and 11, September 1, 21 and 29, and December 7. The company referred to adverse financial conditions at the July 7 meeting and offered to show its books to substantiate its position, but the union declined to inspect. On July 21, the employer submitted its counterproposals and at this meeting agreement was reached on the work day, overtime, and a seniority clause. At the August meetings, the union protested the lowering of wage rates for two employees in May and in early August from $2.10 to $1.80 an hour. On August 16, the company restored the wages to $1.90 per hour and the union dropped the issue in the hope of getting a better contract.

At the September 1 meeting, there was agreement on the maintenance of the current wage scale, on a two-month probationary period, and on a two-year contract with 3 per cent automatic wage increase. However, at the September 9 meeting, the company asked for a five-year contract with a 3 per cent annual increase in wages. On September 21, the major issue was arbitration, with the union wanting the cost to be shared while the company insisted that the party requesting arbitration bear the entire cost. On September 29, there was disagreement on starting wage rates for new employees, with the union asking for a starting rate of $1.40 which had been the company's past practice, and the company insisting upon $1.00 an hour. The employer also insisted upon the right of decreasing any individual's wages when his production and efficiency fell off, despite the contract. A strike vote was taken on October 5 and the strike took place on October 10.

On November 14, the parties exchanged proposals by mail, with the union requesting a union shop, arbitration for grievances with the sharing of cost, two weeks' vacation after five years' employment, a ten-cent an hour increase, a minimum starting rate and minimum wage rates, and a one-year contract term. The company proposed no union shop, no employee eligible for union membership until six months after hiring, arbitration cost borne by requesting party, a 15 per cent per hour reduction of wages for all employees, and a ten-year contract with a 2 per cent annual minimum automatic wage increase plus merit increases at the discretion of the employer.

On December 1, the company sent letters to all strikers notifying them that their jobs would be open until December 7 under the same conditions that prevailed before the strike, but that after December 7 the employees would be subject to replacement. At the December 7 meeting the union representatives walked out, saying that the company's proposals were completely unacceptable.

The region found 8(a)(1) and 8(a)(5) in the unilateral wage changes of eight employees after certification and in the December 1 letter which offered higher wages than those offered to the union. Picketing ceased some time in January, 1961, and the employer signed an informal settlement agreement of the 8(a)(5) charge on January 31 which was approved on February 14.

At the meeting of February 7, 1961, the employer offered wage increases ranging from ten to thirty cents an hour. However, three of the four strikers refused to go back to work. The employer complied with the terms of the settlement agreement; all changes of working conditions have been referred to the union for consultation, and the employer on a number of occasions has requested negotiations. No contract, however, was negotiated, and on October 26, 1961, the employer filed an RM petition. On November 26, the union filed a disclaimer of interest with the result that the RM petition was withdrawn on November 7, 1961.

The last case demonstrates that employer persistence may, on occasion, pay off in ending the union. The employer's bad faith during negotiation does not need much comment. It is clear under existing law that the employer's proposal of a ten-year contract with a 15 per cent per hour reduction of wages for all employees and the unilateral right to decrease any employee's wages is difficult to reconcile with good-faith bargaining. But the effect of the past unfair labor practice survived the employer's compliance with the terms of the settlement agreement in that most of the strikers refused to go back to work. In such conditions, where the union no longer has a majority and where the employer's subsequent conduct is in conformity with the law, the union's abandonment of the situation is not surprising. It need hardly be added that the similarity of this case to other cases where no contract was ever executed is most apparent.

CHAPTER 8 · AN EVALUATION
OF THE DUTY TO BARGAIN

As we have already seen, there exists an almost unanimous consensus of opinion that the duty to bargain as currently interpreted should either be done away with as constituting government interference with free collective bargaining, or drastically amended to make it effective. Although there is some disagreement between those who would abolish and those who would amend, it seems clear that the low esteem of the statute's mandate to bargain is derived from a conclusion about its effectiveness. Now that we have, for the first time, empirical evidence of the operational significance of the duty to bargain, we are in a better position to evaluate it.

The empirical evidence disposes of the view that Section 8(a)(5) is meaningless and ineffective. It is now appropriate to analyze and evaluate the other objections to this section of the act.

We have already seen how the arguments against the board doctrines of good-faith bargaining have arisen directly from a conception of the original congressional intent. Although we have demonstrated the errors in the common view of the legislative purpose, it is most certainly arguable that regardless of what Congress intended, the consequences of the duty to bargain are unwise, undesirable, and pernicious. Perhaps it is appropriate to term this approach "ideological," because it appears to be based upon a value judgment about the role of government in collective bargaining. The genealogy of this line of argument can be traced back to 1916, when the first recommendation was made that the government require employers to bargain with unions. The opposition to this government intervention had a distinctly modern tone. It was primarily based upon the logical ground that in order to be effective, the government would have to go all the way to compulsory arbitration. This view was taken up by employer representatives and academicians during the legislative discussion of the duty to bargain in 1934 and 1935 and is, in my judgment, the heart of the argument against the duty to bargain.

The development of this line of criticism can be traced through the years. At the time of the passage of the Wagner Act, Dean Spencer stated that if the NLRB broke down in administration, it would do so on the question of the enforceability of the duty to bargain. Spencer stated:

It is not thinkable that the government can force employers under threat of penalty to make voluntary, collective agreements with their employees. . . . it may safely be predicted that employers generally, particularly the larger ones, will attempt to defeat collective bargaining by temporizing with the representatives of their employees. They will receive the representatives of their employees and courteously discuss their demands. They will meet the demands by proposing, as the basis of an agreement, "existing rates of pay, wages and hours of employment," or will propose an actual reduction in wages. If the employer stands on such a proposal, insisting that collective bargaining requires no more than this, what can the Board do? The Board can, as it undoubtedly will, rule that the employer must not only bargain, but that he must bargain in good faith. The Board will then in individual cases proceed to pass judgment upon the good faith of the employer. In so doing the Board will certainly and inevitably, directly or indirectly, indicate what it thinks the employer should offer by way of a counterproposal in order to escape its wrath. Undoubtedly in many such cases the employer will to some extent succumb to the pressure, not because he has been persuaded of the justness of the demands of his employees and not because of their collective strength, but because of the fear of incurring a penalty, or to avoid wear and tear of endless wrangling and the losses incident to litigation and bad morale. If the Act has this practical operation, it not only means compulsory arbitration, but it means compulsory arbitration of a unilateral character.[1]

Dean Spencer then took up the hypothetical case of an employer which refuses to comply with a board order directing it to bargain. Because "true bargaining is essentially a matter of exercising discretion and judgment," courts will be disinclined for traditional reasons to interfere with any exercise of discretion. Dean Spencer predicted that a majority of employers would take this position, which "will mean that the National Labor Relations Act, insofar as the Board attempts to induce or force employers into collective agreements with their employees, has broken down in administration."[2]

Opponents of the Wagner Act immediately seized upon this objection. On the day that President Roosevelt signed the bill into law, the National Association of Manufacturers issued a bulletin which termed the duty to bargain "an obvious trouble breeder" and said that if the line of thinking of the NRA labor boards was continued, Section 8(5) would mean

in the last analysis, that the Board is to be the final arbiter as to whether a proposal made by the employees is reasonable; and whether a counterproposal made by the employer is reasonable, and made in good faith. If, therefore, the employees' representatives submit a proposal asking for a substantial wage increase, and the employer submits a counterproposal offering a very small increase, the Board must determine *what, under the circumstances, would be a fair wage. Thus the trend is directly towards wage-fixing by federal boards,* and such a result is inescapable if the principles laid down by the old boards are followed.[3] [Emphasis supplied.]

Within two months, the National Lawyers Committee of the American Liberty League issued a 132-page brief on the Wagner Act in which it stated that "we have no hesitancy in concluding that it is unconstitutional and that it constitutes a complete departure from our constitutional and traditional theories of government."[4] The duty to bargain was described as

almost staggering in its novelty. . . . Illustrations of the length to which this provision may be pressed are sufficient to reveal its hazardous character. Suppose that a group of employees demands a 50% increase in wages, in response to which the employer, at the outset of negotiations, announces that under existing conditions, any increase is impossible. If he continues to adhere to this position and refuses to make any concessions, then it might be justly argued that he had refused to bargain, for the idea of bargaining generally involves a certain amount of yielding on both sides.[5]

The opposition to the duty to bargain has continued until the present to develop and elaborate this line of thought. The animus is centered on the fear of government regulation. For example, Professor Taylor insists not only that the purpose of the Wagner Act "was focused upon organizing for collective bargaining"[6] but that the codification of the Wagner Act's principles of good-faith bargaining in Section 8(d) of the Taft-Hartley Act was ill-advised and "constitutes a vast extension of government regulation."[7] He strongly feels that labor as well as management should have sought the deletion of the duty to bargain in order to guard against this extensive government regulation of collective bargaining.

Professor Cox's objections proceed along the same line. His concern about the consequences of board decisions involving the duty to bargain can be inferred from the questions he raises about the long-term applications of these doctrines. These questions are: (1) Are standards available by which to judge the fairness or unfairness of the course of conduct which a company or union follows in attempting to negotiate an agreement? (2) Can the NLRB effectively regulate the actual conduct of collective negotiations? (3) Would NLRB regulation of the conduct of collective bargaining negotiations affect the relative bargaining power of management and labor? (4) Would NLRB regulation of the conduct of negotiations be a step toward regulation of the substantive provisions of collective bargaining?[8]

Once again, we must note the inconsistency in the objections that the duty to bargain not only is ineffective but also constitutes an overly effective intervention in the collective bargaining process.[9] But, significantly, all major objections to the duty to bargain involve an assumption about its consequences. It is noteworthy that apart from the Textile Workers Union and other labor organizations which registered complaints about the ineffectiveness of the act in legislative hearings, none of the writers in this area have seen fit to produce evidence of any kind to support their assumptions.

Our first task is to evaluate the objections to the duty to bargain on the basis of the available evidence. As a first step, we can reconcile and consolidate the arguments by noting that it is logically possible to assert that the ineffectiveness of the duty to bargain can only be remedied by a process that would lead to greater and greater government regulation of the substantive terms of collective bargaining.

Clearly, the conclusion that the duty to bargain must be ineffective rests upon the assumption that employers will resist compliance with the law's mandate. Indeed, until the sustaining of the constitutionality of the Wagner Act in 1937, the principles of collective bargaining contained in the statute were furiously resisted. Moreover, the opposition to the act did not automatically disappear after *Jones and Laughlin*. One editorial writer issued the following appeal: "Employers ought to refuse to have anything to do with the National Labor Relations Board. They ought to fight it out, and fight it out even if they have to go to jail. Fight it out as one of the fundamental principles of American liberty." [10]

The tone of the attacks on the board even after 1937 is exemplified by one United States Senator's description of the board as a "kangaroo court," by a radio commentator's assertion that a board hearing is comparable to a "drumhead court martial," by the accusation of the former head of the NRA, General Hugh Johnson, that "an employer has as much chance before that Board as an aristocrat had before the French tribunes of the terror," and by the various pejorative names given to the Wagner Act, such as the "Strained-Relations Act" and "an act to increase troubles, to spread unemployment, and to disrupt industry." [11]

In appraising the reaction of employers to the public policy in favor of collective bargaining as expressed in the Wagner Act, due attention must be given to the attitude of most employers to organized labor at the time. The investigations of the La Follette subcommittee in 1937 and 1938 disclosed that the bulk of American employers fought unionism with every weapon at their disposal. An early expression of the position of the National Association of Manufacturers was cited in the committee's hearing. This statement read:

We are not opposed to good unionism, if such exists anywhere. The American Federation brand of unionism, however, is un-American, illegal and indecent because their constitution is simply based on the plan that "we will rule you or ruin you." The manufacturer, therefore, has a right to discriminate against an employee who is affiliated directly or indirectly with an organization that resorts to these methods.[12]

This opposition, in part, resulted in the organization of employer associations such as the National Metal Trades Association, whose membership included many nationally known corporations such as General Motors, Yale and Towne, Chrysler Corporation, Continental Can, and Allis Chalmers. The principal purpose of the National Metal Trades Association was to combat collective bargaining. Among its weapons were the maintenance of an extensive card catalogue and black list of union members, the use of labor espionage, strike guards, and strike-breaking services, and the utilization of economic pressure against businessmen who had expressed approval of collective bargaining.[13] Among the principles to which all members of the association bound themselves was not to deal with striking employees as a body.[14]

Other organizations of employers pursued a similar policy. For example, the Associated Industries of Cleveland not only offered its members espionage and strike-breaking services but set up a collective bargaining service which

was to prevent members of the association from entering into union contracts which would recognize the unions as exclusive bargaining agents. In pursuance of the objective, the association staff devised a form of contract which could be utilized by the company signing it to thwart and obstruct the collective bargaining process.[15]

The committee hearings are replete with evidence of employer hostility to unions. Example after example was given of employers who refused to bargain with the unions representing a majority of their employees, and of the techniques used to break the subsequent strikes.[16]

Given this employer hostility, how are we then to account for the rise in union membership? In 1936, membership in the United States was estimated at 4,164,000. This figure had jumped to 7,218,000 by 1937, and in 1938 membership grew to 8,265,000.[17]

Obviously a relationship exists between the NLRB and the change in labor union membership, and this relationship can be accurately dated from the sustaining of the constitutionality of the Wagner Act in April, 1937.[18] Granting that "since the spring of 1937 the National Labor Relations Act has had a phenomenal effect upon the labor movement," [19] we may ask precisely how the act operated.

It is true that the fact that the labor movement successfully organized millions of new members in 1937–1938 tells us something about the climate of opinion during this period. Success breeds success, and perhaps the growth can be largely explained by a singular combination of events unique to that particular time. These would include the relative prosperity of 1937, the tactics and leadership of the CIO, and the disarray and bewilderment of the business community under the twin blows of Roosevelt's landslide victory in 1936 and the unexpected Supreme Court decision in *Jones and Laughlin*.

But explanations of this kind arise after the event and are basically descriptive rather than analytic. All collective bargaining involves a particular employer operating under specific conditions and confronted with a particular labor organization. While there may be a relationship between broad historical forces and individual employer behavior, there is no reason to expect all employers to react identically. It would seem fruitless to list all the pressures and constraints which influence an employer's attitude to collective bargaining. These would certainly include the state

of the product and labor markets, the extent of unionization among its employees, the depth of their attachment
to the union, the kind of union leadership, etc.

Furthermore, not only are the forces that govern employer behavior specific in character, but they vary in
significance over time for particular employers and as
between employers. It seems difficult to imagine that a
firm would recognize and bargain with a union because
the labor movement had suddenly grown in importance
and strength. In other words, the concept of a climate of
opinion is a useful one which can summarize widely preva-
lent forces, but it cannot entirely explain why many individual employers reversed traditional attitudes towards
unionism.

Broadly speaking, the empirical analysis of refusal-to-
bargain charges in Chapter 7 leads to the conclusion that
the impact of the NLRB upon the individual firm induces
compliance with public policy in two ways: first, by the
imposition of sanctions, and second, by what has been
called "voluntary compliance." It is obvious that these two
categories are not mutually exclusive but intimately related.
However, for expository purposes it may be desirable to
analyze and evaluate them separately.

THE IMPACT OF THE BOARD UPON EMPLOYER BEHAVIOR
IN CASES BEFORE THE BOARD—THE LEGAL SANCTION

The system of legal sanctions, which can also be termed
"enforced compliance," comprises the legal and other consequences imposed upon an employer for violating the act.
As previously stated, the NLRB does not possess any punitive powers and no employer can be fined, imprisoned, or
black-listed from receiving government contracts for vio-

lating the law. An unfair labor practice is not a crime; although properly speaking it can only be regarded as *sui generis,* a useful analogy is that of a public tort.[20]

It is imperative for an understanding of the operations of the board to realize that its orders are not self-enforcing and that enforcement begins only with the issuance of a court decree enforcing a board order. The remedies of board orders for the four major types of employer unfair labor practices are standard and well-known. First, for all violations of the act and specifically for threats, intimidation, surveillance, and all activities which interfere with, restrain, and coerce employees—usually violation of Section 8(a)(1) or 8(a)(3)—the sole remedy is the posting of a notice by the employer. This notice, which is addressed to all employees and usually appears on a plant's bulletin board, is invariably a restatement of the law and an agreement by the employer that he will not engage in specific practices held to be unlawful. The posting of the notice for sixty days and the absence of new violations during this time ordinarily constitute full compliance with the provisions of the act. In the event that new violations take place subsequent to the ending of the sixty days' posting period, the practice of the board, except in unusual circumstances, is to accept and process new charges, even in those cases where a court has enforced a board order. If the employer commits unfair labor practices during the sixty-day period, the sole remedy normally would be an extension of the notice period.

If an employer unlawfully establishes, assists, or dominates a union (normally violations of Section 8(a)(2) of the act), the standard remedy is a withdrawal of such aid or assistance in addition to the posting of a notice. Furthermore, any contracts made with such a union could not lawfully be enforced and these contracts would have no standing in any board proceeding.

Where an employer has discriminatorily discharged or

disciplined employees in order to discourage union activity, in violation of Section 8(a)(3) and, very rarely, of Section 8(a)(4), the remedy is reinstatement with back pay. However, it must be understood that any earnings of a discriminatee in the interim between discharge and the offer of reinstatement are deducted from the back-pay liability.

We have already explained in detail the remedial power of the board for violations of Section 8(a)(5) of the act, which ordinarily consists of an order to bargain in good faith. It should be repeated that such a board order does not usually require an employer to do anything *specific* except in certain categories of cases. These include such conduct as refusal to recognize or meet, refusal to supply information upon request, refusal to sign a contract after an agreement has been reached, and the like. But the true force of a board order lies in the negative injunction of bad-faith bargaining; that is, an employer is ordered to bargain in good faith but the presence of good faith is ordinarily determined by the absence of bad-faith conduct. In other words, compliance with the requirement to furnish information is easily and objectively ascertainable. On the other hand, an employer's course of conduct which leads to an order to bargain in good faith need not ordinarily be corrected by specific acts such as the execution of an agreement. Most importantly, the board does not inquire into the substantive terms of an employer's contract proposal, except in the extreme case where the very terms of the offer are so outrageous as to raise again the inference of bad faith. In any case, our review of NLRB principles of good-faith bargaining and examination of those cases where collective bargaining did not follow a finding of a violation permits, if it does not prove, the conclusion that an employer has ample room to evade the establishment of collective bargaining even in the face of a board order to bargain.

The ultimate test of legal sanctions is what happens to an

employer if he defies the law. Our review of the board's remedial powers reveals that he must in time post notices, avoid supporting a satellite union, reinstate discharged employees with back pay, and avoid certain conduct which would be inconsistent with his legal obligation to bargain. Direct evidence of the efficacy of each of these remedies does not exist, except for that on the duty to bargain cited in Chapter 7. However, it does seem reasonable to hold that the prohibition of company-dominated unions as a method of combatting unionism was effective to the extent of changing the nature and overtness of company favoritism. Additional evidence of the relative effectiveness of the board in this area is the decline of the number of such cases over the years.[21]

It appears plausible to conclude that the basic reason for the effectiveness of the board lies in the nature of the remedy, that is, the requirement that the employer cease certain stipulated acts such as supplying financial assistance, recruiting members, etc.

As for the remedy of posting notices, the prevalence of recidivism and the nature of the remedy itself raise grave doubts of its effectiveness. The universal opinion of experienced NLRB personnel is that it is almost useless as a deterrent.[22]

The most dramatic of all board remedies is the requirement to reinstate discriminatees with back pay. There is widespread agreement that this power "was always the heart of the Act." [23] NLRB publications have always emphasized the number of employees reinstated and the amount of the back-pay awards.[24] However, as a chairman of the board has recently pointed out, the expense of back pay "is regarded in some quarters as not more than a fee for a union-busting license."

The examination of the empirical evidence in Chapter 7

shows how the sanctions of the law work in *compelling* compliance with the duty to bargain. An employer who resists to the end the mandates of the act may under certain circumstances find himself confronted with unfair labor practice strikers. As we have seen, the combination of a heavy back-pay settlement with the enforced reinstatement of strikers can overcome employer recalcitrance and make it very costly. Also, the time interval during which the case is processed serves to increase the back-pay liability and further weaken the employer's position.

But it is important to point out that this kind of compulsion upon an employer depends upon the existence of a certain amount of union strength. If the union lacks sufficient cohesiveness to go out on strike at the time of the refusal to bargain, this kind of sanction is inoperative. During the years required to exhaust the appellate resources of the employer, the unfair labor practices are unexpunged. Employees may become discouraged and disenchanted; the union itself may lose heart, for, after all, the legal outcome of any case is never wholly certain.

In short, an employer who persists in out-and-out opposition to collective bargaining in the form of violations of the law runs certain risks, but these risks are ordinarily known and measurable. Moreover, they may be reduced by a sophisticated accommodation to the well-known remedies of the board; especially, the employer may change the nature of its activities in the event that a prospect of back-pay liability develops. The game may very well be worth the candle, for the reward may be, and frequently is, the union's abandoning a plant despite a bargaining order because it no longer has any strength. An index of the advantages of litigation to the employer is the fact that barely half the discriminatees actually return to their jobs in formal cases, as compared to three-fourths for settled cases.[25]

To put it another way, employers confronted with unionization have a certain freedom of action to fight or not to fight unions, and this freedom includes recourse to methods which are unfair labor practices. The compulsion to cease these unfair labor practices can in practice be deferred for years if an employer elects to litigate the issues to the end. It would seem to follow that an understanding of the impact of the NLRB requires an evaluation of the fully litigated cases to show what happens when employers choose the avenue of complete resistance.

Turning to the Wagner Act experience, we find that for the period 1936–1947, a total of 43,556 unfair labor practice cases were closed, and 39,471 or 90.6 per cent were closed prior to formal action.[26] At least 16,323 of the informally adjusted cases were meritorious and were closed in compliance with the act. During the same period, formal action was taken in 4,085 cases, of which only 2,918 cases were closed after a board decision. Eliminating the number of cases dismissed as without merit by the board and a small number closed for other reasons, we find that for the entire life of the Wagner Act there were only 2,373 cases closed in compliance with formal board decisions and an unknown but probably appreciable number of these were not carried to the courts for enforcement. In other words, 5.4 per cent of all charges filed with the board required a formal order for enforcement.[27]

The Taft-Hartley experience has not substantially changed these figures. For fiscal year 1962, the percentage of unfair labor practice cases closed on compliance after board decision was 4.5 per cent, and the number of cases closed in compliance with court decrees was 1.5 per cent. In other words, 94 per cent of all unfair labor practice charges were closed prior to formal action.[28]

A breakdown of the early years is illuminating. In fiscal

1936 there were only 865 unfair labor practice charges filed, and during that year 636 cases were closed. Of this number only 56 were closed after formal board decision or court review. In fiscal 1937 the filing of unfair labor practices had increased to 2,895, of which only 3 were closed in compliance with board decision. In 1938 filing jumped to 6,807, and again there were only 29 cases closed in compliance with a formal order. The sharp rise in case load was reflected in the cases closed in fiscal 1939; although the filings had dropped to 6,984, the number of cases closed requiring compliance with a board decision had increased to 207. But in this year the total number of cases closed was 4,230, of which 3,833 were closed prior to formal action.[29]

It is obvious that if we define enforced compliance with the act as the invocation of the formal enforcement machinery of the NLRB in correcting employer unfair labor practices, we cannot explain the effect of the act in increasing union membership on the basis of formal case handling alone. Any explanation of board influence must also take into account the fact that most employers did not elect to litigate fully the charges made against them and to make use of their traditional and time-tested weapons for combatting unions.

Moreover, attention must be paid to the slowness with which the board disposed of charges in the early years, due to inadequate appropriations.[30] This was reflected in the extremely high backlog of cases, which was especially marked during the period after 1937. For example, unfair labor practice cases pending at the end of fiscal 1937 totaled 1,373; by the end of fiscal 1938 the figure had risen to 2,486, and it reached 2,874 by the close of fiscal 1939.[31]

The difficulty of imputing the impact of the board to its direct effect upon the parties which are represented before it in cases filed can perhaps best be appreciated by comparing membership growth of unions with elections held. As we have seen, union membership doubled between 1936 and 1938, increasing by over four million. However, in fiscal 1936 there were only thirty-one representation proceedings in which some 7,572 votes were cast, and unions succeeded in winning only twenty-two of these. In fiscal 1937, unions won 250 out of the 265 elections and cross card checks conducted in which 164,146 voters participated. In fiscal 1938, unions won 945 and lost 207 elections in which 343,587 votes were counted. And for fiscal 1939 unions won 574 elections and lost 172; there were 177,215 valid votes cast.[32] The total number of new members so acquired could not have exceeded 500,000.

On the basis of the evidence, it seems difficult to ascribe the enormous increase in union membership to the *direct* consequences of formal board action, that is, the bargaining that followed the board certification of a majority union and the closing of unfair labor practice cases on compliance with the act.

But this statement is in no way intended as a denial of the significance of the act. On the contrary, *although the public policy was carried out through the instrumentality of the board, not all the consequences of the Wagner Act are to be found in the statistics of board activities.* On the basis of the historical and empirical evidence, the achievement of the board can be viewed as, first, the establishment of specific standards and rules of employer conduct in collective bargaining, and second, the implementation of these rules through settlement of cases which appear before the board for action and decision. Legal compulsion can be thought of in several ways. In its broadest sense, the term can be used to describe the appropriate behavioral changes which take place after a law is passed. These necessarily include the changes in conduct which have occurred without any recourse to the administrative and judicial machinery designed to enforce the law. But there is some usefulness in looking at the concept of legal compulsion in the narrower sense. The extent to which a law requires widespread formal enforcement tells us a great deal about the degree to which it is accepted. Accordingly, if we define legal compulsion as conduct specifically required by a direct court order, a violation of which sets in motion specified sanctions, we must conclude that the impact of the board in the promotion of collective bargaining was largely noncompulsive.

It is imperative to point out that the conclusion that the "voluntary" adherence of most employers to NLRB policy is not independent of the possibility of compulsion. For a law to be enforceable, particularly where deep-rooted patterns of behavior are to be changed, some element of coercion must exist. We have already seen that the moral exhortations of the Transportation Act of 1920 broke down under the pressure of employer self-interest, as did the influence of the toothless NRA Labor Boards.[33]

We can go one step further. The *ability* of the board to lay down enforceable rules of conduct depends in the last analysis upon the consequences visited upon respondents who flout the act. And our examination of these consequences in Chapter 7 has revealed that a majority union receives formidable legal support under certain circumstances.

But in noting that board law is enforceable, we have by no means disposed of the question of the past and present meaning of the board. In particular, it is necessary to understand why the vast majority of employers were not required by legal process in the form of a court order to adhere to the national policy. In answering this question, we may also help to show why the prophecies of the 1916 Commission on Industrial Relations and Dean Spencer on the meaning of the duty to bargain were so far off the mark.

THE IMPACT OF THE BOARD UPON EMPLOYER BEHAVIOR IN SITUATIONS WHERE COURT ENFORCEMENT WAS NOT INVOKED

We have been developing a method of looking at the influence of the board in which its operations are regarded as a continuum with one end consisting of board orders enforced by court decrees. It has also been noted that such cases constitute a tiny fraction of all charges filed against employers. In our account of what happens after the filing of a meritorious refusal-to-bargain charge, it has been observed that the overwhelming majority of employees quickly took action to remedy unfair labor practices which usually resulted in the establishment or the continuation of collective bargaining.

Of course, in some cases this change in employer behavior took place under the pressure of an unfair labor practice strike with all its practical and legal implications. However, in most instances compliance with the statute was achieved in the absence of a strike and prior to a formal hearing. In a very important respect, it does not appear inappropriate to term this kind of compliance "voluntary." As a matter of fact, the NLRB has described this area of cases in the following way: "The most important feature of the NLRA is not the grist that gets into the Agency's mill and ultimately is enforced by legal action, but the action which the statute causes to be done voluntarily by the parties." [34]

Judging by numbers alone, most violations of the act are clearly remedied by voluntary settlements. It is also evident that the effective remedy of a refusal-to-bargain violation is set in motion by the filing and preliminary investigation of a charge and the election by most employer respondents not to exercise their legal rights in protracted litigation. In terms of case load and the effect of the board upon the parties represented in cases before it, we have strong evidence in the area of good-faith bargaining of employer acquiescence to board doctrine.

The significance of voluntary settlements in the role of the board cannot be overemphasized. It should not be forgotten that the act of filing a charge tells us something about the parties. The alternatives to filing a refusal-to-bargain charge include the exercise of economic pressures such as strikes, the creation of sources of present and future dissension, and/or the yielding of rights guaranteed by law. In the absence of a speedy disposition of merit charges by voluntary agreement, the alternatives would of necessity come into play. It does seem to a large extent that the major purpose of the act—to minimize strikes—has been carried out in practice, at least for strikes occasioned by violations of public policy.

In addition, informal case disposition plays a critical role in the administrative design of the NLRB. It seems clear that the whole machinery of the act would disintegrate if most employers defied the law and required court-enforced sanctions. After all, in the whole of the United States, there were only eighty-seven fully litigated meritorious cases involving the duty to bargain closed in fiscal 1961.[35] Widespread defiance of the law in the form of increased litigation would not only require an enormous increase in the board's manpower and resources, but would also result in congested court dockets and a heavy backlog of pending cases. The consequences of justice delayed would inevitably make a mockery of board operations and remedies.[36]

It would seem that voluntary compliance is essential to

the functioning of any law. With reference to the Taft-Hartley Act, a high NLRB official has commented:

The vast majority of matters coming before administrative agencies are disposed of informally with the acquiescence of the private interest affected and no formal trial proceedings and "this must be so or Government could not function." If this is true generally in Government, how much more germane is it to the field of labor-management relations. The voluntary adjustment of cases as a means of maintaining industrial peace is necessary to the continued well-being of our national economy.[37]

The prior discussion of the influence of the board has neglected, except inferentially, the impact upon cases which do not result in the filing of charges. Here, in the universe outside board operations, statistics in the normal sense are wanting. The number of unfair labor practices which are committed but for which no charges are filed is simply unknown and unquestionably unknowable.

But information is available which can be used to appraise the significance of the board in shaping employer conduct which does not result in case statistics. To begin with, we have the evidence of the non-meritorious charge. The agency is required to receive and docket any allegation of an unfair labor practice regardless of its apparent or intrinsic lack of merit; and the number of non-merit charges has always exceeded the merit charges. For the twelve-year period of the Wagner Act, the percentage of non-merit charges was 55.4.[38] For fiscal year 1962 the relevant percentage was about 69.[39]

The non-merit charge can best be understood as one made when the employer has not violated the law. In the area of the duty to bargain, for example, it concerns employer conduct which has been consistent with the manifold board requirements for collective bargaining. Looked at in this way, a non-merit refusal-to-bargain charge is evidence that an employer met with the majority representative of his employees, refrained from unilateral action, gave information and other data upon request, did not seek to bypass or undermine the union, and discussed in good faith the mandatory subjects of collective bargaining. The large number of non-merit charges is valid evidence of compliance with the statute and may very well serve as an index to employer conduct in those situations which never resulted in the filing of a charge.[40]

Furthermore, we have additional contemporary evidence at hand concerning potential refusal-to-bargain charges which never materialize. A recent inquiry was made on the number of contracts entered into after a union's certification following the winning of a board-conducted election held in 1960. The results indicated that for five regional offices involved—Atlanta, Pittsburgh, Kansas City, San Francisco, and Boston—unions succeeded in gaining contracts in the vast majority of cases, ranging from 84 per cent to 90 per cent.[41]

The value of this information in ascertaining employer behavior in collective bargaining which is not recorded in the filing of charges is inestimable. There is undoubtedly no greater source of possible refusal-to-bargain charges, at least for initial bargaining relationships, than those unions which have just received board certification. To begin with, we have the fact that a union found it necessary to invoke the board's representation procedure and undergo the trial of election, having been unable to persuade or compel the employer by other means to grant recognition. It must be stressed that certification is by no means required by law and for recognition purposes there are many alternatives which are just as valid and legitimate as the electoral process. The alternatives include a recognition strike, card checks, voluntary balloting including a show of hands, etc.

The advantages of board-conducted elections mainly accrue to the employer in certain statutory protection in the event that a union loses. This protection includes a ban on another election within a twelve-month period and a prohibition against recognition picketing by any union, and is considerably broader than in the absence of the election. As far as the union is concerned, the advantages of certification over recognition based upon other means are minimal, and basically consist of the application of the one-year period during which, absent exceptional circumstances, the employer may not in good faith challenge the union's majority status.

Thus it does not seem likely that a union would come to the board unless it had to. The more powerful a union is, the more reasonable it would seem to expect that it would attempt to acquire recognition outside the board processes in order to avoid the risks, time, and expenses involved. In any case, a strong union has little or no need of the security of the one-year rule.

The fact that the overwhelming majority of certified unions were successful in obtaining contracts tells us a great deal about employer conduct which does not show up in charges filed. It seems difficult to avoid the conclusion that if most unions armed with board certification encounter employers whose behavior leads to the execution of contracts, this fact gives us an insight into management attitudes and practices towards collective bargaining which complements and reinforces our interpretation of the non-merit cases.[42]

Looking at these data from a different angle, we should expect that certified unions would come to the board and file unfair bargaining charges if bargaining broke down, not only because of their limited economic strength but because of their familiarity with board processes which led them to file representation cases in the first place. The statistics of contracts signed are testimony, at least for 1960, of employer conduct which was consistent with the public policy as spelled out in board doctrine in the 8(a)(5) area.

Although comparable data are lacking for the Wagner Act period, we have certain information about employers which is relevant for our purposes. In the first place, we do know that the sustaining of the constitutionality of the Wagner Act resulted in a complete reversal of past policies and practices toward unions by employers' associations and many individual employers. For example, the NAM's industry platform for 1938 set forth an endorsement of "the rights of employees to bargain collectively, either directly or through voluntarily chosen representatives, and to determine the form of their own organization for collective bargaining." [43] The contrast with past pronouncements is not only remarkable but revolutionary.

Furthermore, the files of the NAM after 1937 contain many communications between members in which the principles established by the board are urged as standards of behavior for employers.[44] Of particular interest for our purposes is the analysis by the NAM's law department of board cases concerning the duty to bargain. The case analyses were accurate and were certainly not inconsistent with the new policy of the association.

Subsequent publications of the NAM followed the same approach. A 1943 pamphlet urged employers to conduct their bargaining in good faith and stated that

good faith or the lack thereof is determined after an appraisal of the Board of the entire facts and circumstances surrounding particular negotiating procedures. What the employer does, and what he fails to do, what he says, the manner in which statements are made, and other similar actions are weighed by the Board in determining whether or not the employer has in a very real sense undertaken to discover with the unions such common ground as may exist between the parties. It would seem that a record of previous peaceful relations between the parties would be strong evidence of good faith on the part of an employer. In other words, the fact that an employer had entered into previous contract with representatives of his employees should be a circumstance operating in his favor in the event his good faith is challenged. Good faith can best be described as the absence of conduct felt by the Board as indicative of bad faith.[45]

Other guides for management conduct toward unions issued after 1937 reveal a similar change in employer attitude. One management service stated that

with the passage of the Wagner Act, the simple procedure of management contracting with employees has become a complicated process. The process of collective bargaining is no longer a privilege. It is a right recognized by statute and supervised by administrative board charged with insuring that right against any encroachment whether by positive compulsion or a more subtle form of evasion.[46]

It would seem that *Jones and Laughlin* resulted in a fundamental change in the public position of most American employers with respect to collective bargaining. The behavior of employers in the cases that appeared before the board indicated a widespread willingness to comply with the requirements of the law before the institution of court-enforced orders. The fact that most unfair labor practice and representation cases were informally disposed of in 1937 and 1938 permits no other conclusion than that most employers chose to accept the principles of collective bargaining.

The significance of this voluntary choice is emphasized by the die-hards who held out to the last and exhausted every legal recourse prior to compliance. But it is also important to remember that many of these recalcitrants did in fact not only comply with the legal requirements but made an additional choice ultimately accepting collective bargaining by entering into contractual relations with a union.

In other words, the predictions of the 1916 Commission on Industrial Relations and of Dean Spencer about the response of management to a legal duty to bargain were erroneous. The historical facts indicate that the predicted massive defiance and universal evasion did not take place.

There is considerable historical evidence to support the conclusions based upon the empirical analysis in Chapter 7 that the forces at work can be classified into two categories: voluntary compliance and the imposition of sanctions, particularly by the implications of an unfair labor practice strike.

For example, an examination of the unionization of the steel industry discloses that both of these forces were at work. It is true that the recognition of the union by U. S. Steel occurred prior to *Jones and Laughlin* and was not directly related to any representational proceedings or to a refusal-to-bargain charge.[47] But it must not be forgotten that this recognition was for members only and the renewal of the original contract which was entered into as late as April 14, 1941, did not grant exclusive recognition.[48] It was only after an election conducted under NLRB auspices in which the union won 50 per cent of the votes that exclusive bargaining rights were conceded on September 5, 1942.[49]

Much more dramatic evidence of the effect of board standards in shaping employer conduct is to be found in the unionization of Little Steel. The strike called in May, 1937, against Republic, Youngstown, Bethlehem, and Inland Steel was met and beaten by the employers in a manner similar to the 1919 strike. But what was lost on the picket line was gained through the invocation of board processes. Four years after the strike, during which time the machinery of the board was invoked to reinstate discharged union members with back pay, disestablish company-dominated unions, and remedy other unfair labor practices, the union won elections at all plants. Executed contracts were eventually achieved in August, 1942. The establishment of collective bargaining in the steel industry was a demonstration not so much of union power as of the application of the public policy supporting collective bargaining.

The influence of legal standards on employer behavior was vividly revealed by the testimony in a Senate hearing of T. M. Girdler, Chairman of the Board of the Republic Steel Corporation and acknowledged leader of Little Steel's resistance to the union. Testifying at a time when it was apparent that the union had lost the strike, Girdler repeated constantly that under no condition would he sign a contract with the Steelworkers Union. According to the testimony of Phil Murray, Chairman of the SWOC, the major reason for the Little Steel strikes was the refusal of the companies to sign a contract with the union even if the union represented all of the employees.[50]

When the senators questioned Mr. Girdler concerning compliance with the statute, the following exchange took place:

SENATOR ELLENDER: Mr. Girdler, are you willing to abide by the provisions of the Wagner Act?

MR. GIRDLER: Absolutely.

SENATOR ELLENDER: Do you know that under the Wagner Act if a majority of your employees elected their own officers and appointed from their membership a committee, or even go so far as to appoint an agency to deal with you, that you would have to respect that?

MR. GIRDLER: Absolutely.[51]

Girdler also stated that he gave "instructions to every one of my employees to comply with the Wagner Act in every particular at all times."[52] However, he insisted that the act did not require the execution of a contract. Thereupon he was asked by Senator Ellender if he would sign a contract if the board required him to do so.

Mr. Girdler: I wouldn't care what they ruled on that, because that isn't the law.

Senator Ellender: Well, suppose, let us put it this way, then; suppose that the Board should decide under the Wagner Act, it is necessary that you do sign a contract, and that you under that act would take that to the Supreme Court up here, and let us say that the Supreme Court of the United States should hold that they interpret the act to mean that any agreement between employer and em-employees, must be in writing, would you then sign a contract?

Mr. Girdler: Whenever the law, properly carried through all of its phases, and has gone to the Supreme Court, and says that I have to sign a contract, then I have to sign a contract.

Senator Ellender: Would you refuse to sign it with the CIO?

Mr. Girdler: I wouldn't refuse to sign a contract with the CIO if the Supreme Court of the United States said that I had to sign a contract with the CIO, because I don't deny any law or disobey any law.[53]

Girdler's final word on the question of signing a contract was: "I am trying to tell this distinguished committee that I won't have a contract, verbal or written, with an irresponsible, racketeering, violent, communistic body like the CIO, and until they pass a law making me do it, I am not going to do it."[54]

AN APPRAISAL OF NON-COMPLIANCE

On the basis of the foregoing analysis of the forces which make for compliance with the national policy in collective bargaining, it appears appropriate to evaluate the meaning of non-compliance. Of course, it is true that employer resistance to collective bargaining did not disappear with the judicial approval of the Wagner Act. And the experience of the Textile Workers Union in the South provides ample evidence of the successful frustration of the purposes of the national law.

We have already noted that the most important sanction against an employer if he chooses to violate the law depends upon the existence of a union knowledgeable and strong enough to call an unfair labor practice strike. But as Chairman McCulloch observed:

> Experience has shown that an employer's successful postponement of bargaining pending the year or two it takes to secure judicial enforcement of the Labor Board Order, frequently dissipates the union's majority status and weakens its bargaining power to the extent that it can no longer effectively represent the employees.[55]

Whatever historical methods of opposing or breaking unions may have been employed prior to the Wagner Act, our analysis has demonstrated that the nature and cost of such activities have been changed by the way in which the law operates, particularly by the requirements of the duty to bargain. The way the law works has affected the relative bargaining power of unions in certain specified ways. Of course, a weak union has always been vulnerable to employer pressure, but union strength must now be regarded as reinforced by legal sanctions.

Before 1935, a union was strong to the extent that it could control and restrict the labor supply to an employer. However, since 1935 the exercise of economic power by an employer has been considerably modified. If an employer wishes to engage in a contest with a union subject only to economic pressures, the price that must be paid to minimize his costs is the observance of the law, *provided that the union has sufficient strength.* From this point of view, the durability of collective bargaining in the post-World War II period, in contrast to the sharp decline in union membership in the 1920's, may be explained, in large measure, by the necessity for employers to comply with the NLRA. Put in another way, it is difficult to think of many employers in the last twenty-five years who after having had collective bargaining succeeded in ridding themselves of a union. In other words, the price of breaking a union has been raised by the law in a way which is independent of such economic forces as the availability of strike replacements.

But where a union is weak and unable to go out and stay out on strike in reaction to an employer's unfair labor practices, the practical sanctions of the law are largely minimal. In such circumstances, the time consumed in litigation further weakens the union. Furthermore, as we have already observed, ultimate compliance with a board order and court decree may be met by conduct which stops short of the execution of a contract.

We can only conclude that the law does not ensure collective bargaining and that a union with a precarious majority may be destroyed by persistent employer effort. The relative ease with which employers can defy the law if they are willing to pay the price and take advantage of a union's weakness can be seen by examining the litigated cases. For example, a circuit court enforced a board order requiring an employer to bargain on April 27, 1959, years after the charge was filed. Despite the order, the company ignored or refused all union requests for meetings. A strike took place on July 29, 1959, in which thirty out of the forty-one employees initially participated. The union abandoned the strike on September 15, 1959, as its ranks crumbled. New charges having been filed, the same court enforced a new board order on June 28, 1962, requiring the employer to bargain. The court, which is not distinguished for its hospitality to board doctrines,[56] stated:

The Section 8(a)(5) violation is overwhelmingly supported by substantial evidence. Indeed, a more flagrant case would be difficult to imagine. The company has not even gone through the motions of bargaining. . . Since April 27, 1959, the company has not had a single meeting with the union though repeated requests have been made. . . . [The company's defense] borders on the frivolous . . . [and] is simply unfathomable.[57]

It is not difficult to predict that this employer will not engage in collective bargaining with the union in the foreseeable future.

THE STRATEGIC ROLE OF THE DUTY TO BARGAIN

An additional illustration of the critical role of the duty to bargain is the history of the foremen's unions. Under the Wagner Act, the NLRB vacillated on the issue of whether supervisors were employees within the meaning of the act. When the board ruled that foremen were employees and that an employer must perforce bargain with their majority representative, membership in foremen's unions increased by spectacular numbers. A reverse ruling resulted in stagnation or retrogression in membership.[58]

The significance of the duty to bargain was underscored by the developments after the board ruled in May, 1943, that supervisors were not employees entitled to the protection of the act.[59] The immediate result was that those employers such as the Ford Motor Co. who had already established contractual relations with the leading foremen's union, the Foreman's Association of America, broke off bargaining on the basis that an obligation to bargain no longer existed. Other employers whose supervisory employees had joined the Foreman's Association in substantial majorities refused to recognize the union specifically because there was no legal requirement to bargain.[60]

The consequences were quick, and unexpected only if one assumed that the foremen's unions were not labor organizations. A rash of strikes developed which was described by the Bureau of Labor Statistics as follows:

. . . after the decision in the *Maryland Drydock* case and from July 1, 1943, through November, 1944, there were 20 strikes of supervisory employees; 131,000 employees were involved and 699,156 man-days of work were lost as a result. Over 96% of the man-days lost occurred in strikes for recognition. The basic industries of the nation were affected: shipbuilding, steel, aluminum, brass, automobile, coal mining, airplane products, railroad cars and public utilities.[61]

Impressed and concerned at the effects of *Maryland Drydock*, the board in 1944 partly reversed itself and stated that supervisors were employees within the meaning of Section 8(1) and (3) of the act but not employees within the meaning of Section 8(5) and Section 9(a). This meant that supervisors could not be discriminated against or discharged for their union activities, but that employers were under no obligation to bargain with their unions.[62] The result of this new policy was later described by the board in 1945:

. . . notwithstanding . . . the fact that we have made it clear that nothing in our decisions should be taken to prohibit employers from voluntarily dealing with foremen's organizations, it cannot be denied that most employers have nevertheless refused to accord them recognition and have been strengthened in this position by the belief that this Board would not require them to do so.[63]

In 1945, the board reversed itself once again and decided in the *Packard* cases that supervisors were employees whose labor organizations could be certified and that employers were under a duty to bargain with them.[64] As a result, membership in the Foreman's Association increased by 21,000 in one year, but the overwhelming majority of employers refused to recognize the union until the *Packard* case was reviewed by the courts. The sustaining of the board by the Supreme Court was almost immediately offset by the passage of the Taft-Hartley Act which removed the protection of the act from supervisors.

The consequences of the statutory exclusion of supervisors to the viability of foremen's unions were plain and indisputable. Even the mine foremen's union, which was affiliated with the United Mine Workers, was disbanded "because the Taft-Hartley Act denies the right of collective bargaining to supervisory employees except at the option of the employer, and the coal operators have refused to affirm the right." [65] As for the Foreman's Association, by 1960 its membership had dwindled and it had no written contract in effect with any employer. In the words of one historian, it "was nearly moribund" because of the lack of protective labor legislation.[66]

CONCLUSION

The foregoing historical and operational analysis emphasizes the critical significance of the duty to bargain in the scheme of the act. Unquestionably, the other provisions on unfair labor practices have had important consequences. Certainly the prohibition of discriminatory treatment and discharge of union members and the banning of threats against union activity provided an important stimulus for organizational efforts. But since one of the powerful forces at work was the voluntary compliance of employers with the mandate of the act, it appears clear that the duty to bargain, with all its implications, is the heart of the public policy. In the absence of a duty to bargain, it does not appear at all inevitable that with all the other protection of the act the historical results would have been the same. Employers might very well have ceased interfering with and coercing their employees without taking the final step of establishing collective bargaining.

It is therefore submitted that the most important consequences of federal legislation in support of the principle of collective bargaining flows from the duty to bargain. On this basis, the ideological objections to the duty to bargain as constituting an invasion of free collective bargaining can be summarily dealt with. To the extent that this objection is based upon a misunderstanding of the congressional intent or upon a mistaken evaluation of its operational impact, as in the usual formulation, the evidence indicates the need for a reappraisal.

However, if the objection to government intervention is cast on more general lines, that is, that such government action is objectionable regardless of its source and irrespective of its implications, the question becomes one of subjective values which is outside the scope of this study. All that can be done is to point out that the probable consequence of abandoning the duty to bargain would be a serious weakening of union power.

The objections to government intervention in labor-management relations by establishing and enforcing a compulsory duty for employers to bargain can be summarized as follows:

(1) Initially, the objection was that such a policy would result in the growth and expansion of collective bargaining by unions which were independent of the control of management.

(2) This was followed by a rejection of such a public policy on the basis of its obvious ineffectiveness. This objection was based upon the assumption that employers

would not obey the law and that the courts would not require compliance.

(3) The third objection was related to the others and its echoes are still to be heard in contemporary arguments on the proper role of government. It is that since employers would not voluntarily obey the law, the practical consequences of the enforcement of the duty to bargain would involve the government in collective bargaining to an intolerable extent. The earliest formulations of this approach predicted that the result would be compulsory arbitration with the government fixing the terms and conditions of employment. Not surprisingly, since the prediction did not materialize, this objection has shifted to other grounds. It is often argued at present that the duty to bargain obstructs collective bargaining by imposing unnecessary and undesirable restrictions on the freedom of the parties.

It appears clear that the differing evaluations of public policy follow from various critical assumptions. These assumptions are mainly factual and at times contradictory. It is difficult to see how a proposal can be attacked both because it would spread collective bargaining and because it would be ineffectual. The same weakness vitiates the dual objection of ineffectuality and undue government interference, although it is possible to reconcile them by asserting that government would have to intervene because of the law's weakness.

But this is logic-chopping. It is reasonable to oppose government intervention because of an objection to its purpose, and those employers who rejected the duty to bargain on this basis deserve high marks for their historical vision. On the other hand, given that it is in the public interest to promote collective bargaining, the evidence indicates that the appropriate and effective method of accomplishing this objective is through the establishment and enforcement of the duty to bargain. The predictions about the consequences of such an enforceable duty went wrong because of erroneous assumptions, particularly about employer behavior. Employers did not practice massive defiance and did not engage in widespread evasion of their legal responsibilities. Furthermore, the machinery set up under the act, which included the administrative decisions and policies of the NLRB, was not thwarted by the judiciary. Finally, the rules and standards of collective bargaining set down under board law and enforced by the courts proved over time to be workable, and employers and unions have appeared to adjust their behavior in consonance with the public policy without undue strain.

The main lesson to be derived from the past is an awareness of the danger of an uninformed, oversimplified logic. The roots of the duty to bargain lie deep in American labor history. The peculiar genius of our society is its pragmatic quality and its rejection of ideological extremes. A syllogism is useful for expressing a logical proposition; it is dangerously misleading as a guide to public policy.

NOTES

CHAPTER 1

1. *Singer Manufacturing Co.*, 24 NLRB 463.

2. *Insurance Agents International Union*, 361 U. S. 477, 483.

3. *American National Insurance*, 343 U. S. 395, 402.

4. *The Structure of Collective Bargaining*, ed. Arnold Weber (A publication of the Graduate School of Business, University of Chicago [Glencoe, Illinois: The Free Press, 1961]), p. 348.

5. Harold W. Davey, *Contemporary Collective Bargaining* (2d ed.; Englewood Cliffs, N. J.: Prentice-Hall, Inc., 1959), p. 35.

6. George P. Shultz and John R. Coleman, *Labor Problems: Cases and Readings* (New York: McGraw-Hill Book Company, 1953), p. 363.

7. Charles O. Gregory, *Labor and the Law* (rev. ed.; New York: W. W. Norton & Company, Inc., 1949), p. 472.

8. Archibald Cox and John T. Dunlop, "Regulation of Collective Bargaining by the National Labor Relations Board," in *Harvard Law Review*, LXIII, No. 3 (January, 1950), p. 390; and Herbert R. Northrup and Gordon F. Bloom, *Government and Labor* (Homewood, Ill.: Richard D. Irwin, Inc., 1963), pp. 121–122.

9. "The Public Interest in National Labor Policy," by an independent study group (Committee for Economic Development, 1961), pp. 81–82.

10. "The Operational Impact of the Taft-Hartley Act Upon Collective Bargaining Relationships," in *New Dimensions in Collective Bargaining* (New York: Harper & Brothers, 1959), p. 179. The empirical studies cited are four journal articles of limited scope and one unpublished doctoral dissertation.

11. "Revisions of the Taft-Hartley Act," *Quarterly Journal of Economics*, LXVII, No. 2 (May, 1953), 149.

12. D. V. Brown, "The Impact of Some NLRB Decisions," in *Proceedings*, 13th Annual Meeting of IRRA, Publication No. 26, 1961, pp. 18–19.

CHAPTER 2

1. U. S. Congress, Senate, Commission on Industrial Relations, *Final Report and Testimony*, 64th Congress, 1st Session, Senate Document No. 415, Vol. 1 (Washington, Government Printing Office, 1916), p. 67.

2. U. S. Congress, House of Representatives, 57th Congress, 1st Session, Document No. 380, Vol. XIX (Washington, Government Printing Office, 1902), p. 844.

3. *Report of the Anthracite Coal Strike Commission* (Bulletin of the Department of Labor, No. 46, May, 1903 [Washington: Government Printing Office, 1903]), p. 27.

4. Commission on Industrial Relations, *op. cit.*, p. 266.

5. *Ibid.*, p. 209.

6. *Ibid.*, p. 212.

7. This provision of the Erdman Act was eventually invalidated by the Supreme Court in *Adair v. U. S.*, 208 U. S. 161 (1908), while the state statutes were similarly treated by *Coppage v. Kansas*, 236 U. S. 1 (1915) or by their own judiciary.

8. U. S. Department of Labor, Bureau of Labor Statistics, *Bulletin of the United States*, No. 287 (Washington: Government Printing Office, 1922), p. 32.

9. *Ibid.*, p. 56.

10. *Ibid.*, p. 67.

11. *Ibid.*

12. *Ibid.*, p. 25.

13. Robert P. Reeder, "Analysis of the Awards of the National War Labor Board," in *Reports of the Department of Labor*, 1919, *Report to the Secretary of Labor* and *Reports on Bureaus* (Washington: Government Printing Office, 1920), p. 1214.

14. *Ibid.*, pp. 1214, 1215.

15. *Ibid.*, pp. 1215–1218.

16. *Ibid.*, p. 1211.

17. BLS Bulletin No. 287, pp. 53–56.

18. *Ibid.*, p. 55.

19. *Proceedings of the First Industrial Conference Called by the President, October 6 to 23, 1919* (Washington: Government Printing Office, 1920), pp. 4, 5, 6.

20. *Ibid.*, p. 141.

21. *Ibid.*, p. 82.

22. *Ibid.*, p. 159.

23. *Ibid.*, p. 169.

24. *Ibid.*, p. 159.

25. *Report of Industrial Conference Called by the President, Reports of the Department of Labor, 1920* (Washington: Government Printing Office, 1921), p. 255.

26. United States Congress, *Investigation of Strike in Steel Industry*, 1919, Hearings, Vol. I, p. 163.

27. Statistics from Wolman, *op. cit.*, p. 16.

28. Selig Perlman and Philip Taft, *History of Labor in the United States, 1896–1932* (New York: The Macmillan Company, 1935), p. 524.

29. For a full discussion of the act and its legislative history, see C. O. Fisher, "Use of Federal Power in Settlement of Railway Labor Disputes," in BLS Bulletin No. 303 (Washington: Government Printing Office, 1922), pp. 7–14.

30. Section 6, Act of October 1, 1888.

31. BLS Bulletin No. 303, p. 11.

32. Philip Taft, *The AF of L in the Time of Gompers* (New York: Harper & Brothers, 1957), p. 77.

33. BLS Bulletin No. 303, p. 19.

34. The bill passed the Senate by a vote of 47 to 3 and the House by a vote of 226 to 5. BLS Bulletin No. 303, p. 24.

35. National Mediation Board, *First Annual Report* (Washington: Government Printing Office, 1935), p. 59.

36. *American Federationist*, III (February, 1897), 258.

37. BLS Bulletin No. 303, p. 24.

38. *Ibid.*, p. 25. The reason for Gompers' opposition appeared to be purely ideological, based upon a fear and distrust of government intervention. See Taft, *op. cit.*, p. 462. On the other hand, the Republican Party's 1908 campaign textbook called the Erdman Act "one of the most commendable accomplishments of the present administration." BLS Bulletin No. 303, p. 41.

39. *Adair v. United States*, 208 U. S. 161.

40. The controversy about whether unions should be incorporated which resulted in the passage of the 1886 statute (an act to legalize the incorporation of National Trade Unions, ch. 567, U. S. Stat. L. Vol. 24) ended on a ludicrous note. This act was repealed in 1932 after a congressional inquiry found out that not only had no trade union ever utilized the act but that its sole use had been by twenty-eight Texas insurance companies whose primary if not exclusive function was to insure married couples against divorce. See National Mediation Board, *op. cit.*, p. 60.

41. BLS Bulletin No. 303, pp. 31–32.

42. *Ibid.*, p. 32.

43. National Conference on Industrial Conciliation, under the auspices of the National Civic Federation (December, 1901), as cited in BLS Bulletin No. 303, p. 38.

44. *Ibid.*, p. 44.

45. *Ibid.*

46. *The Railway Age Gazette*, L, No. 17 (1911), 979.

47. BLS Bulletin No. 303, p. 45.

48. For a useful summary of contemporary views on the process of arbitration see U. S. Congress, House of Representatives, *Hearings on National Arbitration Bill*, H.R. 9491; for government fixing of railroad wages see the majority report of the Board of Arbitration on Eastern Railroads and the Brotherhood of Locomotive Firemen and Enginemen (1912) as reported in BLS Bulletin No. 303, pp. 45–46. It is also noteworthy that a minority report by the labor member of the board was severely critical of compulsory arbitration. *Ibid.*

49. For a synopsis of the Newlands Act, see Harry E. Jones, *Historical Background of Machinery Set Up for the Handling of Railroad Labor Disputes, 1888–1940* (no publisher, no date; printed in New York for Eastern Committee of the National Railroad Adjustment Board), pp. 401–402.

50. National Mediation Board, *op. cit.*, p. 61.

51. U. S. Board of Mediation and Conciliation, *Report on Operations, 1913–1919*, pp. 24, 25, as cited in BLS Bulletin No. 303, p. 51. However, it must be remembered that in 1917 the railroads were taken over by the government. For the four-year period before the government control and the establishment of machinery to handle wartime disputes, the board adjusted fifty-eight out of the seventy disputes submitted. *Ibid.*, pp. 50, 51.

52. One case which angered the unions was the selection and retention, as a neutral arbitrator, of an attorney who was a trustee in an estate the assets of which included bonds in one of the railroads involved in the dispute. The award was bitterly attacked not only for its substance but for the use of admittedly inaccurate statistics. BLS Bulletin No. 303, pp. 52, 53, and 64.

53. *The Railway Age Gazette*, LVII (August 7, 1914), 252.

54. *Report of the Eight Hour Commission* (1918), p. 10, as cited in BLS Bulletin No. 303, p. 66. Differences over the application of the agreement were to be determined by a joint labor management committee. See Jones, *op. cit.*, p. 19, Appendix.

55. *Wilson v. New*, 243 U. S. 332.

56. *The Railway Age Gazette*, LXII, 612, as quoted in BLS Bulletin No. 303, p. 68.

57. Senate Document No. 549, 64th Congress, 1st Session, pp. 5–15, as cited in BLS Bulletin No. 303, p. 61.

58. U. S. Congress, Senate, Committee on Interstate Commerce, *Hearings on S. 2906, The Prevention of Strikes*, pp. 47, 51. Testimony of Warren S. Stone, as cited in BLS Bulletin No. 303, p. 63.

59. U. S. Congress, House of Representatives, Committee on Interstate and Foreign Commerce, *Hearings on H.R. 19730*, 64th

Congress, 2nd session, p. 71, Testimony of W. G. Lee, as cited in BLS Bulletin No. 303, p. 63.

60. Gompers said in part, "Has the court permanently abandoned the field of justice, to play into the hands of the employing class, the wealth producers of our country, by taking away from the working people the only effective power they possess to compel a decent regard for their rights, their freedom, the American standard of life?" *American Federationist*, XXIV (April, 1917), 291.

61. Section 5 of General Order No. 8, issued on February 21, 1918; see U. S. Railroad Administration, *Bulletin No. 4* (revised 1919), p. 167.

62. U. S. Railroad Administration, *Annual Report, 1918–1919, Division of Labor*, p. 7. Prior to federal operation of the railroads, the brotherhoods had about 80 per cent of total employees. When the lines were restored to private ownership in 1920, the percentage of union membership had increased to 90 per cent. For non-operating personnel, the increase was far more dramatic: from 20 per cent to 80 per cent. See H. D. Wolf, *The Railway Labor Board* (Chicago: University of Chicago Press, 1927), p. 58.

63. See U. S. Railroad Administration, *Report of the Railway Wage Commission*, April 30, 1918.

64. National Mediation Board, *op. cit.*, pp. 62, 63.

65. *Ibid.*, p. 63.

66. *Ibid.*

67. L. A. Lecht, *Experience Under Railway Labor Legislation* (New York: Columbia University Press, 1954), p. 35.

68. U. S. Railroad Administration, *Bulletin No. 4* (revised 1919), pp. 178, 300, 340.

69. U. S. Department of Labor, Bureau of Labor Statistics, *Monthly Labor Review*, XI (1920), p. 41; Lecht, *op. cit.*, p. 33; BLS Bulletin No. 303, pp. 73, 74.

70. W. D. Hines, Director General of Railroads, report to the President for the fourteen months ending March 1, 1920, p. 15, as cited in BLS Bulletin No. 303, p. 74.

71. U. S. Railroad Administration, Director of Railroads, Division of Labor, *Annual Report for 1919* (Washington: Government Printing Office, 1919), p. 50.

72. BLS Bulletin No. 303, pp. 74–75.

73. *Ibid.*, pp. 71, 72.

74. Taft, *op. cit.*, p. 468.

75. *Ibid.*, p. 470.

76. U. S. Congress, Senate, Committee on Interstate Commerce, *Hearings on S. Res. 23*, 67th Congress, 1st Session, p. 410, 1921, as cited in BLS Bulletin No. 303, p. 75.

77. Senator La Follette commented on the wide scope of the ban on strikes by noting that anyone supplying food to the family of a striker would also be guilty of a crime. *S. Rept. No. 304*, 66th Congress, 1st Session, Part 2, p. 10, as cited in BLS Bulletin No. 303, p. 71.

78. U. S. Stats. 456 (1920).

79. National Mediation Board, *op. cit.*, p. 63.

80. Decision No. 119 (1921), as cited in Frank B. Ward, *The United States Railroad Labor Board and Railway Labor Disputes* (Ph.D. thesis in economics, University of Pennsylvania, 1929), pp. 23–24.

81. *Ibid.*, pp. 28–30.

82. II RLB 251.

83. Wolf, *op. cit.*, pp. 230–231.

84. The method was contained in Decision No. 218, II RLB 207 (1921). The facts in the case indicated that the railroad refused to confer with the union on the basis that there was no evidence that the union represented a majority of employees. In order to ascertain the majority representative, the carrier desired an election. The union refused to participate on the grounds that the railroad insisted upon a ballot which would not name the union but individuals who must also be employees. The ballot also did not allow for system representation but for regional representation only. The board held that the carrier was not justified in refusing to permit the name of the union to be placed on the ballot or in insisting that representatives must be actual employees, and had no legal authority to divide the system into regions for the purpose of the election. The actual voting on the company ballot was boycotted by the union and 89.5 per cent of the employees refused to vote. See Ward, *op. cit.*, pp. 37–42.

85. *Pennsylvania Railroad Company v. Railway Labor Board*, 282 Fed. 693.

86. 261 U. S. 72, 79, 80.

87. Decision No. 2, I RLB 13, p. 17.

88. Lecht, *op. cit.*, pp. 40, 41.

89. *Ibid.*, p. 41.

90. III RLB 404 ff, as cited in Wolf, *op. cit.*, pp. 227, 228.

91. For a full discussion see Wolf, *op. cit.*, pp. 166–213.

92. For a review of the strike's history, see Wolf, *op. cit.*, pp. 214–265; Taft, *op. cit.*, pp. 471–474. Many non-union employees and some operating personnel joined the strike and by mid-July between 600,000 and 700,000 employees were on strike. Wolf, *op. cit.*, p. 242.

NOTES TO PAGES 39 TO 47

93. Hearings of the Railroad Labor Board, Docket 2387, p. 50, as cited in Wolf, *op. cit.*, p. 236.

94. Wolf, *op. cit.*, p. 239.

95. This part of the resolution was described as "practically calling upon the railroads to organize company unions. As a result, between July 1, 1922, when the strike began, and October 14 of the same year, 16 roads formed independent unions among their shopmen." Twentieth Century Fund, *Labor and the Government* (New York: McGraw-Hill Book Company, 1935), p. 181. For colorful accounts of the origins of some of these company unions, see U. S. Congress, Senate, *Hearings Before the Committee on Interstate Commerce*, 73rd Congress, 2nd Session (Washington: Government Printing Office, 1934), *passim* and particularly p. 120 which quotes a statement by a prominent company union officer that following the strike his organization was founded by "Dicks and Spies."

96. III RLB 1139.

97. Wolf, *op. cit.*, p. 239.

98. *Ibid.*, pp. 244–246.

99. *Ibid.*, p. 249.

100. *Ibid.*, p. 253.

101. *Ibid.*, pp. 253–256.

102. Taft, *op. cit.*, p. 474.

103. *Senate Reports*, 69th Congress, 1st Session, Vol. 1 (Washington: Government Printing Office, 1926), Report No. 222, pp. 2, 3.

104. Donald R. Richberg, *The Rainbow* (New York: Doubleday, Doran and Company, Inc., 1936), p. 49.

105. Senate Report No. 222, p. 2. It was supported by the AF of L and opposed by the NAM. Taft, *The AF of L from the Death of Gompers to the Merger* (New York: Harper & Brothers, 1959), pp. 68–70.

106. U. S. Congress, House of Representatives, *House Reports*, 69th Congress, 1st Session, Report No. 328, Vol. 1 (Washington: Government Printing Office, 1926), p. 4.

107. Public Law No. 257, 69th Congress, 1926.

108. Senate Report No. 222, p. 5.

109. *Ibid.*

110. C. O. Fisher, "The New Railway Labor Act," *American Economic Review*, XVII (1927), 177–187.

111. Senate Report No. 222, p. 6.

112. Section 77, Paragraphs o, t, and q, Public Law No. 420, 72nd Congress, 1933. For background see Taft, *The AF of L from the Death of Gompers to the Merger*, pp. 42–43.

113. Section 7 and Section 10, Paragraph A, Public Law No. 68, 73rd Congress, 1933. For a discussion see Lecht, *op. cit.*, p. 77 ff.

114. See testimony of George M. Harrison, Senate Hearings on S. 3266, pp. 27–38. Without question, the ending of union security and checkoff helped the national unions. "Commencing in 1922 . . . the carriers introduced both the closed shop (or more accurately the union shop) and the checkoff as means to insure the maintenance of company unions which they had organized after the shopmen strike of that year. In addition, many of the carriers developed the practice of compensating company union officials for time spent away from their jobs on union business and gave other financial aid to the administration of these organizations. In other words, what is 'union security' in industry generally became an anti-union device in the railroad relations with non-operating unions." Herbert R. Northrup, "Unfair Labor Practice Prevention Under the Railway Labor Act," *Industrial and Labor Relations Review*, III, No. 3 (April 1950), 330–331. The activities of some of these company unions had a comic opera air. For example, the head of the company union of train dispatchers on the Santa Fe Railroad was also the vice president in charge of personnel. An unfriendly critic commented: "As Vice President of the railroad, he addresses to himself a letter demanding that he agree to reduction in the rates of pay of train dispatchers; as general chairman representing the employees he receives and acknowledges the letter, and then advises himself whether or not he is disposed to accede to his own demands. After a desperate controversy with himself, he probably arrives at an amicable settlement of a dispute." Senate Hearings on S. 3266, p. 166.

115. National Mediation Board, *op. cit.*, pp. 1–2.

CHAPTER 3

1. We shall not discuss here the significance of the Norris-LaGuardia Act (Act of March 23, 1932, 47 Stat. 70) which severely limited and, for all practical purposes, ended the exercise of the injunctive power on the application of employers by the federal courts in labor cases. One author has observed, "The point of this Act is not what it does for organized labor but is what it permits organized labor to do for itself without judicial interference." (Gregory, *op. cit.*, p. 186.) In any event, the aid given to the trade union movement by this act was submerged by the importance of the succeeding New Deal legislation.

2. 308 U. S. 401, 408.

3. *Appalachian Electric Company*, 93 F. 2d 985 (CCA 4).

4. Support for this view is given in the two bound volumes published by the National Labor Relations Board on the legislative history of the National Labor Relations Act, 1935, which reproduces the 1934 bills and discussion. In accordance, see Irving Bernstein,

The New Deal Collective Bargaining Policy (Berkeley: University of California Press, 1950), *passim,* and particularly the preface.

5. 48 Stat. L. 214.

6. Lewis L. Lorwin and Arthur Wubnig, *Labor Relations Boards* (Washington: The Brookings Institution, 1935), p. 48.

7. Paul F. Brissenden, "Genesis and Import of the Collective Bargaining Provisions of the Recovery Act," in *Economic Essays in Honor of W. C. Mitchell* (New York: Columbia University Press, 1935), p. 62.

8. *Ibid.,* p. 46.

9. Bernstein, *op. cit.,* p. 39.

10. Brissenden, *op. cit.,* p. 47.

11. Raymond S. Rubinow, *Section 7(a): Its History, Interpretation and Administration* (Office of National Recovery Administration, Division of Review, Labor Studies Section, March, 1936 [mimeo]), p. 19.

12. Rubinow, *op. cit.,* p. 27.

13. *Ibid.,* pp. 28–29.

14. William H. Spencer, *Collective Bargaining Under Section 7(a) of The National Industrial Recovery Act* (Studies in Business Administration, The School of Business [Chicago: The University of Chicago, 1935]), p. 5.

15. NRA Bulletin No. 1, "Statement by the President of the United States of America outlining Policies of The National Recovery Administration," June 16, 1933 (Washington: Government Printing Office, 1933), pp. 2–3.

16. Lorwin and Wubnig, *op. cit.,* p. 54; and Spencer, *op. cit.,* p. 18.

17. Bernstein, *op. cit.,* p. 57.

18. Lorwin and Wubnig, *op. cit.,* p. 95.

19. Spencer, *op. cit.,* p. 19.

20. *In the Matter of National Lock Company,* I NLB 19.

21. *Ibid.,* pp. 19, 20.

22. *Matter of S. Dresner and Son,* I NLB 26, 27.

23. *Matter of Edward G. Budd Manufacturing Company,* 1 NLB 59. Here the employer had also formed a company union and summarily rejected the demands of a committee of workers. The board said in part, "Once the employees determine the nature and extent of the organization which they are forming, it is incumbent upon the employer to meet for the purposes of collective bargaining those who represent a majority of the class of employees which their organization is designed to cover." (P. 61.)

24. 1 NLB 73.

25. *Ibid.,* p. 74.

26. *Matter of the Harriman Hosiery Mills,* 1 NLB 68.

27. *Matter of Eagle Rubber Company,* 2 NLB 33.

28. *Matter of Hall Baking Company,* 1 NLB 83.

29. Among the cases so holding are *Edward G. Budd,* I NLB 58; *Philadelphia Rapid Transit,* 1 NLB 66; *Cleveland Knitting Mills,* 1 NLB 69; *Norge Corporation,* 1 NLB 82, *Republic Steel,* 1 NLB 88; *Berkeley Woolen Mills,* 1 NLB 5; *A. Roth and Company,* 1 NLB 75.

30. Petroleum Labor Policy Board, *Magnolia Petroleum Company,* Decision on Appeal, February 28, 1934, cited in *National Labor Board Principles with Applicable Cases* (mimeo., August 21, 1934), p. 6.

31. *Bender Tramway Corporation,* I NLB 64; *Houde Engineering Corporation,* I NLB 87.

32. *Reading Hosiery,* 1 NLB 1; *Tierson Manufacturing Company,* 1 NLB 53; *Harriman Hosiery,* 1 NLB 68; *Connecticut Coke,* 2 NLB 88.

33. *Norge Corporation,* 1 NLB 82; *Republic Steel,* 1 NLB 88; *Bee Line Bus,* 2 NLB 24.

34. Executive Order of February 1st, 1934 (No. 6580) as cited in Rubinow, *op. cit.,* p. 159.

35. *Ibid.,* p. 160.

36. Leon H. Keyserling, "The Wagner Act: Its Origin and Current Significance," in the *George Washington Law Review,* XXIX, No. 2 (December, 1960), 200.

37. National Labor Relations Board, *Legislative History of the National Labor Relations Act, 1935,* Vol. I (Washington: Government Printing Office, 1949), p. 3, hereafter referred to as *I Legis. Hist.* The second volume will be cited as *II Legis. Hist.*

38. *Ibid.,* p. 15.

39. *Ibid.,* pp. 16, 17.

40. *Ibid.,* p. 89.

41. *Ibid.,* pp. 147, 148.

42. *Ibid.,* pp. 173, 174, 175.

43. *Ibid.,* p. 222.

44. *Ibid.,* p. 264.

45. *Ibid.,* p. 380.

46. *Ibid.,* p. 540.

47. For a summary of these reasons, see Bernstein, *op. cit.,* pp. 71–75.

48. For a discussion of this, see Bernstein, *op. cit.,* p. 72. Keyserling calls Walsh "enigmatic and uncertain in his attitude and action" and states that the Walsh report "would have provoked an extremely narrow construction of the legislation by the courts."

This attitude apparently resulted in an agreement by Senator Wagner to support Public Resolution 44 and wait until 1935 to offer a stronger bill. Keyserling, *op. cit.*, p. 208.

49. *I Legis. Hist.*, p. 1124.

50. The Walsh report is Senate Report No. 1184, contained in *I Legis. Hist.*, pp. 1099–1112.

51. Bernstein, *op. cit.*, pp. 76–83.

52. Lorwin and Wubnig, *op. cit.*, p. 261.

53. Keyserling, *op. cit.*, p. 203.

54. *I Legis. Hist.*, p. 1192.

55. *Ibid.*, p. 1195.

56. *Ibid.*, p. 1204.

57. *Ibid.*, p. 1203.

58. *Ibid.*, pp. 1207–1208.

59. *Ibid.*, p. 1209.

60. *Ibid.*, pp. 1241–1242.

61. Bernstein, *op. cit.*, p. 84.

62. The citations for the Labor Board included *Eagle Rubber Company, National Aniline and Chemical Company,* and *Connecticut Coke Company;* citation for the Petroleum Board was *Magnolia Petroleum Company.*

63. *Houde Engineering Corporation,* I NLB 87, pp. 35–36.

64. *Ibid.*, p. 38.

65. *Ibid.*, p. 39.

66. *Ibid.*, p. 39.

67. *Ibid.*, p. 44.

68. *Ely and Walker Dry Goods Company,* 1 NLRB 97.

69. *National Aniline and Chemical Company,* 1 NLRB 115.

70. *Ibid.*, p. 116.

71. *Atlanta Hosiery Mills,* 1 NLRB 145.

72. *Ibid.*, p. 146.

73. *Eagle Rubber Company,* 1 NLRB 157.

74. *Resnick Brothers,* 2 NLRB 214.

75. *Fine Rough Hat Company,* 2 NLRB 411.

76. *Resnick Brothers,* 2 NLRB 214.

77. *Claire Knitting Mills, Inc.,* 2 NLRB 472.

78. *Clifton Wright Hat Company,* 2 NLRB 453.

79. *Globe Gabbe Corporation,* 2 NLRB 60.

80. *Samson Tire & Rubber Corporation (Division of the United States Rubber Company),* 2 NLRB 504.

81. *I Legis. Hist.*, p. 1469.

82. Testimony of John L. Lewis, *I Legis. Hist.*, p. 182. For several other examples see Twentieth Century Fund, *op. cit.*, p. 80.

83. Testimony of Robert F. Wagner, *I Legis. Hist.*, p. 10. (Cor-

roboration is also evident in the rise of trade union membership in 1933 and 1934. See Wolman, *op. cit.*, pp. 43–74.)

84. Twentieth Century Fund, *op. cit.*, p. 79. This was only 1,700,000 fewer than that for trade union membership. *Ibid.*, p. 80.

85. U. S. Congress, Senate, Subcommittee of the Committee on Education and Labor, *Hearings*, 75th Congress, Part 17 (Washington: Government Printing Office, 1938), p. 7576.

86. *I Legis. Hist.*, p. 1311.

87. *Ibid.*, p. 1312.

88. *Ibid.*, p. 1414.

89. *Ibid.*, p. 1415.

90. *Ibid.*, p. 1419.

91. *Ibid.*

92. *Ibid.*, pp. 1420–1421.

93. *Ibid.*, p. 1455.

94. *Ibid.*, pp. 1455, 1456.

95. *Ibid.*, p. 1517.

96. *Ibid.*, p. 1519.

97. *Ibid.*, p. 1612.

98. Mr. Lippman considered the bill unworkable, the ACLU thought it an invasion of individual freedom, and the Communist Party considered it a typically capitalistic subterfuge.

99. *II Legis. Hist.*, p. 2243.

100. Bernstein, *op. cit.*, p. 112.

101. *II Legis. Hist.*, p. 2312.

102. *Ibid.*, p. 2301.

103. *Ibid.*

104. *Ibid.*, pp. 2303–2304.

105. *Ibid.*, p. 2313.

106. *Ibid.*, p. 2321.

107. *Ibid.*, p. 2332.

108. *Ibid.*, p. 2336.

109. *Ibid.*

110. Bernstein, *op. cit.*, p. 117.

111. *II Legis. Hist.*, p. 2371.

112. *Ibid.*, p. 2373, 2374.

113. *Ibid.*, p. 2392.

114. *Ibid.*, p. 2393.

115. *Ibid.*

116. Bernstein, *op. cit.*, p. 117.

117. *II Legis. Hist.*, p. 2910.

118. *Ibid.*, p. 2911.

119. *Ibid.*, p. 2912.

120. *Ibid.*, p. 2915.

121. *Ibid.*, p. 2927.
122. *Ibid.*, pp. 3102–3110.
123. *Ibid.*, p. 3113.
124. *Ibid.*
125. *Ibid.*, p. 3183.
126. *Ibid.*, p. 3269.

CHAPTER 4

1. II Legis. Hist., p. 2373.
2. *Report of the Special Committee to Investigate the N.L.R.B.*, submitted by Mr. Smith of Virginia (Washington: Government Printing Office, 1941), p. 87.
3. *Ibid.*, p. 88.
4. Millis and Brown, *op. cit.*, p. 50. For an objective appraisal of the board during the Wagner Act administration, see Walter Gellhorn and S. L. Linfield, "Politics and Labor Relations—N.L.R.B. Procedure," *Columbia Law Review*, 39 (1939), pp. 339–395.
5. U. S. Congress, Senate, Committee on Education and Labor, *Hearings*, 76th Congress, 4th Session, Part 3, April 26, 1939 (Washington: Government Printing Office, 1939), pp. 507–508.
6. Sylvester Petro, *The Labor Policy of a Free Society* (New York: The Ronald Press Company, 1957), pp. 254–255.
7. Russell A. Smith, "The Evolution of the 'Duty to Bargain' Concept in American Law," *Michigan Law Review*, XXXIX, No. 7 (May, 1941), 1065–1108.
Moreover, one recent labor economics textbook went to the length of asserting, "It should be noted incidentally, however, that the one new feature of the Wagner Act, which did not have precedent in earlier public policy, was the provision making it an unfair labor practice to refuse to bargain collectively." L. Reed Tripp, *Labor Problems and Processes* (New York: Harper & Brothers, 1961), p. 237.
8. *Ibid.*, p. 1084.
9. *Ibid.*, p. 1089.
10. *Ibid.*
11. Sylvester Petro, "The Employer's Duty to Bargain," 3 *Labor Law Journal* 515 (1952).
12. George W. Taylor, *Government Regulation of Industrial Relations* (New York: Prentice-Hall, Inc., 1948).
13. Taylor asserted that the duty to bargain "has been one of the greatest mistakes [in] public policy in this area." See *The Structure of Collective Bargaining*, ed. Arnold Weber (A Publication of the Graduate School of Business, University of Chicago [Glencoe, Ill.: The Free Press, 1961]), p. 348.

14. Archibald Cox and John T. Dunlop, "Regulation of Collective Bargaining by the National Labor Relations Board," *Harvard Law Review*, LXIII (January, 1950), 389–432.

15. *Ibid.*, p. 394.

16. *Ibid.*, p. 395.

17. *Ibid.*, p. 396.

18. *Ibid.*, p. 400.

19. *Ibid.*, p. 418.

20. *Ibid.*, p. 432.

21. For a further exposition of their misunderstanding of board doctrine, see David P. Findling and William Colby, "Regulations of Collective Bargaining by the National Labor Relations Board—Another View," *Columbia Law Review*, LI (1951), p. 170.

22. Cox and Dunlop, *op. cit.*, p. 396.

23. *Ibid.*, p. 396.

24. R. W. Fleming, "The Significance of the Wagner Act," in *Labor and the New Deal*, ed. Milton Derber and Edwin Young (Madison: University of Wisconsin Press, 1961), pp. 148–149.

25. R. W. Fleming, "The Obligation to Bargain in Good Faith," in *Public Policy and Collective Bargaining*, ed. Joseph Shister, Benjamin Aaron, and Clyde W. Summers (New York and Evanston: Harper & Row, 1962), p. 6.

26. Archibald Cox, "The Duty to Bargain in Good Faith," *Harvard Law Review*, LXXI (1958), pp. 1401–1442. The cited cases were in *NLRB v. Insurance Agents Union*, 361 U. S. 477.

27. *Ibid.*, pp. 1406–1407.

28. *Ibid.*, p. 1416.

29. *Ibid.*, pp. 1339–1440.

30. *The Public Interest in National Labor Policy*, pp. 81–82.

31. *Ibid.*, p. 82.

32. 356 U. S. 342, 354.

33. 361 U. S. 477, 484.

34. John Chamberlin, *Collective Bargaining and the Law* (Ann Arbor: University of Michigan Law School, 1959), p. 47.

35. Northrup and Bloom, *op. cit.*, p. 121.

36. See, for example, Nathan P. Feinsinger, "The National Labor Relations Act and Collective Bargaining," in Chamberlin, *op. cit.*, p. 9.

37. *II Legis. Hist.*, pp. 2374–2392.

38. *I Legis. Hist.*, p. 3.

39. *Ibid.*, pp. 16–17.

40. Senator Walsh stated, "The bill indicates the method and manner in which employees may organize, and method and manner of selecting their representatives or spokesmen, and leads them to

the office door of their employer with the legal authority to negotiate for their fellow employees. The bill does not go beyond the office door. It leaves the discussion between the employer and employee, and the agreements which they may or may not make, voluntary and with the sacredness and solemnity to a voluntary agreement with which both parties to an agreement should be enshrouded." *Ibid.,* p. 1124.

41. *Ibid.,* p. 1195.
42. *Ibid.,* pp. 1207–1208.
43. *Ibid.*
44. *Ibid.,* p. 1421.
45. *II Legis. Hist.,* p. 2312.
46. *I Legis. Hist.,* p. 1209; see also pp. 15–19 and *passim.*

CHAPTER 5

1. NLRB, First Annual Report (Washington: Government Printing Office, 1936), pp. 1, 14, 21, 29.
2. *Globe Mail Service, Inc.,* 2 NLRB 610, 621; *Suburban Lumber Co.,* 3 NLRB 194, 203; *Sheba Ann Frocks, Inc.,* 5 NLRB 12, 16, 17.
3. *Sheba Ann Frocks,* 16.
4. *Lorillard Co.,* 16 NLRB 684, 703; *Martin Brothers Box Company,* 35 NLRB 217, 239.
5. *Matter of Inland Steel Company,* 9 NLRB 783.
6. 1 NLRB 714.
7. *Lorillard,* p. 696.
8. *Matter of Biles-Coleman Lumber Company,* 4 NLRB 690, 700.
9. *Louisville Refining Company,* 4 NLRB 861.
10. *American Hawaiian S. S. Company,* 10 NLRB 1361–1366; *Tomlinson of High Point, Inc.,* 74 NLRB 127.
11. *Rollway Bearing Company, Inc.,* 1 NLRB 659.
12. *Scandore Paper Box Co.,* 4 NLRB 918.
13. *The Stolle Corporation,* 13 NLRB 382.
14. *Griswold Manufacturing Company,* 6 NLRB 307; see also *Tishomingo County Electric Power Association,* 74 NLRB 135.
15. *McNeely & Price Company,* 6 NLRB 811. For other cases, see *Consolidated Machine Tools,* 67 NLRB 95; *American Creosetting,* 4 NLRB 240.
16. *Atlantic Refining Company,* 1 NLRB 368; cf. *Westinghouse Air Brake Co.,* 25 NLRB 1312.
17. See *Mooresville Cotton Mills,* 2 NLRB 955, where the refusal to bargain was dismissed because of the absence of a majority showing; and *North American Aviation, Inc.,* 44 NLRB 604, 611, where the board said, "Grievances and grievance procedure are normal and proper subjects of collective bargaining."

18. *Rapid Roller Co.*, 33 NLRB 589. See also *NLRB v. Newark Morning Ledger Company* (CCA 3), enforced as mod. *Newark Morning Ledger*, 21 NLRB 988, as cited by the board in *Rapid Roller*, pp. 587–588.

19. *NLRB v. Sands Manufacturing Co.*, 306 U. S. 332.

20. *J. H. Allison & Company*, 70 NLRB 378.

21. *Timken Roller Bearing Company*, 70 NLRB 506.

22. *Singer Manufacturing Company*, 24 NLRB 460.

23. *Ibid.*

24. *Ibid.*, p. 470.

25. 72 NLRB 676.

26. *Matter of S. L. Allen & Company*, 1 NLRB 714.

27. *Ibid.*, 1 NLRB 727.

28. But see *NLRB v. Sands Manufacturing Co.*, 96 F. (2d) 721, 725 (CCA 6) setting aside 1 NLRB 546, affirmed 306 U. S. 442, where the court applied frequency of negotiations as one of the tests of good faith.

29. 2 NLRB 39, 48.

30. NLRB, Third Annual Report (Washington: Government Printing Office, 1939).

31. NLRB 10.

32. *Ibid.*

33. *Matter of M. H. Birge & Sons*, 1 NLRB 739.

34. *Matter of National Licorice Company*, 7 NLRB 551.

35. See the board's Third Annual Report, p. 97.

36. *Matter of Singer Manufacturing Company*, 24 NLRB 463.

37. *Ibid.*, p. 464.

38. For early board decisions expressing this view, see *Matter of H. J. Heinz Company*, 10 NLRB 963; *Matter of Inland Steel Company*, 9 NLRB 783; *Matter of St. Joseph Stockyards Company*, 2 NLRB 39. For court confirmation of this position see *Consolidated Edison Company v. NLRB*, 305 U. S. 197, 236, where the Supreme Court said, "The Act contemplates the making of contracts with labor organizations. That is the manifest objective in providing for collective bargaining." Another Supreme Court decision to the same end was *NLRB v. The Sands Manufacturing Company*, 59 S. Ct. 508, 513, 514, where the court said, "The legislative history of the Act goes far to indicate that the purpose of the statute was to compel employers to bargain collectively with their employees to the end that employment contracts binding on both parties should be made."

39. *Matter of Highland Park Manufacturing Company*, 12 NLRB 1248, 1249.

40. *Matter of Edward E. Cox, Printer, Inc.* 1 NLRB 600.

41. *Globe Cotton Mills v. NLRB*, 103 F. (2d) 94 (CCA 5) enforcing 6 NLRB 461.

42. *Matter of Wilson and Company,* 19 NLRB 1000.
43. *Matter of Capital Broadcasting Company,* 30 NLRB 164.
44. *Ibid.,* p. 165.
45. *Matter of Easton Publishing Company,* 19 NLRB 389.
46. *Ibid.,* p. 397.
47. *Montgomery Ward & Co.,* 39 NLRB 240.
48. *S. L. Allen & Co., Inc.,* 1 NLRB 728.
49. *Pioneer Pearl Button Co.,* 1 NLRB 843.
50. 24 NLRB 444.
51. *Aluminum Ore Co.,* 39 NLRB 1297.
52. *Montgomery Ward & Co.,* 39 NLRB 240, 241.
53. *Compton-Highland Mills, Inc.,* 70 NLRB 207. For a similar case, see *Pool Manufacturing Co.,* 70 NLRB, where the board affirmed an intermediate report on the same issue.
54. *Hanson-Whitney Machine Company,* 8 NLRB 159.
55. 12 NLRB 1002.
56. *Ibid.,* 1011.
57. *Hancock Brick & Tile Co.,* 44 NLRB 933.
58. *Inland Lime,* 119 F. 2d 20, 22 (CCA 7).
59. *Western Printing Co.,* 34 NLRB 202.
60. *Libby, McNeill and Libby,* 65 NLRB 873.
61. *George E. Carrol,* 56 NLRB 935, 937–938.
62. The board does not police contracts, for to do so would be inconsistent with the practice of collective bargaining. See *Consolidated Aircraft Corp.,* 47 NLRB 694.
63. Ruth Weyand, "Majority Rule in Collective Bargaining," in *Columbia Law Review,* XLV, No. 4 (July, 1945), p. 583.
64. *Matter of General Motors Corporation,* 59 NLRB 205, enforced June 20, 1945 (CCA 3).
65. *Western Felt Works,* 10 NLRB 407, 415, 416; *Hopwood Retinning Co.,* 4 NLRB 922; *Stolle Corporation,* 13 NLRB 370, 381–382; *Bussmann Manufacturing Co.,* 14 NLRB 322.
66. *NLRB v. Acme Air Appliance Company, Inc.,* 117 F. (2d) 417 (CCA 2) 420.
67. *J. I. Case Company v. NLRB,* 321 U. S. 322 (1944).
68. *Medo Photo Supply Corp.,* 43 NLRB 997, 998.
69. *John S. Doane Company,* 63 NLRB 1403; *Montgomery Ward,* 133 F. (2d) 676, 681, 687 (CCA 9), where the court held that the employer violated Section 8(5) of the act by notifying strikers that operations were continuing and that their jobs were open for them as an attempt to deal with individual employees and thus bypass the union.
70. *Atlas Mills, Inc.,* 3 NLRB 10, 18; *United Dredging Company,* 30 NLRB 118.
71. *Ford Motor Company,* 29 NLRB 873.

72. *Bradford Dyeing Association,* 4 NLRB 604, 615; *Crown Can Company,* 42 NLRB 1160; *Fansteel Metallurgical Corp.,* 5 NLRB 930.

73. *Sorg Paper Co.,* 25 NLRB 946.

74. *Dixie Motor Coach,* 128 F. (2d) 201, 202–203 (CCA 5).

75. *Pilling,* 119 F. (2d) 32, 38 (CCA 3).

76. *Saldway Process,* 117 F. (2d) 83, 86 (CCA 5).

77. *Texas Mining,* 117 F. (2d) 86, 88 (CCA 5).

78. *Express Publishing Company,* 312 U. S. 437.

79. *Pilling,* 119 F. (2d) 32, 35–36 (CCA 3); *Great Southern Trucking,* 127 F. (2d) 180, 184–185 (CCA 4).

80. *Beckerman Shoe Corporation,* 21 NLRB 1222; *Out West Broadcasting Co.,* 40 NLRB 1367; *Southern Prison Company,* 46 NLRB 1268.

81. NLRB, Third Annual Report, p. 95 and cases cited therein.

82. *Matter of Sunshine Mining Company,* 7 NLRB 1252.

83. *Franks Bros. Co. v. NLRB,* 64 S. C. 817; for a discussion of this see NLRB, Ninth Annual Report (Washington: Government Printing Office, 1944), p. 54.

84. 2 NLRB 74.

85. *Cullom and Ghertner Company,* 14 NLRB 270; *Reading Batteries, Inc.,* 19 NLRB 249.

86. *Matter of Globe Cotton Mills,* 6 NLRB 461.

87. *Globe Cotton Mills v. NLRB,* 103 F. (2d 91).

88. *Express Publishing Company,* 13 NLRB 1223.

89. *Ibid.,* p. 1224.

90. *National Licorice Company,* 309 U. S. 350, 358.

91. *Agwilines,* 87 F. (2d) 146, 153 (CCA 5).

92. *Griswold Manufacturing Company,* 106 F. (2d) 713, 723 (CCA 3).

93. *Rapid Roller Co.,* 126 F. (2) 452, 459–460 (CCA 7).

94. *Singer Manufacturing Co.,* 119 F. (2d) 131, 136 (CCA 7).

95. *Wilson and Company, Inc.,* 30 NLRB 314.

96. *Singer Manufacturing Company v. NLRB,* 119 F. (2d) 134 (CCA 7).

97. *Ibid.,* 133.

98. *Ibid.,* 133, 134.

99. *Mooresville Cotton Mills v. NLRB,* 94 F. (2d) 61, 65, modifying 2 NLRB 952.

100. *Clifford M. Dekay,* 2 NLRB 231.

101. *Elbe File and Binder Company,* 2 NLRB 906.

102. *Clarksburg Publishing Company,* 120 F. (2d) 976, 980 (CCA 4).

103. *Concordia Ice Company,* 51 NLRB 1068, and compare *Green Colonial Furnace Company,* 52 NLRB 161.

104. *Burnside Steel Foundry*, 7 NLRB 714.

105. *McNeely*, 6 NLRB 800.

106. *Hamilton-Brown Shoe Company*, 9 NLRB 1073; also see discussion in the NLRB's Fourth Annual Report, pp. 105–106.

107. *Hugh Leather Company*, 11 NLRB 394.

108. *Chicago Apparatus Company*, 12 NLRB 1002.

109. *Whittier Mills*, 15 NLRB 457, enforced in *NLRB v. Whittier Mills*, 111 F. (2d) 474 (CCA 5); *Lennox Furniture Company*, 20 NLRB 93.

110. *Bausch and Lomb*, 69 NLRB 1104.

111. *Edward E. Cox, Printer, Inc.*, 1 NLRB 594, 598.

112. *Atlas Mills, Inc.*, 3 NLRB 1014, 15; *Biles-Coleman Lumber Company*, 4 NLRB 679, 688, 689.

113. *Hancock Brick and Tile Company*, 44 NLRB 920.

114. *Denver Automobile Dealers Association, et al.*, 10 NLRB 1173; *Rollway Bearing Company, Inc.*, 1 NLRB 651, 655.

115. *I. Spiewack and Sons*, 71 NLRB 770.

116. *Bethlehem Steel Company*, 73 NLRB 277; *Harris-Woodson Company, Inc.*, 70 NLRB 956, enforced 162 F. (2d) 97 (CCA 4).

117. *Motor Valve and Manufacturing Company*, 58 NLRB 1057, enforced 149 F. (2d) (CCA 6).

118 *Franks Brothers*, 321 U. S. 702, 705.

119. *Appalachian Electric Company*, 140 F. (2d) 217, 221 (CCA 4).

120. *NLRB v. Dadourian Export Corporation*, 138 F. (2d) 891 (CCA 2).

121. *NLRB v. Capital Greyhound Lines*, 140 F. (2d) 754 (CCA 6), cert. den. 64 S. Ct. 1285.

122. *Ben Samuels d/b/a National Bag Company*, 65 NLRB 1078; *Simmons Engineering Company*, NLRB 1373.

123. *Norfolk Southern Bus Corporation*, 66 NLRB 1165.

124. *Midland Steamship Line*, 66 NLRB 836.

125. *Polish National Alliance*, 136 F. (2d) 175 (CCA 7).

126. *Biles-Coleman*, 98 F. (2d) 18, 22 (CCA 9).

127. *McQuay-Norris*, 116 F. (2d) 748, 752 (CCA 7).

128. *National Motor Bearing*, 105 F. (2d) 652, 660 (CCA 9).

129. *National Silver Company*, 50 NLRB 570; *Spicer Manufacturing Corporation*, 51 NLRB 679.

130. *Matter of Whittier Mills Company, etc.*, 15 NLRB 457, enforced *NLRB v. Whittier Mills Company*, 111 F. (2d) 474 (CCA 5).

131. NLRB, Fourth Annual Report, pp. 89–90.

132. *American Federation of Labor v. NLRB*, 308 U. S. 401, 408–411; *Pittsburgh Plate Glass v. NLRB*, 313 U. S. 154.

133. *Pittsburgh Plate Glass v. NLRB*, 313 U. S. 165.

CHAPTER 6

1. Millis and Brown, *op. cit.*, p. 333.

2. *Ibid.*, p. 343.

3. 57 Stat. 163.

4. The importance of the rash of postwar strikes should not be underestimated. In winding up the case for his bill, Senator Taft began his argument by stating that the public demanded an end to abuses. "They had been deluged with a series of strikes. They had been deluged with strikes ordered for men who did not desire the strikes. They had been deluged with strikes against companies which had settled all differences with their own men. They had been deluged with strikes in violation of existing collective bargaining agreements . . . there was a demand that we act." Congressional Record, Senate, June 23, 1947 (93 Cong. Rec. 7690).

5. H.R. 3020, 80th Congress, 1st Session (1947), Vol. 1, *Legislative History of the L.M.R.A.* (Washington: Government Printing Office, 1949), p. 159, hereafter cited as *I. Legis. Hist. L.M.R.A.* The second volume will be referred to as *II Legis. Hist. L.M.R.A.*

6. *Ibid.*, pp. 236–237.

7. *Ibid.*, p. 176.

8. *Ibid.*, pp. 166–167.

9. *Ibid.*, p. 205.

10. *Ibid.*, p. 164.

11. *Ibid.*, p. 166.

12. *Ibid.*, pp. 187–188.

13. House Report No. 245, 80th Congress, 1st Session, *I Legis. Hist. L.M.R.A.;* p. 292.

14. *Ibid.*, p. 298.

15. *Ibid.*

16. *Ibid.*, p. 301.

17. *Ibid.*, p. 310.

18. *I Legis. Hist. L.M.R.A.*, p. 310. This portion of the report received a number of Supreme Court references. For example, in one case the Supreme Court stated: "In 1947, the fear was expressed in Congress that the Board 'has gone very far, in the guise of determining whether or not employers had bargained in good faith, in setting itself up as a judge of what concessions an employer must make and of the proposals and counter-proposals that he may or may not make.' Accordingly, the Hartley Bill, passed by the House, eliminated the good faith test and expressly provided that the duty to bargain collectively did not require submission of counterproposals." *American National Insurance*, 343 U. S. 404. Another justice of the Supreme Court cited this report in defense of his position. *Borg-*

Warner, 356 U. S. 342, 355. The purpose of relying upon the House report was to limit the scope of the duty to bargain.

19. T. R. Iserman, *Industrial Peace and the Wagner Act* (New York: McGraw-Hill Book Company, Inc., 1947), pp. 31–35; Harold W. Metz, *Labor Policy of the Federal Government* (Washington: The Brookings Institution, 1945), p. 73. The use of these books as sources for textbooks has been fairly widespread. For example, one labor textbook, relying upon Dr. Metz's book, states, "The National Labor Relations Act, as amended, gives the Board the right and duty to pass on the desirability of the proposals of both sides, and to determine whether either party fails to bargain in good faith. The refusal to provide for abitration of differences may be adjudged by the Board evidence of bad faith." Albion G. Taylor, *Labor Problems and Labor Law* (2d ed.; New York: Prentice-Hall, Inc., 1950), p. 359. It need hardly be added that no documentation for this statement was presented, since none exists.

20. *Op. cit.*, p. 33.

21. *Op. cit.*, p. 72.

22. 1 NLRB 499.

23. 1 NLRB 185.

24. 9 NLRB 127, 128.

25. 26 NLRB 696, 697.

26. 71 NLRB 1148.

27. *I Legis. Hist. L.M.R.A.*, p. 310.

28. 14 NLRB 426.

29. 44 NLRB 847.

30. *I Legis. Hist. L.M.R.A.*, pp. 301–311.

31. 21 NLRB 1254, 1255.

32. 39 NLRB 119, 120.

33. A later book by Dr. Metz written with Meyer Jacobstein contains many similar inaccuracies. For example, "The employer's refusal to accept a closed shop may not be advanced as an argument against the proposed agreement." Sweeping condemnations were made without documentation upon board policy, such as the charge that "In cases where the workers entered a complaint against the employer for failure to bargain collectively, the Board frequently adjudged the employer guilty on unsubstantial evidence . . ." and "The Board has used its wide discretionary power to pass on the question as to whether or not the terms demanded by the union or the counterproposals offered by the employer would best carry out the purposes of the Act." Metz and Jacobstein, *A National Labor Policy* (Washington: The Brookings Institution, 1947), pp. 100–102. This book received the following endorsement from Dr. Harold Moulton, President of the Brookings Institution: "The authors, Dr.

Metz and Dr. Jacobstein, have had long experience in this field. The book has had, in addition to their joint thinking, the collaboration of a committee of the institution, so that the conclusions at which they arrive may fairly be said to represent the Brookings Institution point of view with respect to the labor policies of the government and what might be done to improve the labor situation." This testimony by Dr. Moulton was given during his appearance before the House Committee on Education and Labor as cited in Irving G. McCann, "Why the Taft-Hartley Law?" (New York: Committee for Constitutional Government, Inc., 1950), p. 65. Mr. Iserman was also the source of information on NLRB for Professor Edward H. Chamberlin, who stated that Iserman "documents exhaustively his contention that the NLRB used its broad discretionary powers consistently to 'make unions grow' rather than to provide 'full freedom' for employees." See "The Economic Analysis of Labor Union Power" (Washington: American Enterprise Association, 1958), p. 19.

34. *I Legis. Hist. L.M.R.A.*, pp. 311–312.

35. See "The Legislative History of the Taft-Hartley Act," in the *George Washington Law Review*, XXIX, No. 2 (December, 1960), 297.

36. *I Legis. Hist. L.M.R.A.*, p. 408.

37. *I Legis. Hist. L.M.R.A.*, p. 430.

38. Reilly, *op. cit.*, p. 298.

39. *I Legis. Hist. L.M.R.A.*, p. 546.

40. *I Legis. Hist. L.M.R.A.*, p. 538.

41. *II Legis. Hist. L.M.R.A.*, pp. 1653, 1655.

42. 61 Stat. 136.

43. Section 8(d): "For the purposes of this section, to bargain collectively is the performance of the mutual obligation of the employer and the representative of the employees to meet at reasonable times and confer in good faith with respect to wages, hours, and other terms and conditions of employment, or the negotiation of an agreement, or any question arising thereunder, and the execution of a written contract incorporating any agreement reached if requested by either party, but such obligation does not compel either party to agree to a proposal or require the making of a concession . . ." It should be noted that the language of Section 8(5) remained unchanged but because of the inclusion of union unfair labor practices, its designation is now 8(a)(5).

44. NLRB, Thirteenth Annual Report for the fiscal year ending June 30, 1948 (Washington: Government Printing Office, 1948, 1949), p. 59.

45. NLRB, Fourteenth Annual Report for the fiscal year ending 1949 (Washington: Government Printing Office, 1950), p. 73.

46. This policy was affirmed as being within the allowable area of the board's discretion in *Ray Brooks*, 204 F. 2d 899; 348 U. S. 96.

47. *Westfolk Cut Glass Company*, 90 NLRB 944.

48. *Arnolt Motor*, 173 F. 2d 597; (CCA 7); *Samuel Bingham's Sun Manufacturing*, 227 F. 2d 751 (CCA 6).

49. *Ray Brooks*.

50. *Krantz Wire and Manufacturing Company*, 97 NLRB 971.

51. *Henry Heide*, 107 NLRB No. 258.

52. *National Waste Material Corporation*, 93 NLRB 477.

53. *Celanese Corporation of America*, 95 NLRB 664.

54. *Old Line Life Insurance Co.*, 96 NLRB 499.

55. *John H. Barr Marketing Co.*, 96 NLRB 675.

56. *Taormina Co.*, 207 F 2d 251 (CCA 5).

57. *Hexton Furniture Company*, 111 NLRB 342. In this case under the board's contract bar rules, a representation petition would not have been entertained in view of existing contract. Hence the employer was under a continuing obligation to bargain.

58. *International Broadcasting Corp.*, NLRB No. 25.

59. *Krimm Lumber Co.*, 97 NLRB 1574.

60. *Dallas Concrete*, 212 F (2d) 98 (CCA 5); *Harris Langenberg Hat Corp.*, 216 F (2d) 146 (CCA 8).

61. *Clerostat Mfg. Co.*, 216 F (2d) 525 (CCA 1); *Foreman N. Clark, Inc.*, 215 F (2d) 396 (CCA 9).

62. *American Steel Buck Co.*, 227 F (2d) 927 (CCA 2).

63. *Esquire, Inc.*, 222 F (2d) 253 (CCA 7).

64. *Reeder Motor Co.*, 96 NLRB 831.

65. *Leader News Co., Inc.*, 98 NLRB 119.

66. *Crown Zellerbach Corp.*, 95 NLRB 753.

67. NLRB, Fourteenth Annual Report, p. 78, citing *Allied Mills, Inc.*, 82 NLRB No. 99.

68. *Otis Elevator*, 208 F (2d) 176 (CCA 2).

69. *Bemis Bros. Bag Co.*, 206 F (2) 33 (CCA 5).

70. *Leland-Gifford Co.*, 95 NLRB 1306.

71. *Dorsey Trailers, Inc.*, 80 NLRB No. 89, at 486.

72. The earliest such case was *Pioneer Pearl Button Co.*, 1 NLRB 837.

73. *Whitin Machine Works*, 108 NLRB No. 223.

74. *Associated Unions of America*, 200 F (2d) 52 (CCA 7).

75. *Leland-Gifford*, 200 F (2d) 620 (CCA 1).

76. *Item Company*, 220 F (2d) 956 (CCA 5); *Boston Herald-Traveler*, 223 F (2d) 58 (CCA 1).

77. *Truitt Mfg. Co.*, 110 NLRB 856.

78. 351 U. S. 152, 153. Frankfurter dissented on the basis that the decision rested upon a per se theory of violation. Justice Frank-

furter stated, "These Sections [Sections 8(a)(5) and 8(d) of the act] obligate the parties to make an honest effort to come to terms; they are required to try to reach an agreement in good faith. Good faith means more than merely going through the motions of negotiating; it is inconsistent with a predetermined resolve not to budge from an initial position. But it is not necessarily incompatible with stubbornness or even with what to an outsider may mean unreasonableness. A determination of good faith, or of want of good faith normally can rest only on an inference based upon more or less persuasive manifestations of another's state of mind. The previous relations of the parties, antecedent events explaining behavior at the bargaining table, and the course of negotiations can constitute the raw facts for reaching such a determination. . . . The totality of the conduct of the negotiation was apparently deemed irrelevant to the question; one fact alone disposed of the case . . . this is to make a rule of law out of one item—even if a weighty item—of the evidence. There is no warrant for this."

79. *Item Company,* 220 F (2d) 956 (CCA 5).
80. *Niles-Bement-Pond Co.,* 97 NLRB 165.
81. *Bemis Brothers Bag Co.,* 96 NLRB 728.
82. *United Shoe Machinery Corp.,* 96 NLRB 1309.
83. *National Gas Co.,* 99 NLRB 44.
84. *Reed and Prince Mfg. Co.,* 96 NLRB 850.
85. *Bickford Shoes, Inc.,* 109 NLRB 1346.
86. *Diaper Jean Mfg. Co.,* 109 NLRB 1045.
87. *Bethlehem Steel Co.,* 89 NLRB 341; *Shell Oil Co.,* 77 NLRB 1306.
88. *American National Insurance Co.,* 89 NLRB No. 19.
89. *NLRB v. American National Insurance Co.,* 343 U. S. 395.
90. *Ibid.,* 409.
91. 343 U. S. 402, 403, 404.
92. *Ibid.,* 408.
93. *Ibid.,* 411, 412.
94. *NLRB v. Insurance Agents Union,* 45 L.R.R.M. 2704.
95. *NLRB v. Katz,* 47 L.R.R.M. 2967.
96. *NLRB v. Katz, et al.,* 50 L.R.R.M. 2182.
97. *Associated Unions of America,* 200 F 2d 52 (CCA 7).
98. *International Furniture Company,* 212 F 2d (CCA 5).
99. *National Shoes,* 208 F 2d 688 (CCA 2).
100. *NLRB v. Reed and Prince Manufacturing Company,* 205 F (2d) 13, 134 (CCA 1).
101. *L. L. Majure Transport Company,* 95 NLRB No. 43 (28 L.R.R.M. 1317).
102. *Ibid.*

103. *Majure Transport Company v. NLRB* 198 F 2d 735 (CCA 5) 30 L.R.R.M. 2441.

104. *Herman Sausage Company*, 122 NLRB No. 23 (43 L.R.R.M. 1091).

105. 275 F 2d 229 (CCA 5) 45 L.R.R.M. 2830.

106. *Ibid.*

107. *Lion Oil Co.*, 109 NLRB 680, 221 F 2d 231 (CCA 8).

108. *Blackstone Mills*, 109 NLRB 772.

109. *Bethlehem Steel Co.*, 89 NLRB No. 33, at 334.

110. *Dalton Telephone Co.*, 187 F 2d 811 (CCA 5).

111. *American Laundry Machinery Co.*, 174 F 2d 124 (CCA 6).

112. *Pecheur Lozenge Co.*, 98 NLRB 496, enforced, 209 F 2d 393 (CCA 2).

113. *Wade and Paxton*, 96 NLRB 650.

114. 113 NLRB 1288, *NLRB v. Wooster Division of Borg-Warner*, 356 U. S. 342.

115. 113 NLRB 1288, 1291, 1292.

116. *Ibid.*, at 1295.

117. *Ibid.*, at 1293.

118. Cox and Dunlop, "Regulation of Collective Bargaining by the National Labor Relations Board," *Harvard Law Review*, LXIII (1950), 389; Cox and Dunlop, "The Duty to Bargain Collectively During the Term of an Existing Agreement," *Harvard Law Review*, LXIII (1950), 1097.

119. 113 NLRB 1306.

120. *Ibid.*, p. 1306.

121. *NLRB v. Wooster Division of Borg-Warner Corporation*, 356 U. S. 342, 346, 347.

122. *Ibid.*, at 351, 352.

123. Donald H. Wallett, "The Borg-Warner Case and the Role of the NLRB in the Bargaining Process" (*Proceedings* of New York University 12th Annual Conference on Labor [New York: Matthew Bender & Co., 1959]), p. 46.

124. Northrup and Bloom, *op. cit.*, pp. 120–121.

CHAPTER 7

1. For statistics on the time lag in the past, see U. S. Congress, Senate, Committee on Labor and Public Welfare, *Hearings*, 83rd Congress, 1st Session, Part I (1953), pp. 548–557; for current statistics see the annual Summary of Operations, Office of the General Counsel, NLRB, beginning with calendar year 1961, pp. 11–27, and for calendar year 1962, pp. 8–21. For a full explanation of the current statistics and a further breakdown see the testimony of General Counsel Rothman in the Pucinski subcommittee hearings (Hearings

before the Subcommittee on National Labor Relations Board, Committee on Education and Labor, House of Representatives, 87th Congress, 1st Session, Part 2, pp. 1076–1233.)

2. U. S. Congress, Senate, Committee on Labor and Public Welfare, *Hearings*, 81st Congress, 2nd Session, Part 2, p. 145.

3. Report to the Senate Committee on Labor and Public Welfare by the advisory panel on Labor-Management Relations Law (Cox Report), Document No. 80, 86th Congress, 2nd Session, 1960, pp. 1–2.

4. Pucinski hearings, p. 194.

5. U. S. Congress, Senate, *Hearings*, 83rd Congress, 1st Session, Part 1, pp. 553–554; for additional examples of other protracted hearings see p. 554 ff.

6. U. S. Congress, Senate, Subcommittee on the Judiciary, *Hearings*, 75th Congress, 3rd Session, 1938.

7. U. S. Congress, Senate, Committee on Education and Labor, *Hearings*, 76th Congress, 1st Session, on S. 1000, S. 1392, S. 1264, S. 1550, S. 1580, and S. 2123, Bills to amend the National Labor Relations Act (24 volumes), 1939.

8. U. S. Congress, House of Representatives, Special Committee, *Report on the Investigation of the National Labor Relations Board,* 76th Congress, 2nd Session (30 volumes), 1939.

9. U. S. Congress, House of Representatives, Committee on Labor, *Hearings, Proposed Amendments to the NLRA,* 76th Congress, 1st Session, 1939.

10. U. S. Congress, Senate, Committee on Labor and Public Welfare, *Hearings, Labor Relations Program,* 80th Congress, 1st Session, 1947; and House of Representatives, Committee on Education and Labor, *Hearings, Amendments to the NLRA,* 80th Congress, 1st Session, 1947.

11. U. S. Congress, Joint Committee on Labor Management Relations, *Hearings on Operation of Labor-Management Relations Act,* 1947, 80th Congress, 2nd Session, 1948.

12. U. S. Congress, House of Representatives, Committee on Education and Labor, Hearings on H.R. 2032, NLRA of 1949, 81st Congress, 1st Session, 1949; Senate, Committee on Labor and Public Welfare, *Hearings on S. 249, Labor Relations,* 81st Congress, 1st Session, 1949; Senate, Committee on Labor and Public Welfare, *Hearings,* 83rd Congress, 1st Session, 1953.

13. U. S. Congress, *Labor Management Relations, Report of the Joint Committee on Labor-Management Relations,* 1948, p. 99.

14. U. S. Congress, *Labor-Management Relations, Minority Views of the Joint Committee on Labor-Management Relations,* 1948, p. 25.

15. U. S. Congress, Report of the Senate Committee on Labor and Public Welfare, 81st Congress, 1st Session, Report No. 99, p. 3.

16. U. S. Congress, House of Representatives, Committee on Education and Labor, Minority Report, 81st Congress, 1st Session, Report No. 317, p. 3.

17. NLRB, Twenty-sixth Annual Report, p. 220.

18. *Ibid.*, p. 221.

19. "Revision of the Taft-Hartley Act," *Quarterly Journal of Economics*, LXVII, No. 2 (May, 1953), 149.

20. Senate Hearings, 81st Congress, 2nd Session, p. 82.

21. *Ibid.*, p. 114.

22. *Ibid.*

23. *Ibid.*, p. 118.

24. U. S. Congress, Senate, Committee on Labor and Public Welfare, 83rd Congress, 1st Session, *Hearings on Proposed Revisions of the Labor-Management Relations Act, 1947*, part 1, p. 463.

25. *Ibid.*, p. 464.

26. *Ibid.*, p. 586.

27. *Ibid.*, p. 508.

28. Cox Report, pp. 1–2.

29. *Ibid.*, p. 12.

30. Pucinski hearings, p. 535.

31. *Ibid.*, p. 155.

32. *Ibid.*, p. 190.

33. *Ibid.*

34. NLRB, Sixth Annual Report, p. 2.

35. "Final Report of the Attorney General's Committee on Administrative Procedure," p. 35, cited in NLRB, Sixth Annual Report, p. 2.

36. Testimony of Stuart Rothman in the Pucinski hearings, part 2, p. 1287.

37. NLRB, Twenty-sixth Annual Report, p. 226.

38. *Ibid.*

39. Emily C. Brown, *Studies of the Results of National Labor Relations Board Activities, a Summary of Operations Analysis, 1942–1944* (Washington: Government Printing Office, 1946).

40. *Ibid.*, p. 6.

41. *Ibid.*, p. 9.

42. *Ibid.*, p. 37.

43. The leading decision is *NLRB v. Mackay Radio and Telegraph Co.*, 304 U. S. 333, enforcing 1 NLRB 201; the limitations and qualifications of economic strikers are spelled out in *NLRB v. Fansteel Metallurgical Corp.*, 306 U. S. 240; *Southern Steamship v. NLRB*, 316 U. S. 312; *NLRB v. Sands Manufacturing Co.*, 306 U. S.

332; *Republic Steel Corp. v. NLRB,* 107 F 2d, 472 (CCA 3), modified in other respects, 311 U. S. 7; *Mastro Plastics Corp. v. NLRB,* 350 U. S. 270, 278; *Local 833, U.A.W. v. NLRB (Kohler Co.),* 49 L.R.R.M. 2485 (CA–D.C.)

44. See note 43, particularly the Mackay case.

45. The information for the case histories was obtained from an examination of the case files located in the board's various regional offices.

CHAPTER 8

1. William H. Spencer, "The National Labor Relations Act," in *The Journal of Business of the University of Chicago,* VIII, No. 4 (October, 1935), 21, 22–24. Copyright 1935 by the University of Chicago. All rights reserved. Published October 1935.

2. *Ibid.,* p. 27.

3. Law Bulletin of the National Association of Manufacturers (July 5, 1935).

4. National Lawyers Committee of the American Liberty League, *Report on the Constitutionality of the National Labor Relations Act* (Pittsburgh: Smith Bros. Co., 1935), p. xi.

5. *Ibid.,* p. 42.

6. Taylor, *Government Regulation of Industrial Relations,* p. 283.

7. *Ibid.,* p. 284.

8. Cox, *op. cit.,* pp. 1435–1442.

9. We may note again in passing that the opposition by employers to the duty to bargain rests upon the same basis. For example, the president of General Motors in his testimony before the Senate asserted that the removal of the duty to bargain "would have the great advantage of removing the necessity for defining the legal requirement of collective bargaining and of eliminating any interference by the NLRB in and during the actual process of collective bargaining. This would leave the matter of the actual bargaining to the parties themselves. This is the most effective way to remove from the Government the responsibility for policing the process of collective bargaining in detail, an administrative job of great magnitude and one of very doubtful value. It would make the parties responsible for their own negotiations and restore real collective bargaining." (Statement of C. E. Wilson before U. S. Senate Committee on Labor and Public Welfare, Feb. 5, 1947; reproduced in pamphlet form by General Motors, no date, p. 11.) It should also be pointed out that President Truman's Labor-Management Conference broke down on the issue of the proper subjects of collective bargaining. Management representatives insisted that a number of subjects be excluded from collective bargaining including the "de-

termination of job content . . . the allocation and assignment of work to workers . . . establishment of quality standards and judgment of workmanship required; and the maintenance of discipline and control and use of the plant operations; and the schedule of operations and the number of shifts." U. S. Department of Labor, Division of Labor Standards, *The President's National Labor-Management Conference, Nov. 5–30, 1945*, Bulletin No. 77 (Washington: Government Printing Office, 1946), p. 58.

10. Lewiston (Maine) *Sun*, February 4, 1938, as cited in Gellhorn and Linfield, "Politics and Labor Relations—NLRB Procedure," p. 339.

11. *Ibid.*, p. 340. It must not be forgotten that the National Lawyers Committee which sponsored the report of the American Liberty League issued on September 5, 1935, advised the public unequivocally that the Wagner Act was unconstitutional. The membership of this committee included some of the most successful and eminent lawyers of the day, among them a former Attorney General of the United States and two former Solicitors General of the United States. The chairman of the National Labor Relations Board has stated that "the effect of the advice upon the thousands of lesser lawyers who look for leadership to the distinguished lawyers of the committee, was what might be expected. Many of them regarded themselves as being in the fortunate position of engaging in a holy crusade, with pay, when they were employed to frustrate the efforts of the Board to administer the new law. And there was a place for judges in the ranks of the devout." J. Warren Madden, "The Origin and Early History of the National Labor Relations Board," *George Washington Law Review*, XXIX, No. 2 (1960), 243.

12. U. S. Congress, Senate, Subcommittee of the Committee on Education and Labor, *Hearings*, 75th Congress, 3rd Session, Part 17 (Washington: Government Printing Office, 1938), p. 7398.

13. *Ibid.*, pp. 108–113.

14. *Ibid.*, p. 17.

15. U. S. Congress, Senate, Committee on Education and Labor, *The Associated Industries of Cleveland*, 76th Congress, 4th Session, Report No. 6, Part 5 (Washington: Government Printing Office, 1939), pp. 184–185.

16. U. S. Congress, Senate, Committee on Education and Labor, *Republic Steel Corporation*, 76th Congress, 1st Session, Report No. 6, Part 2 (Washington: Government Printing Office, 1939), pp. 116–201.

17. Millis and Brown, *op. cit.*, p. 77.

18. The NLRB asserted in its annual reports that its effectiveness started with *Jones and Laughlin*. Third Annual Report, p. 1.

19. Taft, "Organized Labor and the New Deal," p. 9.

20. Interestingly enough, an unfair labor practice under the 1934 Railway Labor Act amendments is a crime. However, there has been only one indictment issued and no convictions under this penalty. See Northrup, *op. cit.*, p. 331.

21. For the period 1938–1947, there were 1,709 company unions disestablished; the numbers of such unions disestablished in 1945, 1946, and 1947 were 54, 54, and 36 respectively. NLRB, Twelfth Annual Report, p. 88.

22. Interviews with NLRB compliance officers in Washington, D. C. and in the regional offices in Boston, New York, Pittsburgh, San Francisco, Los Angeles, Kansas City, and Atlanta.

23. Millis and Brown, *op. cit.*, p. 78.

24. The board's annual reports invariably contain this information and the recent summary reports of General Counsel Stuart Rothman prominently highlight these data.

25. Office of General Counsel, *Summary of Operations, Fiscal Year 1962*, dated June 30, 1962, p. 26.

26. About 15,000 of these involved an allegation of a refusal to bargain. In the early years of the board, almost one-half of all charges contained this allegation. See the board's annual reports.

27. NLRB, Twelfth Annual Report, 1947 (Washington: Government Printing Office, 1948), p. 86.

28. Office of the General Counsel, *Summary of Operations, Fiscal Year 1962*, p. 17.

29. *Ibid.* This figure also reflected a conscious effort by the NLRB to close cases which were "stale" and represented in some cases a compromise with the principles of the act. Millis and Brown, *op. cit.*, pp. 48, 49.

30. Congressional hostility to the board during the Wagner Act period customarily took the form of exiguous appropriations. For a discussion of this see Millis and Brown, *op. cit.*, pp. 33–34.

31. NLRB, *Historical Digest*, June 1959, p. C–1. For specific examples in the delay in processing representation and unfair labor practice cases during this period see statement of Lee Pressman, General Counsel, CIO, in U. S. Congress, Senate, Hearings Before the Committee on Education and Labor, 76th Congress, 1st Session, Part 2 (Washington: Government Printing Office, 1939), pp. 4282–4288.

32. NLRB, Twelfth Annual Report, pp. 89, 90. The percentage of votes to those eligible was almost 90.

33. The importance of compulsion in inducing compliance was brought out by Senator Taft in a colloquy with Senator Ives in 1953 in discussing an amendment to Taft-Hartley. Senator Ives stated,

in reference to one suggestion on emergency strikes: "I do not think it has to be enforced by a court." To which Senator Taft replied: "If it is disobeyed, it has to be." Senator Ives: "I have a procedure in one of the bills I introduced which does not force it before a court." Senator Taft: "Then it is no good, and it would be defied by either one side or the other." U. S. Congress, Senate, *Taft-Hartley Act Revisions*, Hearings Before the Committee on Labor and Public Welfare, 83rd Congress, 1st Session, Part 1 (Washington: Government Printing Office, 1953), pp. 140–141.

34. Office of the General Counsel, *Summary Report*, Operational Activities, NLRB, Fiscal Year 1961, July 26, 1961, p. 16.

35. NLRB, Twenty-sixth Annual Report, p. 221.

36. The present import of this can be appreciated by realizing that the case load of the board has risen 56 per cent over the period 1958–1962.

37. General Counsel Stuart Rothman, "Voluntary Adjustments as a Way of Life Under the National Labor Relations Act," Release 866, May 17, 1962, p. 11.

38. NLRB, Twelfth Annual Report, p. 86.

39. Office of the General Counsel, *Summary of Operations*, NLRB, Fiscal Year 1962, June 30, 1962, p. 14.

40. We must, however, note that the proportion of non-merit charges has changed significantly over time, particularly with changes in the national administration. It has already been observed that the legal requirement to bargain did not change in any substantial way with the Taft-Hartley amendments and with the decisions of the Eisenhower Labor Board. The impact of the board upon the disposition of cases did, however, show a trend. For example, the proportion of all unfair labor practice cases in which there was a finding of merit was only 18.5 per cent in calendar year 1955 and rose to over 30 per cent by 1962. (Office of the General Counsel, *Summary Report*, NLRB, Calendar Year 1961, Dec. 29, 1961, p. 27.) It was not the change in legal doctrine which accounted for this difference but the quantum of evidence which different general counsels thought necessary to prove violations.

41. Inquiries made by the writer to the Regional Directors. See also address by Chairman Frank McCulloch to the American Bar Association, August 7, 1962, Board Release, R-879.

42. While no detailed information is available about what happened in these cases when no contract was reached, we do know that very few unions in this situation filed subsequent refusal-to-bargain charges.

43. U. S. Congress, Senate, Hearings before a Subcommittee of the Committee on Education and Labor, 75th Congress, 3rd Session,

Part 18 (Washington: Government Printing Office, 1938), p. 7860.

44. *Ibid.*, pp. 8129–8151.

45. "Collective Bargaining, Management Obligations and Rights," issued by the Law Department, NAM (New York: November, 1943), pp. 7–14.

46. International Statistical Bureau, Inc., *How to Bargain With the Labor Union* (New York: Forward, 1944). For other sources of similar advice see Harvey B. Rector, "Solving the Employers Labor Problem Under New Deal Legislation" (2nd ed.; Cincinnati: Law Research Service, 1942), p. 72; L. R. Greenman and E. B. Greenman, *Getting Along With Unions* (New York: Harper & Brothers, 1947), p. 3.

47. For a discussion of the background of U. S. Steel and SWOC relations, see Walter Galenson, "The Unionization of the American Steel Industry," in *International Review of Social History*, Vol. 1 (1956), and the same author's *The CIO Challenge to the AFL* (Cambridge: Harvard University Press, 1960), pp. 75–122.

48. Galenson, *The CIO Challenge to the AFL*, p. 117.

49. *Ibid.*, p. 119.

50. Girdler confirmed Murray's evaluation of the causes of the strike by testifying: "The difficulties in the present dispute arise from the fact that the company will not enter into a contract, oral or written, with an irresponsible party and the CIO as presently constituted, is wholly irresponsible." U. S. Congress, Senate, Hearings Before the Committee on Post Offices and Post Roads on S. Res. 140, *A Resolution Authorizing an Investigation of Delivery or Non-Delivery of Mail to Establishments Where Industrial Strife is in Progress*, 75th Congress, 1st Session (Washington: Government Printing Office, 1937), p. 208. Murray's testimony is at *ibid.*, pp. 42–44.

51. *Ibid.*, p. 215.

52. *Ibid.*, p. 242.

53. *Ibid.*, p. 243. Note the similarity with the NAM bulletin issued to all members on April 16, 1937, which began: "The Supreme Court of the United States has sustained the validity and application of the National Labor Relations Act to the field of employment in local manufacture to an unprecedented extent. It is the law of the land. Our problem now is to ascertain the nature and extent of our obligations." Statement of John C. Gall, Counsel of NAM, in Hearings before a Subcommittee on Education and Labor, Part 18, p. 7871.

54. Senate, Hearings Before the Committee on Post Offices and Post Roads, p. 244.

55. Address by Frank W. McCulloch, "New Problems in the

Administration of the Labor-Management Relations Act: The Taft-Hartley Injunction," Nov. 3, 1961, R. 11, p. 23.

56. The chief judge of the Fifth Circuit has had occasion to criticize severely the failure of a majority of his colleagues to accept the findings of the board which were supported by substantial evidence. *White v. NLRB*, F. 2d, 564, 570–573 (CCA 5).

57. *American Aggregate Co., Inc.* and *Featherlite Corp.* in the U. S. Court of Appeals for the Fifth Circuit, No. 19109 (June 28, 1962).

58. Charles P. Larrowe, "A Meteor on the Industrial Relations Horizon: The Foreman's Association of America," in *Labor History*, II, No. 3 (Fall, 1961).

59. *Matter of Maryland Drydock Co.*, 49 NLRB 733.

60. Larrowe, *op. cit.*, p. 279.

61. *Ibid.*, p. 282.

62. 56 NLRB 353.

63. Larrowe, *op. cit.*, p. 284.

64. 61 NLRB 4; 64 NLRB 1217.

65. President McAlpine of the UMW foremen's union, as cited in Larrowe, *op. cit.*, p. 289.

66. *Ibid.*, p. 293.

SELECTED BIBLIOGRAPHY

BOOKS, PERIODICALS, PAMPHLETS, AND SPEECHES

Bernstein, Irving. *The Lean Years. A History of the American Workers, 1920–1933*. Boston: Houghton Mifflin Company, 1960.

———. *The New Deal Collective Bargaining Policy*. Berkeley: University of California Press, 1950.

Berman, Edward. *Labor and the Sherman Act*. New York: Harper & Brothers, 1930.

———. "Studies in History, Economics, and Public Law," *Labor Disputes and the President of the United States*, CXI, 2 (1924).

Brissendon, Paul F. "Genesis and Import of the Collective Bargaining Provisions of the Recovery Act," *Economic Essays in Honor of W. C. Mitchell*. New York: Columbia University Press, 1935.

Brown, D. V. "The Impact of Some NLRB Decisions," *Proceedings of 13th Annual Meeting of I.R.R.A.*, Publication No. 26 (no publisher), 1961.

Chamberlin, John. *Collective Bargaining and the Law*. Ann Arbor: University of Michigan Law School, 1959.

Committee for Economic Development. *The Public Interest in National Labor Policy*. New York, 1961.

Cox, Archibald. "The Duty to Bargain in Good Faith," *Harvard Law Review*, LXXI (1958).

Cox, Archibald, and Dunlop, John T. "The Duty to Bargain Collectively During the Term of an Existing Agreement," *Harvard Law Review*, LXIII (1950).

———. "Regulation of Collective Bargaining by the National Labor Relations Board," *ibid*.

Davey, Harold W. *Contemporary Collective Bargaining*. Englewood Cliffs, N. J.: Prentice-Hall, Inc., 1959.

Findling, David P. and Colby, William. "Regulations of Collective Bargaining by the National Labor Relations Board—Another View," *Columbia Law Review*, LI (1951).

Fisher, C. O. "The New Railway Labor Act," *American Economic Review*, LVII (1927).

Fleming, Robben W. "The Obligation to Bargain in Good Faith," *Public Policy and Collective Bargaining*, edited by Joseph Shister, Benjamin Aaron, and Clyde W. Summers. New York and Evanston: Harper & Row, 1962.

———. "The Significance of the Wagner Act," *Labor and the New Deal*, edited by Milton Derber and Edwin Young. Madison: University of Wisconsin Press, 1961.

Frankfurter, Felix, and Greene, Nathan, *The Labor Injunction*. New York: Macmillan Company, 1930.

Galenson, Walter. *The CIO Challenge to the AFL*. Cambridge: Harvard University Press, 1960.

———. "The Unionization of the American Steel Industry," *International Review of Social History*, I (1956).

Gellhorn, Walter, and Linfield, S. L. "Politics and Labor Relations—N.L.R.B. Procedure," *Columbia Law Review*, XXXIX (1939).

Gregory, Charles O. *Labor and the Law* (2nd rev. ed.). New York: McGraw-Hill, Inc., 1932.

Humphrey, Helen F. "The Government at the Bargaining Table—Has the American National Insurance Company Case Liberated the Parties From the National Labor Relations Board?" *Syracuse Law Review*, VI, No. 1 (Fall, 1954).

Industrial Relations Research Association. *New Dimensions in Collective Bargaining* (Publication No. 21). New York: Harper & Brothers, 1959.

International Statistical Bureau, Inc. *How to Bargain With the Labor Union*. New York: Forward, 1944.

Jones, Harry E. *Historical Background of Machinery Set Up for the Handling of Railroad Labor Disputes, 1888–1940*. No publisher, no date; printed in New York for Eastern Committee of the National Railroad Adjustment Board.

Keyserling, Leon H. "The Wagner Act: Its Origin and Current Significance," *George Washington Law Review*, XXIX, No. 2 (December, 1960).

Larrowe, Charles P. "A Meteor on the Industrial Relations Horizon: The Foreman's Association of America." *Labor History*, II (1961).

Lecht, L. A. *Experience Under Railway Labor Legislation*. New York: Columbia University Press, 1954.

"Legislative History of the Taft-Hartley Act," *George Washington Law Review*, XXIX, 1960.

Lorwin, Lewis L., and Wubnig, Arthur. *Labor Relations Boards*. Washington: The Brookings Institution, 1935.

Madden, J. Warren. "The Origin and Early History of the National Labor Relations Board," *George Washington Law Review*, XXIX, No. 2 (December, 1960).

McCulloch, Frank. "A Tale of Two Cities," NLRB Release 879, August 7, 1962.

———. "New Problems in the Administration of the Labor-Management Relations Act: The Taft-Hartley Injunction," NLRB Release 811, November 3, 1961.

Millis, Harry, and Brown, Emily. *From the Wagner Act to Taft-Hartley*. Chicago: University of Chicago Press, 1950.

Millis, Harry A., and Montgomery, Roy E. *Organized Labor*. New York, 1945.

NAM Law Department. "Collective Bargaining, Management Obligations and Rights," New York: November, 1943.

National Lawyers Committee of the American Liberty League. *Report on the Constitutionality of the National Labor Relations Act*. Pittsburgh: Smith Bros. Co., 1935.

Northrup, Herbert R., and Bloom, Gordon F. *Government and Labor*. Homewood, Illinois: Richard D. Irwin, 1963.

Perlman, Selig, and Taft, Philip. *History of Labor in the United States, 1896–1932*. New York: The Macmillan Company, 1935.

Petro, Sylvestro. "The Employer's Duty to Bargain," 3 *Labor Law Journal* 515 (1952).

Richberg, Donald R. *The Rainbow*. New York: Doubleday, Doran and Company, Inc., 1936.

Rothman, Stuart. "The Duty to Bargain in a Noncompulsory Society," NLRB Release 747, October 27, 1960.

———. "Voluntary Adjustments as a Way of Life Under the National Labor Relations Act," NLRB Release 866, May 17, 1962.

Rubinow, Raymond S. *Section 7(a): Its History, Interpretation and Administration*. Office of National Recovery Administration, Division of Review, Labor Studies Section, March, 1936 (mimeo.).

Samoff, Bernard. "Research on National Labor Relations Board Decisions," *Industrial and Labor Relations Review* (October, 1956).

Shultz, George P., and Coleman, John R. *Labor Problems: Cases and Readings*. New York: McGraw-Hill, 1953.

Slichter, Sumner. "Revision of the Taft-Hartley Act," *Quarterly Journal of Economics*, LXVII, No. 2 (May, 1953).

Smith, Russell A. "The Evolution of the 'Duty to Bargain' Concept in American Law," *Michigan Law Review*, XXXIX, No. 7 (May, 1941).

Spencer, William H. *Collective Bargaining Under Section 7(a) of the National Industrial Recovery Act*. Studies in Business Administration, The School of Business, The University of Chicago, 1935.

———. "The National Labor Relations Act," in *The Journal of Business of the University of Chicago*, VIII, No. 4 (October, 1935).

Taft, Philip. *The AF of L in the Time of Gompers.* New York: Harper & Brothers, 1957.

———. *The AF of L From the Death of Gompers to the Merger.* New York: Prentice-Hall, Inc., 1948.

Taylor, George W. *Government Regulation of Industrial Relations.* New York: Prentice-Hall, Inc., 1948.

———. *The Structure of Collective Bargaining,* edited by Arnold R. Weber. Glencoe: The Free Press, 1961.

Tripp, L. Reed. *Labor Problems and Processes.* New York: Harper & Brothers, 1961.

Twentieth Century Fund. *Labor and the Government.* New York: McGraw-Hill, 1935.

Ward, Frank B. *The United States Railroad Labor Board and Railway Labor Disputes.* Ph.D. Thesis in Economics, University of Pennsylvania, Philadelphia, 1929.

Watkins, Gordon L. "Labor Problems and Labor Administration in the United States During the World War," *University of Illinois Studies in the Social Sciences,* VIII.

Weber, Arnold (ed.), *The Structure of Collective Bargaining.* (A Publication of the Graduate School of Business.) Glencoe, Ill.: University of Chicago, The Free Press, 1961.

Weyand, Ruth. "Majority Rule in Collective Bargaining," *Columbia Law Review,* XLV, No. 4 (July, 1945).

Witte, Edwin E. *The Government in Labor Disputes.* New York: McGraw-Hill, 1932.

Wolf, H. D. *The Railway Labor Board.* Chicago: University of Chicago Press, 1927.

Wollet, Donald. "The Borg-Warner Case and the Role of the NLRB in the Bargaining Process," 12, *New York University Conference of Labor,* 39, 1959.

Wolman, Leo. *Ebb and Flow in Trade Unionism.* New York: National Bureau of Economic Research, 1936.

PUBLIC DOCUMENTS

Bureau of Labor Statistics. *Bulletin of the United States.* "History of the Shipbuilding Labor Adjustment Board, 1917–1919," 283 (1921).

———. "National War Labor Board," 287 (1922).

National Labor Relations Board. *Annual Reports: First (1936) to Twenty-sixth (1961).*

———. *Historical Digest.* June, 1959.

———. *Legislative History of the Labor Management Relations Act, 1947.* 2 vols. Washington, 1948.

———. *Legislative History of the National Labor Relations Act, 1935.* 2 vols. Washington, 1949.

———. *Studies of the Results of National Labor Relations Board Activities.* Washington, 1946.

———. *Summary Report, Operational Activities, Fiscal Year 1961.* Office of the General Counsel, July 26, 1961.

———. *Summary of Operations, Fiscal Year 1962.* Office of the General Counsel, June 30, 1962.

National Mediation Board. *First Annual Report.* Washington, 1935.

National Recovery Administration. "Statement by the President of the United States of America Outlining Policies of the National Recovery Administration," Washington, 1933.

U. S. Congress. *Hearings on National Arbitration Bill.* H. R. 9491.

———. *Labor-Management Relations, Minority Views of the Joint Committee on Labor-Management Relations,* 1948.

———. *Labor-Management Relations, Report of the Joint Committee on Labor-Management Relations,* 1948.

———. *Report of the Special Committee to Investigate the N.L.R.B.,* submitted by Mr. Smith of Virginia. Washington, 1941.

U. S. Congress, House of Representatives.

Committee on Education and Labor. *Hearings, Amendments to the NLRA.* 80th Congress, 1st Session, 1947.

———. *Hearings on H. R. 2032, NLRA of 1949.* 81st Congress, 1st Session, 1949.

———. *Hearings on Operation of Labor-Management Relations Act, 1947.* 80th Congress, 2nd Session, 1948.

———. *Final Report of the Industrial Commission.* Document No. 380. 57th Congress, 1st Session, 1902.

———. *Minority Report.* Report No. 317. 81st Congress, 1st Session, 1949.

Committee on Labor. *Hearings, Proposed Amendments to the NLRA.* 76th Congress, 1st Session, 1939.

House Reports. Report No. 328, Vol. I, 69th Congress, 1st Session, 1926.

Special Committee. *Report on the Investigation of the National Labor Relations Board.* 76th Congress, 2nd Session (30 volumes), 1939.

U. S. Congress, Senate.

Committee on Education and Labor. *Hearings,* General Counsel, CIO. 76th Congress, 1st Session, 1939.

———. *Hearings on S. 1000, S. 1392, S. 1550, S. 1580, and S. 2123, Bills to amend the National Labor Relations Act.* 76th Congress, 1st Session (24 volumes), 1939.

———. *Republic Steel Corporation*. Report No. 6, Part 2. 76th Congress, 1st Session, 1939.

———. *Hearings*. 76th Congress, 4th Session, Part 3, April 26, 1939.

———. *The Associated Industries of Cleveland*. 76th Congress, 4th Session, Report No. 6, Part 5, 1939.

———. Commission on Industrial Relations. *Final Report and Testimony*, Senate Document 415, Vol. 1, 64th Congress, 1st Session, 1916.

Subcommittee of the Committee on Education and Labor. *Hearings*. 75th Congress, 3rd Session, Parts 17, 18, 1938.

Committee on Interstate Commerce. *Hearings*. 73rd Congress, 2nd Session, 1934.

———. *Hearings*. Testimony on S. 3266 of Louis R. Gwyn, Vice President of Railway Express Agency. 73rd Congress, 2nd Session, 1934.

Committee on Labor and Public Welfare. *Hearings, Labor Relations Program*. 80th Congress, 1st Session, 1947.

———. *Report No. 99*. 81st Congress, 1st Session, 1949.

———. *Hearings on S. 249, Labor Relations*. 81st Congress, 1st Session, 1949.

———. *Hearings on Proposed Revisions of the Labor-Management Relations Act*. 33rd Congress, 1st Session, Part 1, 1947.

———. *Hearings, Taft-Hartley Act Revisions*. 83rd Congress, 1st Session, 1953.

———. *Report by the Advisory Panel on Labor-Management Relations Law*, Document No. 80, 86th Congress, 2nd Session, 1960.

Committee on Post Offices and Post Roads. *Hearings on S. Res. 140, A Resolution Authorizing an Investigation of Delivery or Non-Delivery of Mail to Establishments Where Industrial Strife is in Progress*. 75th Congress, 1st Session, on S. Res. 140, 1937.

———. *Report No. 222, Vol. 1*. 69th Congress, 1st Session, 1926.

Subcommittee on the Judiciary. *Hearings*. 75th Congress, 3rd Session, 1938.

———. *Hearings, Investigation of Strike in Steel Industry,* Vol. 1, 1919.

U. S. Department of Labor, Bureau of Labor Statistics. *Monthly Labor Review*, XI (1920).

———. *Proceedings of the First Industrial Conference Called by the President, October 6 to 23, 1919*. Washington, 1920.

———. Robert P. Reeder, "Analysis of the Awards of the National War Labor Board," in *Reports of the Department of Labor, 1919, Report of the Secretary of Labor and Reports on Bureaus*. Washington, 1920.

————. *Report of Industrial Conference Called by the President.* Washington, 1921.

————. "Use of Federal Power in Settlement of Railway Labor Disputes," Bulletin No. 303. Washington, 1922.

Secretary of Labor. *Eighth Annual Report.* Washington, 1921.

U. S. Department of Labor, Division of Labor Standards. *The President's National Labor-Management Conference, November 5–30, 1945.* Bulletin No. 77. Washington, 1946.

————. Bulletin. *Report of the Anthracite Coal Strike Commission.* Washington, 1903.

U. S. Railroad Administration. *Annual Report, 1918–1919,* Division of Labor.

————. *Bulletin No. 4* (rev.), 1919.

————. *Report of the Railway Wage Commission.* April 30, 1918.

MAJOR CASES CITED

Adair v. United States, 208 U. S. 161 (1908).
Agwilines, 87 F. (2d) 146 (CCA 5).
Allen, S. L., & Company, 1 NLRB 714.
Allison, J. H., & Company, 70 NLRB 378.
Aluminum Ore Co., 39 NLRB 1297.
American Aggregate Co., Inc. and Featherlite Corp. in the U. S. Court of Appeals for the Fifth Circuit, No. 19109 (June 28, 1962).
American Creosetting, 4 NLRB 240.
American Federation of Labor v. NLRB, 308 U. S. 401.
American Hawaiian S. S. Company, 10 NLRB 1361-66.
American Laundry Machinery Co., 174 F 2d 124 (CCA 6).
American National Insurance Co., 89 NLRB No. 19; 343 U. S. 395.
American Steel Buck Co., 227 F (2d) 927 (CCA 2).
American Steel Foundries v. The Tri-City Central Trades Council et al., The United States Supreme Court, 42 S. C. R.
Appalachian Electric Company, 93 F. 2d 985 (CCA 4).
Arnolt Motor, 173 F. 2d 597; (CCA 7).
Associated Unions of America, 200 F (2d) 52 (CCA 7).
Atlanta Hosiery Mills, 1 NLRB 145.
Atlantic Refining Company, 1 NLRB 368.
Atlas Mills, Inc., 3 NLRB 1014, 15.
Barr, John H., Marketing Co., 96 NLRB 675.
Bausch and Lomb, 69 NLRB 1104.
Beckerman Shoe Corporation, 21 NLRB 1222.
Bee Line Bus, 2 NLB 24.
Bemis Bros. Bag Co., 206 F (2d) 33 (CCA 5).
Bender Tramway Corporation, 1 NLB 64.
Berkeley Woolen Mills, 1 NLB 5.
Bethlehem Steel Company, 73 NLRB 277, 89 NLRB 341.
Bickford Shoes, Inc., 109 NLRB 1346.
Biles-Coleman Lumber Company, 4 NLRB 679.
Birge, M. H., & Sons, 1 NLRB 739.
Blackstone Mills, 109 NLRB 772.

Borg-Warner, 113 NLRB 1288, 356 U. S. 342.
Boston Herald-Traveler, 223 F (2d) 58 (CCA 1).
Bradford Dyeing Association, 4 NLRB 604.
Budd, Edward G., 1 NLB 58.
Burnside Steel Foundry, 7 NLRB 714.
Bussman Manufacturing Co., 14 NLRB 322.
Capital Broadcasting Company, 30 NLRB 164.
Carrol, George E., 56 NLRB 935, 937.
Case, J. I., Company v. NLRB, 321 U. S. 322 (1944).
Chicago Apparatus Company, 12 NLRB 1002.
Claire Knitting Mills, Inc., 2 NLRB 472.
Clark, Foreman N., Inc., 215 F (2d) 396 (CCA 9).
Clarksburg Publishing Company, 120 F. (2d) 976 (CCA 4).
Clerostat Manufacturing Co., 216 F (2d) 525 (CCA 1).
Cleveland Knitting Mills, 1 NLB 453.
Clifton Wright Hat Company, 2 NLRB 453.
Compton-Highland Mills, Inc., 70 NLRB 207.
Concordia Ice Company, 51 NLRB 1068.
Connecticut Coke, 2 NLB 88.
Consolidated Aircraft Corp., 47 NLRB 694.
Consolidated Edison Company v. NLRB, 305 U. S. 197, 236.
Consolidated Machine Tools, 67 NLRB 95.
Coppage v. Kansas, 236 U. S. 1 (1915).
Cox, Edward E., Printer, Inc., 1 NLRB 594.
Crown Can Company, 42 NLRB 1160.
Crown Zellerbach Corp., 95 NLRB 753.
Cullom and Ghertner Company, 14 NLRB 270.
Dallas Concrete, 212 F (2d) 98 (CCA 5).
Dalton Telephone Co., 187 F 2d 811 (CCA 5).
Dekay, Clifford M., 2 NLRB 231.
Denver Automobile Dealers Association, et al., 10 NLRB 1173.
Diaper Jean Mfg. Co. 109 NLRB 1045.
Dixie Motor Coach, 128 F. (2d) 201, (CCA 5).
Doane, John S., Company, 63 NLRB 1403.
Dorsey Trailers, Inc., 80 NLRB No. 89.
Dresner, S., and Son, 1 NLRB 26.
Eagle Rubber Company, 1 NLRB 157.
Easton Publishing Company, 19 NLRB 389.
Elbe File and Binder Company, 2 NLRB 906.
Ely and Walker Dry Goods Company, 1 NLRB, 97.
Esquire, Inc., 222 F (2d) 253 (CCA 7).
Express Publishing Company, 13 NLRB 1223.
Fansteel Metallurgical Corp., 5 NLRB 930.
Fine Rough Hat Company, 2 NLRB 411.

Ford Motor Company, 29 NLRB 873.
Franks Bros. Co. v. NLRB, 64 S.C. 817.
General Motors Corporation, 50 NLRB 205, enforced June 20, 1945
(CCA 3).
Globe Cotton Mills v. NLRB, 103 F. (2d) 94 (CCA 5) enforcing
6 NLRB 461.
Globe Gabbe Corporation, 2 NLRB 60.
Globe Mail Service, Inc., 2 NLRB 610.
Great Southern Trucking, 127 F. (2d) 180 (CCA 4).
Green Colonial Furnace Company, 52 NLRB 161.
Griswold Manufacturing Company, 6 NLRB 307.
Hall Baking Company, 1 NLRB 83.
Hamilton-Brown Show Company, 9 NLRB 1073.
Hancock Brick and Tile Company, 44 NLRB 920.
Hanson-Whitney Machine Company, 8 NLRB 159.
Harriman Hosiery Mills, 1 NLB 68.
Harris-Woodson Company, Inc., 70 NLRB 956, enforced, 162 F.
(2d) 97 (CCA 4).
Heide, Henry, 107 NLRB No. 258.
Heinz, H. J., Company, 10 NLRB 963.
Herman Sausage Company, 122 NLRB No. 23 (43 L.R.R.M. 1091).
Hexton Furniture Company, 111 NLRB 342.
Highland Park Manufacturing Company, 12 NLRB 1248.
Hitchman Coal and Coke Co., v. Mitchell, 245 U. S. 299 (1917).
Hopwood Retinning Co., 4 NLRB 922.
Houde Engineering Corporation, 1 NLB 87.
Hugh Leather Company, 11 NLRB 394.
Inland Lime, 119 F. 2d 20, (CCA 7).
Inland Steel Company, 9 NLRB 783.
Insurance Agents Union, 119 NLRB 768.
International Broadcasting Corp., NLRB No. 25.
International Furniture Company, 212 F 2d (CCA 5).
Item Company, 220 F (2d) 956 (CCA 5).
Krantz Wire and Manufacturing Company, 97 NLRB 971.
Krimm Lumber Co., 97 NLRB 1574.
Langenberg, Harris, Hat Corp., 216 F (2d) 146 (CCA 8).
Leader News Co., Inc., 98 NLRB 119.
Leland-Gifford Co., 95 NLRB 1306.
Lennox Furniture Company, 20 NLRB 93.
Libby, McNeill and Libby, 65 NLRB 873.
Lion Oil Co., 109 NLRB 680, 221 F. 2d 231 (CCA 8).
Local 833, U.A.W. v. NLRB, (Kohler Co.), 49 L.R.R.M. 2485
(CA–D.C.).
Lorillard Co., 16 NLRB 684, 703.

Louisville Refining Company, 4 NLRB 861.
Majure Transport Company v. NLRB, 198 F 2d 735 (CCA 5) 30 L.R.R.M. 2441.
Martin Brothers Box Company, 35 NLRB 217.
Maryland Drydock Co., 49 NLRB 733.
Mastro Plastics Corp., v. NLRB, 350 U. S. 270.
McNeely, 6 NLRB 800.
McNeely & Price Company, 6 NLRB 811.
McQuay-Norris, 116 F. (2d) 748, (CCA 7).
Medo Photo Supply Corp., 43 NLRB 997.
Midland Steamship Line, 66 NLRB 836.
Montgomery Ward & Co., 39 NLRB 240.
Mooresville Cotton Mills v. NLRB, 94 F. (2d) 61.
Morand Brothers Beverage Company, 99 NLRB 1488.
Motor Valve and Manufacturing Company, 58 NLRB 1057, enforced 149 F. (2d) (CCA 6).
National Aniline and Chemical Company, 1 NLRB, 115.
National Gas Co., 99 NLRB 44.
NLRB v. Acme Air Appliance Company, Inc., 117 F. (2d) 417 (CCA 2) 420.
NLRB v. American National Insurance Co., 343 U. S. 395.
NLRB v. Capital Greyhound Lines, 140 F. (2d) 754 (CCA 6), cert. 64 SCT 1285.
NLRB v. Dadourian Export Corporation, 138 F. (2d) 891 (CCA 2).
NLRB v. Fansteel Metallurgical Corp., 306 U. S. 240.
NLRB v. Insurance Agents Union, 361 U. S. 477.
NLRB v. Mackay Radio and Telegraph Co., 304 U. S. 333.
NLRB v. Newark Morning Ledger Company, (CCA 3).
NLRB v. Reed and Prince Manufacturing Company, 205 F (2d) 13, 134 (CCA 1).
NLRB v. Sands Manufacturfing Co., 306 U. S. 332.
NLRB v. Whittier Mills, 111 F. (2d) 474 (CCA 5).
NLRB v. Wooster Division of Borg-Warner Corporation, 356 U. S. 342.
National Licorice Company, 7 NLRB 551.
National Lock Company, 1 NLB 19.
National Motor Bearing, 105 F. (2d) 652 (CCA 9).
National Shoes, 208 F (2d) 688 (CCA 2).
National Silver Company, 50 NLRB 570.
National Waste Material Corporation, 93 NLRB 477.
Niles-Bement-Pond Co., 97 NLRB 165.
Norfolk Southern Bus Corporation, 66 NLRB 1165.
Norge Corporation, 1 NLB 82.
North American Aviation, Inc., 44 NLRB 604, 611.

Old Line Life Insurance Co., 96 NLRB 499.
Otis Elevator, 208 F (2d) 176 (CCA 2).
Out West Broadcasting Co., 40 NLRB 1367.
Pecheur Lozenge Co., 98 NLRB 496, enforced, 209 F 2d 393 (CCA 2).
Pennsylvania Railroad Company v. Railway Labor Board, 282 Fed. 693, 261 U. S. 72.
Philadelphia Rapid Transit, 1 NLB 66.
Pilling, 119 F. (2d) 32, 35–36 (CCA 3).
Pioneer Pearl Button Co., 1 NLRB 837.
Pittsburgh Plate Glass v. NLRB, 313 U. S. 154.
Polish National Alliance, 136 F. (2d) 175 (CCA 7).
Pool Manufacturing Co., 70 NLRB.
Quaker State Oil Refining Corporation, 121 NLRB 334, 337.
Rapid Roller Co., 33 NLRB 589.
Reading Batteries, Inc., 19 NLRB 249.
Reading Hosiery, 1 NLB 1.
Reed and Prince Mfg. Co., 96 NLRB 850.
Reeder Motor Co., 96 NLRB 831.
Republic Aviation Corporation v. National Labor Relations Board, 324 U. S. 793, 65 Sup. Ct. 982 (1945).
Republic Steel Corp. v. NLRB, 107 F. 2d., 474 (CCA 3).
Resnick Brothers, 2 NLRB 214.
Rollway Bearing Company, Inc., 1 NLRB 659.
Roth, A., and Company, 1 NLB 75.
St. Joseph Stockyards Company, 2 NLRB 39.
Saldway Process, 117 F. (2d) 83, (CCA 5).
Samson Tire & Rubber Corporation (Division of the United States Rubber Company), 2 NLRB 504.
Samuels, Ben, d/b/a National Bag Company, 65 NLRB 1078.
Scandore Paper Box Co., 4 NLRB 918.
Sheba Ann Frocks, Inc., 5 NLRB 12.
Shell Oil Co., 77 NLRB 1306.
Simmons Engineering Company, NLRB 1373.
Singer Manufacturing Company, 24 NLRB 460.
Sorg Paper Co., 25 NLRB No. 104.
Southern Prison Company, 46 NLRB 1268.
Southern Steamship v. NLRB, 316 U. S. 312.
Spicer Manufacturing Corporation, 51 NLRB 679.
Spiewack, I., and Sons, 71 NLRB 770.
Stolle Corporation, 13 NLRB 370.
Suburban Lumber Co., 3 NLRB 194, 203.
Sunshine Mining Company, 7 NLRB 1252.
Taormina Co., 207 F 2d 251 (CCA 5).

Texas Mining, 117 F. (2d) 86 (CCA 5).
Tierson Manufacturing Company, 1 NLB 53.
Timken Roller Bearing Company, 70 NLRB 506.
Tishomingo County Electric Power Association, 74 NLRB 135.
Tomlinson of High Point, Inc., 74 NLRB 127.
Truax v. Corrigan, 257 U. S. 312 (1921).
Truitt Mfg. Co., 110 NLRB 856.
United Dredging Company, 40 NLRB 118.
United Shoe Machinery Corp., 96 NLRB 1309.
Wade and Paxton, 96 NLRB 650.
Western Felt Works, 10 NLRB 407.
Western Printing Co., 34 NLRB 202.
Westfolk Cut Glass Company, 90 NLRB 944.
Westinghouse Air Brake Co., 25 NLRB 1312.
Whatcom County Dairymen's Association, 1 NLB 73.
White v. NLRB, 225, F. (2d) 564 (CCA 5).
Whitin Machine Works, 108 NLRB No. 223.
Whittier Mills, 15 NLRB 457.
Wilson and Company, Inc., 19 NLRB 1000, 30 NLRB 314.
Wilson v. New, 243 U. S. 332.

INDEX

Act of 1888, 19–20
Adamson, Congressman, 26
Adamson Act, 25–28
Alabama, case history from, 221
Allen, S. L., & Company, Matter of, 104, 108
Allis Chalmers, 237
Amalgamated Butchers Union, 213–214
American Civil Liberties Union, 77
American Federation of Labor, 21, 27, 28, 32, 36, 51
American Liberty League, 234
American National Insurance Co., 157–158, 160, 161, 167–168, 176
"American Plan," 17
American Railway Association, 26
American Railway Union, 20
American Telephone and Telegraph Company, 16
Associated Industries of Cleveland, 237
Atlanta (NLRB region), 183, 251
Atlas Mills, Inc., Matter of, 110

Ball Committee, 172, 173
Baltimore and Ohio Railroad, 27
Bankruptcy Act (1933), 47
Baruch, Bernard, 15
Bernstein, Irving, 78
Bethlehem Steel, 255
Biddle, Francis, 70, 74–75
Bituminous Coal Labor Board, 59
Bloom, Gordon F., 5
Board of Mediation (under Railway Labor Act of 1926), 45–46
Board of Mediation and Conciliation (under Newlands Act), 24–25, 26

Board of Railroad Wages and Working Conditions (during World War I), 29
Borg-Warner, 92, 95, 164–169
Boston (NLRB region), 183, 251
Brennan, Justice, 95
Brookings, Robert S., 15
Brotherhood of Locomotive Engineers, 28
Brotherhood of Locomotive Firemen and Enginemen, 24, 31
Brotherhood of Railroad Trainmen, 28
Brown, D. V., 7
Brown, Emily C., 180–182
Building Service Employees Union, 212

California, case histories from, 185–187, 193–200, 207–210, 211, 212, 213, 215–216, 222–224
California Conciliation Department, 209
Case, Congressman, 133
Case, J. I., Company, Matter of, 141–142
Chicago Apparatus Company, 119
Chrysler Corporation, 237
Circuit Court of Appeals, 113, 126–127, 161, 162, 179, 186, 187
Clark, E. E. 23
Cleveland, Grover, 19
Coleman, John R., 4
Colombian Enameling and Stamping Company, Matter of, 139–140
Commission on Industrial Relations (1916), 8, 9–10, 248, 255

Committee for Economic Development, 5–6, 94–95

Communist Party, 77

Congress, U.S.; *see also* House of Representatives, Senate
hearings and debates in
on Adamson Act, 26
on bills to amend Wagner Act, 133
on Erdman Act, 20
on National Industrial Recovery Act, 50–51
on Railway Labor Act of 1926, 42–43, 46
on Taft-Hartley Act, 133–148, 172
on Wagner Act, 49–86
investigations of NLRB by, 172–173
legislative intent of
in Taft-Hartley Act, 158, 166, 231
in Wagner Act, 2, 6, 89, 96–100, 109
regulation of interstate commerce by, 18

Congress of Industrial Organizations (CIO), 176, 238

Congressional Record, 99

Connecticut, case histories from, 188–193, 204, 208, 219–220

Connery, Congressman, 85

Connery bill, 84; *see also* Wagner Bill

Consumers Research Inc., 124

Continental Can, 237

Cox, Archibald, 4, 90–94, 96, 99, 234–235

Cox Panel, 177

Cummins bill, 33

Dallas Cartage Company, Matter of, 142

Davey, Harold, 4, 6

Democratic Party, 71, 133, 173

Department of Labor, 53, 85, 86

Depression, 47

Director General of Railroads (during World War I), 28, 29, 30, 32

Dunlop, John T., 4, 90–93, 96, 99

Easton Publishing Company, Matter of, 114

Eliot, Charles W., 15

Ellender, Senator, 256–257

Emergency Transportation Act (1933), 47

Emery, James, 77–78

Erdman Act, 10–11, 20–23, 43, 45

Executive Orders of 1934 (on National Labor Board), 56, 61, 67

Fair Labor Standards Act, 117, 204

Farmer (chairman of NLRB), 166

Federal Mediation and Conciliation Service, 223

Federation of Independent Salaried Employees, 193

Fish, Frederick P., 16

Fleming, R. W., 93

Foreman's Association, 262

Furuseth, Andrew, 22

Garrison, Lloyd, 75–77

Gary, Elbert H., 15, 17

General Motors, 237

Georgia, case histories from, 215, 217, 220–221

Girdler, T. M., 256–257

Globe Cotton Mills v. NLRB, 113

Goldberg, Arthur J., 175–177

Gompers, Samuel, 15, 21–22, 28

Grable (union president), 39

Green, William, 51

Greenwood, Congressman, 85

Gregory, Charles O., 4

Griswold, Congressman, 85, 89

Haas, Francis J., 58–59

Handler, Milton, 77

Harding, Warren G., 40, 42

Harlan, Justice, 95, 167

Hartley Bill (H.R. 3020), 134, 135–137, 147; *see also* Taft-Hartley Act
House report accompanying, 137–145, 167

Hines, W. D., 31

Houde Engineering Corporation, 65, 67, 72, 77, 100
House of Representatives, U.S.; *see also* Congress, Senate, congressmen by name
  hearings and debates of
    on bills to amend Wagner Act, 133, 134
    on National Industrial Recovery Act, 51
    on National Labor Relations Act, 172
    on Taft-Hartley Bill, 134, 135–137, 147
    on Wagner-Connery Bill, 84–86, 97, 99
  Labor Committee, 134
  report on NLRB, 137–145, 167
  Ways and Means Committee, 50–51
Humphrey, Hubert, 177

Industrial Commission (1902), 8
Industrial Workers Federation of Labor, 195–198
Inland Steel Company, 103, 166, 255
Insurance Agents Union; see NLRB v. . . .
International Association of Machinists (IAM), 204–206, 209–210, 217, 221, 222–224
International Filter Company, Matter of, 139
International Ladies' Garment Workers' Union (ILGWU), 217, 220–221
Interstate Commerce Commission, 20, 25, 26
Iserman, T. R., 138, 142, 145

Jackson Daily News, Matter of, 140
Jasper Blackburn Products Compay, Matter of, 143–144
Johnson, Hugh, 236
Joint Resolution; *see* Public Resolution No. 44
Jones and Laughlin, 138, 236, 238, 254

Kansas, case histories from, 206–207, 213–214, 218
Kansas City (NLRB region), 183, 251
Kelly, Congressman, 51
Kerr, Clark, 5
Krantz Wire and Manufacturing Company, 150

La Follette, Senator, 63, 64, 76, 98, 236
Laborers Union, 224–227
Landrum-Griffin Act, 1
Lapp, John A., 59
Leiserson, William, 60
Lewis, John L., 59
Lippman, Walter, 77
Little Steel, 255–256
Lorillard Co., 103, 104
Los Angeles (NLRB region), 183, 184

Machinist Union, 32
McClellan Committee, 134
McCulloch, Frank W., 258
Massachusetts, case history from, 210–211
Metal Mouldings Corporation, Matter of, 144–145
Metz, Harold W., 139, 142, 145
Minton, Justice, 158
Missouri, case history from, 204–206
Murray, Phil, 256

National Association of Manufacturers, 60, 71, 77–78, 233–234, 236, 253–254
National Chamber of Commerce, 15
National Industrial Conference Board, 15, 16
National Industrial Recovery Act (NIRA), Section 7(a), 49–57, 63, 65, 68–69, 70, 71, 79, 95; *see also* National Labor Board
National Labor Board (under National Industrial Recovery Act, *q.v.*), 52–57, 58, 59, 60, 61, 62, 63, 64, 70, 77, 84, 97, 98; *see*

also National Recovery Administration

National Labor Relations Act; *see* Wagner Act

National Labor Relations Board (first board, 1934–1935), 64–71, 74, 75, 79, 85, 86

National Labor Relations Board (NLRB), 1935–present; *see also* Taft-Hartley Act, Wagner Act
annual reports of, 173–174, 180
Brown study on, 180–182
case histories of, 138–142, 184–230
congressional investigations of, 172–173
disposition of cases by, 179–180, 244–246, 250
studies on, 180–230
doctrines and policies of, 2, 6, 87, 88, 100
criticisms of, 94, 133, 166
effectiveness of, 182–183, 246–265
criticisms of, 174–175, 177–178, 232–233, 235
House of Representatives report on, 137–145, 167
powers of, 170, 239–244
regional offices of, 183
under Taft-Hartley Act, 146, 148–169, 244, 250
under Wagner Act, 101–132, 137, 151, 152, 159, 166, 232–233, 244–245, 250, 253

NLRB v. Insurance Agents Union, 159

NLRB v. Reed and Prince, 189

NLRB v. Sands Manufacturing Co., 107

National Lawyers Committee (American Liberty League), 234

National Metal Trades Association, 237

National Recovery Administration (NRA), 57, 236
Industrial Advisory Board, 52
Labor Advisory Board, 52

Labor Boards, 63, 98, 99, 100, 233–234, 247

National War Labor Board, 11–14, 66, 79, 80

New Deal, 49–86

Newlands Act, 23, 24–25, 26, 45

Norris-LaGuardia Act, 47, 51

Norris, Senator, 47

Northrup, Herbert R., 4

Office Employees Union, 215–216

Operating Engineers, 212–213

Order of Railway Conductors, 23

Packard, 262

Painters Union, 185–187

Pennsylvania, case history from, 221–222; 227–229

Pennsylvania Railroad, 36

Petro, Sylvester, 89

Petroleum Labor Policy Board, 56, 60

Pittsburgh (NLRB region), 183, 251

Plumb Plan, 32

Pollock (TWU president), 178

Public Resolution No. 44, 62–64, 65, 80, 98

Pucinski Committee, 172, 177

Pullman strike, 20

Railroad Administration (during World War I), 31, 32, 43

Railroad Boards of Adjustments (during World War I), 30, 31

Railroad Labor Board; *see* U.S. Railroad Labor Board

Railway Labor Act of 1926, 42–47, 51, 60, 61, 64, 97
amendments to, 47–48, 80

Reed and Prince; see NLRB v. . . . .

Regional Labor Boards (under National Industrial Recovery Act), 59; *see also* National Labor Board

Register Publishing Company, Matter of, 142–143

Reilly, Gerald, 146

Republic Steel Corporation, 255, 256

Republican Party, 133, 173

Resnick Brothers, 69
Retail Clerks Union, 198–200, 206–207
Retail, Wholesale and Department Store Union, 210–211, 227–229
Richberg, Donald, 51
Richfield Oil, 166
Rockefeller, John D., Jr., 15
Roosevelt, Franklin D., 52, 62, 86, 233, 238

St. Joseph Stockyards, 109
Sands case; *see NLRB v. Sands Manufacturing Co.*
San Francisco (NLRB region), 183, 251
Selvin, Mrs. Edwin, 195–197, 207–208
Senate, U.S.; *see also* Congress, House of Representatives, senators by name
    Committee on Education and Labor, 78
    Committee on Finance, 51
    hearings and debates in
        on anti-union bill, 133
        on bills to amend Wagner Act, 134
        on Southern Textile industry, 172, 174–175
        on steel strike, 256–257
        on Taft-Hartley Bill, 134, 135, 148
        on Wagner bill (first), 57–62
        on Wagner Bill, 71–84, 97, 99, 101, 172
    investigation of NLRB, 172
    investigation of Taft-Hartley Act, 173, 176
    Labor Committee, 134
    majority report on Taft-Hartley Bill, 146–148
    Subcommittee on Labor and Labor-Management Relations, 177
Senate bill 2926; *see* Wagner bill (first)
Senate Bill 1958; *see* Wagner Bill
Shroyer, Thomas B., 146

Shultz, George P., 4
Singer Manufacturing Company, 116
Slichter, Sumner, 7, 58, 60, 174
Smith, Congressman (Virginia), 133
Smith, Russell A., 89–90, 93, 98, 100
Smith Committee, 87–88, 172
Smith-Connally Act, 133
South, collective bargaining in, 174–175, 178, 258
Southern Pacific Railroad, 26
Spencer, William H., 52–53, 232–233, 248, 255
Steel Workers Organizing Committee (SWOC), 256
Supreme Court, U.S.; *see also* cases by name
    on Adamson Act, 27
    on Erdman Act, 22
    on duty to bargain, 3, 93, 95, 107, 121, 122–123, 155, 156–159, 166–167, 176
    on NLRB, 132, 138
    on Transportation Act of 1920, 36–37
    on Wagner Act, 49, 138, 238, 262
System Federation No. 90, 36

Taft, Senator, 147
Taft, William Howard, 32
Taft-Hartley Act, 1; *see also* Taft-Hartley Bill
    congressional hearings on, 172, 173
    NLRB under, 146, 148–169, 244, 250
    proposed amendments to, 172
    Section 8(a)(5), duty to bargain, 133–169, 174, 181
        criticisms of, 174–179, 183, 231–232, 234
        violations of, 181–230
Taft-Hartley Bill
    House version of, 134, 135–137, 147
    Senate version of, 146–148
Taylor, George, 4, 90, 234
Teamsters Union, 185–187, 209–210, 213, 215

Tennessee, case history from, 217

Textile Workers Union (TWU), 174–175, 178, 183, 200, 235, 258

Times Publishing Company, 108

Transportation Act of 1920, 32–42, 67, 95, 247

Truman, Harry S., 133, 148

Uhlich and Company, Matter of, 141

United Automobile Workers of America (UAW), 188–193

United Brotherhood of Maintenance-of-Way Employees and Railroad Shop Laborers, 39

United Electrical, Radio and Machine Workers of America (UE), 211, 212, 219–220

United Mine Workers of America, 70, 221–222, 262

United Packinghouse Workers of America, 218

U.S. Attorney General, 41
    Committee on Administrative Procedure, 179

U.S. Commissioner of Labor, 19, 20, 25

U.S. Railroad Labor Board (under Transportation Act of 1920), 33, 34–42, 47, 80

U.S. Secretary of the Interior, 26–27

U.S. Secretary of Labor, 27

U.S. Secretary of the Treasury, 28

U.S. Steel, 255

United Steelworkers Union of America, 177–178

Upholsterers Union, 207–208

Vandenberg, Senator, 82

Wabash Railroad, 23

Wagner, Robert F., Senator, 51, 52, 57, 58, 64
    and Wagner Bill, 71–74, 80–81, 97, 98, 99, 100

Wagner Act (National Labor Relations Act)
    bills to amend, 88, 133, 172
    congressional intent in, 96–100
    constitutionality of, 236, 238, 258
    criticisms of, 138, 234, 236
    importance of, 1–2, 246–247, 258–259
    legislative history of, 49–86, 89, 90
    NLRB under, 101–132, 137, 151, 152, 159, 166, 232–233, 244, 250, 253
    Section 8(5) (duty to bargain), 88, 89, 98, 99
    Taft-Hartley amendment to, 134, 135, 147, 148

Wagner bill (first, S. 2926), 57–62, 63, 72, 88, 97, 98
    Walsh amendments to, 60–62, 63, 72, 74

Wagner Bill (S. 1958), 49, 71–86, 97, 98, 99

Walsh, Senator
    on Wagner bill (first), 60–62, 63
    on Wagner Bill (S. 1958), 73, 75, 78, 82–83, 96–97, 99
        citations of his remarks, 87, 88-89, 90, 93, 94–95, 167

War Labor Board, 181

Welch, Congressman, 85, 89

West Virginia, case history from, 224–227

Whatcom County Dairymen's Association, Matter of, 55

White, Chief Justice, 27

Wilson, Woodrow, 14, 26–27

Wilson and Company, Matter of, 113

Wilson v. New, 28

World War I
    administration of railroads during, 28–32, 43
    collective bargaining during, 10–18, 181

Wyle, Benjamin, 178–179

Yale and Towne, 237

Youngstown Steel, 255